The Legal and Economic Aspects of Gray Market Goods

THE LEGAL AND ECONOMIC ASPECTS OF GRAY MARKET GOODS

Seth E. Lipner

QUORUM BOOKS
New York • Westport, Connecticut • London

Library of Congress Cataloging-in-Publication Data

Lipner, Seth E.
　　The legal and economic aspects of gray market goods / Seth E.
Lipner.
　　　　p.　　cm.
　　ISBN 0–89930–466–4 (lib. bdg. : alk. paper)
　　　1. Black market—United States.　2. Marketing—Law and
legislation—United States.　3. Foreign trade regulation—United
States.　4. Marketing—Law and legislation.　5. Black market.
I. Title.
KF1609.L57　1990
343.73'084—dc20
[347.30384]　　　90–30008

British Library Cataloguing in Publication Data is available.

Library of Congress Catalog Card Number: 90–30008
ISBN: 0–89930–466–4

First published in 1990

Quorum Books, 88 Post Road West, Westport, CT 06881
An imprint of Greenwood Publishing Group, Inc.

Printed in the United States of America

The paper used in this book complies with the
Permanent Paper Standard issued by the National
Information Standards Organization (Z39.48–1984).

10 9 8 7 6 5 4 3 2 1

to my Parents

Contents

Acknowledgments

I first became interested in the gray market when, in 1982, I read an article by Tamar Lewin in *The New York Times*. Since then, I have been writing about the subject on a regular basis, producing three law review articles as well as several other pieces. Those articles, "The Legality of Parallel Imports: Trademark, Antitrust or Equity" (19 Texas Int'l L. Rev. 553 [1984]); "Gray Market Goulash: The Problem of At-The-Border Restrictions on Importation of Genuine Trademarked Goods" (20 Cornell Int'l L. J. 103 [1987], reprinted in 77 Trademark Rep. 77 [1987]); and "Gray Market Controversies: The 1980s and Beyond" (1989 Fletcher Forum 307 [1989]), helped me to understand and evaluate the problems caused by gray market importation and led to many of the ideas set forth in this work. I wish to express my appreciation to all who helped me with those articles, especially Helene Banks, Lawrence Schiffman, and Jonathan Schecter, but also the many law students and law review editors who assisted in editing and publishing the articles.

For his assistance with the preparation of this manuscript, I also wish to acknowledge the invaluable assistance of my graduate research assistant, Brian Lipner (no apparent relation), who struggled not only to learn the law in this area but also to write footnotes, perform legal research, and edit the text. I am also indebted to Murray Franck, who is responsible not only for preparing Chapter 5 of this book, but also for commenting on some of the chapters and for keeping me intellectually honest.

This book was the product of many long hours of writing. I am therefore most indebted to my wife, Judith Rosen, for her encouragement and for her forbearance during the weekends and evenings we could not spend together while I undertook this project.

The Legal and Economic Aspects of Gray Market Goods

1

A Primer on the Gray Market

INTRODUCTION

The term "gray market goods" is a loosely used expression intended to connote any goods sold outside normal, authorized distribution channels. All gray market goods are genuine trademarked goods and are either imported or sold without the permission of the local trademark owner. Such goods must be distinguished from those goods that are counterfeit, so-called "black market" goods. Importation into the United States and sale of counterfeit goods clearly violate the rights of the trademark owner and are actionable under state and federal trademark statutes. Indeed, the Customs Service will halt such importation at the border, impound the goods, and possibly subject the importer to civil and perhaps criminal penalties.

The meaning of the term "genuine" was once the subject of legal dispute, but semantic questions of this kind have fallen to the wayside as courts moved on to the merits of the issues in the gray market. In the early 1980s, in a gray market case, the U.S. International Trade Commission addressed the semantical question of whether gray market goods were "genuine."

Genuine goods are goods produced or selected by the owner of a trademark, to which the owner of that trademark affixes the trademark or in connection with which the owner of the trademark uses the trademark (as in advertising). The phrase simply serves to distinguish the goods so produced and marked from goods marked with a trademark by someone not authorized to use the mark (i.e., someone other than the owner or licensee of the owner). [1]

While questions have arisen in cases where there were allegations that the gray market versions were either inferior to or different from the authorized counterparts, the "genuineness" question must now be deemed settled. As one court recently stated: "Any contention that only equipment sold through [a U.S. trademark owner] should be considered genuine is meritless." [2]

The legal status of gray market goods is quite different from that of counterfeit goods. Because these gray market goods are genuine, that is, they were manufactured either by or under the authority of the trademark owner, doubt has arisen about whether trademark infringement exists. Similarly, until recently, there was considerable doubt about whether Customs was required to bar the importation of such goods. Because the gray market phenomenon is of recent origin, the law in this area continues to evolve. Courts have now had approximately ten years of experience with the legal issues of gray market sales, and a substantial body of law now exists to determine whether gray market importation and sale is lawful.

The opponents of the gray market have employed a wide variety of theories to combat these sales. In addition to claims for trademark infringement, trademark dilution, and violation of the Tariff Act, trademark owners have alleged copyright infringement, unfair trading practices, fraud, and trafficking in stolen goods. These theories have met with a checkerboard of successes and failures. In spite of the fact that there are now decisions in numerous cases, outcomes continue to depend on a combination of forum choice and unique fact situations.

The goal of this book is to explore and expound upon the history of and future for gray market litigation, and to analyze the various judicial decisions and legislative actions that bear upon the legality of gray market sales. In order to appreciate fully the context of gray market litigation, one must first examine the sources of and economic reasons for the existence of the gray market. That task will be accomplished in the remainder of this chapter.

THE BUSINESS OF THE GRAY MARKET

Gray market goods, by definition, were manufactured by the trademark owner or his authorized representative, and thus their features and quality are usually similar to their authorized counterparts. Gray market goods, however, are sold outside the normal distribution channels and, in some cases, were not intended for sale in the United States. Gray market sales nevertheless constitute a vigorous industry. Initially, the source of these goods was shrouded in mystery, but, as research has been done and as litigation records have developed, a great deal has been learned about the sources of gray market goods.

Before examining these sources, however, a crucial distinction must be drawn between the international gray market and the domestic gray market. In the latter scenario, which has been the subject of a recent article in the *Harvard Business Review*,[3] the gray market phenomenon is the result of overproduction, distress merchandise, and technological improvements that have caused authorized sellers to cease selling older models and to "dump" their inventory onto the open market. The goods in these cases, either manufactured domestically or manufactured abroad and lawfully imported into the United States, are now being sold outside authorized channels.

In addition to this type of goods and these causes of the gray market, the international trading environment creates additional variables that influence the flow of gray market goods. Because of a variety of factors, including price and quality differentials, exchange rates, free riding, and perhaps even smuggling, it has become profitable to import goods outside the normal chain of distribution and sell them here. In all cases, whether domestic or international, the gray market survives because sellers are able to obtain or sell goods at prices below those being charged by authorized distributors. Consumers frequently take advantage of these price differentials, although it is sometimes claimed that they are deceived or otherwise harmed because they purchased outside the authorized distribution system.

The existence of the international gray market is in some sense a 1980s phenomenon. While isolated instances of gray market sales existed before that time, the meteoric rise in the value of the U.S. dollar in 1981 and 1982 caused gray market importation to become a lucrative business. During this time, it was not unusual to see prices for gray market goods one third lower than the price of their authorized counterparts. As the U.S. dollar declined in value in 1987 and 1988, the profitability of international gray market sales was undoubtedly reduced. The international gray market, however, continues to exist, although on a smaller, more focused scale. The domestic gray market continues to flourish, unaffected by these marked currency fluctuations. The following is a brief exploration of some available data about the source of gray market goods.

UNCOVERING GRAY MARKET CHANNELS

As has already been stated, for many years gray market transactions were cloaked in secrecy. Gray market sellers have gone to great lengths to conceal the sources of their goods. For example, in a 1984 case, the defendant gray market importer accepted a court's unfavorable finding rather than respond to certain questions about the source of his wares. Adding to this paucity of information is the fact that portions of judicial opinions dealing with gray market transactions have been redacted from published reports, and some consent decrees have been sealed by court order. More than one gray market seller has accepted evidentiary sanctions and a negative finding rather than reveal the source of goods. Finally, of course, many cases either were never litigated or were settled at early stages, depriving observers of published opinions and judicial findings of fact. There are numerous magazine and journal articles about gray market sales, but the stories tend to be either anecdotal or based upon unverified research.

Another reason for the lack of public information on the details of gray market channels of distribution is the fact that some manufacturers, while publicly opposed to gray market sales of their products, privately do little to inhibit their flow and in some instances even go so far as to encourage these transactions. Such practices, for example, may help improve the bottom line of a foreign subsidiary, which may make sales abroad knowing that the goods sold will eventually be imported into the United States. In this way, the foreign subsidiary (not to mention the salesperson) can, in essence, make sales that could not otherwise be made, that is, to customers outside its allotted territory. The domestic parent may even turn a blind eye to such sales as a method of discriminating in price in the U.S. market or covering fixed costs in a foreign market. Only when an authorized U.S. distributor makes a complaint will the domestic parent try to halt these "sanctioned" gray market sales.

In recent litigation about gray market pharmaceuticals, the defendant-importers raised the defense of manufacturer (or at least authorized dealer) complicity in the initial sale. A motion for summary judgment on these grounds was rejected by the court, and sanctions were imposed against the defendant on the grounds that the claim was without merit. While that may have been true in this case, it cannot be doubted that there are instances in which such complicity exists.

Recent litigation has, however, revealed some details about gray market transactions. Foremost among these litigations is a series of cases brought by Johnson & Johnson, Inc. (hereinafter J&J), the giant manufacturer and distributor of household products and proprietary medications. The first such case is *J&J v. Quality King*,[4] decided by the Third Circuit Court of Appeals. The goods in *Quality King* (toothbrushes and baby powder) began their travels with negotiations between J&J Ltd. (a European subsidiary of the American parent) and DAL International Trading Co. (hereinafter DAL), an entity of the Polish government. Unable to purchase for hard currency, DAL, J&J Ltd., and a company called Wendexim negotiated a barter transaction in which Wendexim received Polish lumber in exchange for its cash payment to J&J. Almost as an afterthought, and probably in response to mild urging from the parent, J&J Ltd.'s salesman asked for and received oral assurances that the goods in question would not be resold outside of Poland. Nothing to that effect was put in writing and the invoices, packing cartons, and goods in question did not reflect this oral representation.

At about the same time the DAL transaction was being negotiated, Cubro Trading Company, Ltd., a British firm, inquired of J&J Ltd. as to whether it could purchase quantities of toothbrushes and baby powder similar to those ordered by DAL. That transaction was never consummated. Meanwhile, the goods shipped to DAL never entered Poland. Instead, they were turned around at the border, destined for Belgium, where they were loaded onto ships headed for New Jersey. Evidently, Cubro had purchased the goods from DAL, who in turn resold them to Tereza Merchandise, Inc., a gray market dealer. Tereza eventually resold the goods to Quality King, a drug chain that operates through several well-known tradenames. By the time Quality King had received the goods, shipping codes and batch numbers had been removed from the packing containers in an effort (ultimately unsuccessful) to obscure their origin.

The facts in the second J&J litigation, *Ortho Pharmaceutical v. Sona Distributors, Inc.*[5] are essentially similar, involving a Hong Kong dealer selling goods supposedly destined for the People's Republic of China. The defendants were Sona, the ultimate U.S. buyer, and Elmcrest Trading, the firm that allegedly perpetrated the fraud. The goods in question were a skin treatment known as Retin-A, available in the United States only by prescription. The facts of *Sona* differ from *Quality King* in that the two entities involved in *Sona* (Elmcrest and Sona) were both owned by the same individual, and the original fraud was thus directly traceable to the ultimate U.S. seller.

These two cases involve goods that might be denominated "unintended" goods, because the manufacturer did not wish them to be sold in the United States. As will be seen in Chapter 3, one reason for this desire frequently lies in differences in the goods themselves or in the packaging of the goods when compared with their authorized counterparts. Unintended goods are sometimes referred to as "parallel imports," a term that has perhaps broader application and less descriptiveness than does the term "unintended." While unintended goods are usually manufactured outside the country where they are ultimately sold on the gray market, that need not be the case. A category of goods does exist that might be denominated "exported goods reimported," but such goods would clearly be a subset of unintended goods.

Without regard to the question of differences, certain generalities can be drawn about unintended goods. First, the U.S. seller obtained them either at favorable prices or in circumstances where they were unavailable locally. *Quality King* is certainly an example of the former, while *Sona* seems to be an example of the latter. Second, the diverter purchases or obtains a large quantity of goods that were originally destined elsewhere. The J&J cases notwithstanding, the diverter might not have to commit fraud to obtain these goods; it is likely that in some cases no false representation was made, either because none was solicited or because some authorized dealer was in complicity with the diverter.

Unintended goods probably make up the large bulk of gray market sales. The second largest category involves goods that are manufactured either abroad or in the United States pursuant to a trademark license. For some reason the manufacturer (or perhaps a diverter farther down the distribution chain), bypasses the normal route and sells to a gray marketer. In some situations, the manufacturer or diverter can get a better price for the goods or is unable to sell them through ordinary channels. For example, *El Greco Leather Products Company, Inc. v. Shoe World Inc.*[6] involved the sale of gray market shoes with the mark "CANDIE'S" affixed to them. The plaintiff, El Greco, was owner and licensor of the U.S. trademark and was the exclusive distributor of "CANDIE'S" shoes in the United States. El Greco had licensed Solemio, a Brazilian shoe manufacturer, to manufacture the shoes according to its specifications. Either because of inferior quality or because of production delays, the licensor became dissatisfied with Solemio's performance. El Greco cancelled the remainder of the contract, and El Greco's agent in Brazil refused to certify the quality of the shoes. El Greco gave Solemio no instructions about how to dispose of the shoes, and Solemio eventually sold them to defendant Shoe World at very low prices.

Licensed goods might also be diverted from their normal channels for any of the reasons that might motivate a diverter in the case of unintended goods. Those cases aside, the goods in *El Greco* must be distinguished from those involved in the J&J litigation because the shoes were originally intended to be sold in the United States. These goods might also be different from their authorized counterparts, that is, if the cancellation was due to inferior quality. For reasons that will become apparent in subsequent chapters, significant legal distinctions exist between unintended goods and cancelled-license goods. In licensed-goods cases, the licensor of course has the option of terminating the license and bringing suit against the manufacturer for breach. For jurisdictional and other reasons, however, most of these actions are brought against firms which, like Shoe World, were found to be in possession of the goods. The Plaintiff seeks an injunction, replevin, and damages for trademark infringement.

A third category of goods, typically involving the domestic gray market, is "distress" goods, dumped onto the market, often in large quantity, by an authorized dealer. That dealer might be experiencing cash flow difficulties, might have over ordered, or might have excess quantities of an older or out-of-date version of the goods. Distress goods might also be unintended goods if the authorized dealer operated in a foreign market and the goods were ultimately diverted to an unintended destination.

Regardless of the category of gray market goods, authorized U.S. sellers have an incentive to fight this new form of competition. Conversely, consumers, at least in certain instances, have a great stake in sustaining the flow of such imports. The very competition that the trademark owners and authorized dealers abhor benefits consumers in the form of greater choice and lower prices. Consumers, however, do need protection from poor quality goods and from features of gray market goods that diminish or otherwise affect their value or utility.

Consequently, sound jurisprudential policy requires a delicate balancing among these diverse interests; the result is a tangled body of law. Untangling this web is the subject of this book.

Except where distinctions are important, this text uses the term "gray market goods" to denote all genuine, unauthorized goods regardless of their source. The term "gray market" can be deemed somewhat pejorative, however no such connotation is intended. As one court wrote recently

> Appellants in the present case note that the term "gray-market" unfairly implies a nefarious undertaking by the importer, and that the more accurate term for the goods at issue is "parallel import." We agree that the term "parallel import" accurately describes the goods and is, perhaps, a better term because it is devoid of prejudicial suggestion. . . . [W]e also employ the term [gray market] . . . for better or worse, [because] it has become the commonly accepted and employed reference.[7]

By contrast, the European Community, also faced with an unauthorized importation problem, chose the term "parallel imports" instead of "gray market." This text, however, adopts the U.S. terminology.

THE ECONOMICS OF THE GRAY MARKET

While it is clear that an active gray market cannot exist without price differentials, the source of these differentials is not quite so apparent. Depending on the type of goods involved and the character of the market for the product, price differentials can be the result of a variety of factors, several of which are likely to exist in every case. These factors can range from honest enterprise, such as the diverter who takes advantage of favorable foreign currency exchange rates and engages in a sort of product arbitrage, to a manufacturer who attempts to discriminate in price in different (usually foreign) markets. Of course, successful price discrimination requires the presence of certain economic conditions. In certain cases, however, the ability to exploit price differentials might result in the creation of a gray market.[8] Finally, the sale of quality, cancelled-license or distress goods can also be considered an arguably honest endeavor that places goods onto the gray market.

A more questionable endeavor is free-riding, the practice of selling goods identical to those sold by full-service dealers without incurring the expenses attributable to the promoting and servicing of the product. Such free-riding falls into two categories: advertising free-riding and point-of-sale service free-riding. An advertising free rider takes advantage of the advertising and marketing efforts of authorized sellers, reaping the consumer recognition and other benefits that flow from advertising without incurring the attendant expense.

The second but distinct form of free-riding, point-of-sale service free-riding, is the failure to provide various ancillary services that consumers desire. Such services range from product instruction to the maintenance of an inventory of spare and auxiliary parts to the provision of warranty or repair services. Another type of free rider in this category sells trademarked goods without taking sufficient safeguards to ensure product integrity by compromising on packing, transportation, storage, or inspection costs in order to keep the price of goods lower.[9]

Where free-riding exists, the distinction between trademark and point-of-sale service free-riding may be of little consequence to the party attempting to fight the gray market. Yet in subtle ways this distinction affects the outcome of litigated cases. That is a subject to which we will return in Chapter 3. Indeed, whether such free-riding is actionable as trademark infringement remains the subject of substantial controversy.

Certainly the most pernicious source of gray market involves cases of outright dishonesty. Needless to say, *Sona* is an example of such a case, as perhaps is *Quality King*, although to a lesser degree. The sale of decidedly inferior, different, or not up-to-date goods can also be characterized as dishonest, particularly if done through concealment or without full disclosure. Also, cases of outright smuggling, for instance, without the payment of applicable duties, certainly exist. There is little question that sales in this third area offend some law, whether based upon fraud, consumer protection, or customs practice. The clearest instances of such illegality are beyond the scope of this work, although certain questions (as they affect the gray market) will be considered in detail.

The success of any suit to combat individual cases of gray market importation and sale is likely to depend upon, at least in part, where on this spectrum the defendant lies. The bulk of cases fall within the second category. In the most typical scenario, the owner of the U.S.

trademark, alleging infringement, sues a gray market seller. In the international context, the trademark owner might be affiliated with or owned by the foreign manufacturer of the goods, or it might be an independent U.S. corporation. The suits often arise when authorized dealers put pressure on the trademark owner to shield them from gray market competition. In many cases, these dealers are contractually bound to engage in point-of-sale promotion and service and thus cannot compete on an equal basis with free-riding gray marketers. These authorized dealers are thus caught between whether to maintain prices in the face of lost sales or to cut profit margins in order to compete with gray market prices.

In most cases, the trademark owner earnestly complies and brings suit, expecting to benefit from the reduction of intrabrand (i.e., gray market) competition and the renewed incentive for dealers to promote and service its products. There are some cases, as already indicated, in which suits are brought by the same entity that was responsible, either directly or indirectly, for the original diversion of the goods. Nevertheless, such trademark owners initiate suit to assuage their dealers, at the same time continuing to do business with diverters and gray market sellers.

History has proven that most cases, after substantial and costly litigation, result in either injunctions or settlements that prohibit the defendant from further gray market sales of the plaintiff's product. This action may put a temporary halt to specific gray market sales but is likely to have limited long-range effect, especially when the conditions that caused the original gray market trade continue to exist. Virtually all attempts to employ legal theories that would bar all gray market sales of a specific product have met with little success. The only instance of successful litigation involves the importation of cancelled-license goods, in which the Supreme Court ruled that such imports are barred by Section 526 of the Tariff Act.

Needless to say, questions remain about gray market causes, gray market sources, and the marketing issues raised by gray market sales. These are important subjects, but the answers to these questions are generally beyond the scope of this work. Rather, the focus will be on the legal and economic issues raised by gray market sales. The final resolution of most of the legal issues discussed herein will have to await future judicial and/or legislative action. A comprehensive exploration of these issues, their current status, and the prospects for the future is overdue.

NOTES

1. *In re Certain Alkaline Batteries*, 225 U.S.P.Q. 823, 834 (ITC 1984).

2. *Yamaha Corp. of America v. ABC International Traders, Corp.*, 703 F.Supp. 1398 (C.D.Calif. 1988).

3. Cespedes, Corey and Rangan, "Gray Markets: Causes and Cures," *Harvard Business Review*, July–August, 1988.

4. 798 F. 2d 100 (3rd Cir. 1986).

5. 663 F.Supp. 64 (S.D.Fla. 1987). This case, as well as the case last cited, are discussed in greater depth in Chapter 7.

6. 599 F.Supp. 1380 (E.D.N.Y. 1984), rev'd, 806 F.2d 392 (2d Cir. 1986), cert. denied, 108 S.Ct. 71 (1987).

7. *Weil Ceramics & Glass, Inc. v. Dash*, No. 86–5187, slip op., July 5, 1989 (3rd Cir.), cert den., ___U.S. ___(1989).

8. The economic causes of the gray market have been the subject of two recent law review articles. These articles, which reach opposite conclusions, are important material for anyone endeavoring to study and understand the gray market.
See J. T. McDermott, "The Gray Market in the United States: Law, Policy and Myth," 2 Conn. J. Int'l L. 1, 53–55 (1986); R. Staaf, "The International Gray Market: The Nexus of Vertical Restraints, Price Discrimination and Foreign Law," 19 U. Miami Inter-Am. L. Rev. 37, 49–52 (1987).

9. The matter of free-riding is discussed further in Chapter 4.

2

A Historical Perspective

While the gray market is for all intents and purposes a 1980s phenomenon, the law in this area has early antecedents. Sporadic outbreaks of gray market commerce led to a handful of cases that continue to influence current cases and issues. Some of those cases, notably *A. Bourjois & Co. v. Katzel*,[1] arose from fact situations that differ markedly from many modern gray market scenarios; nevertheless these early judicial decisions endure as important precedent, and a detailed review is thus required.

EARLY ANTECEDENTS: *APOLLINARIS* TO *PERRY*

The first gray market case to arise was *Apollinaris Co. v. Scherer*,[2] decided by the Southern District of New York in 1886. The *Apollinaris* decision, for the most part lost to history, was founded on legal principles that are deemed dubious today. The plaintiff was the exclusive U.S. and British distributor of mineral water sold under the trademark "HUNYADI JANOS." The owner of the mark (as well as the spring from which the water originated), was Andreas Saxlehner. Saxlehner continued to market his water on the European continent, although his bottles contained a legend warning that importation into the United States and Britain was prohibited.

The defendants had obtained bottled water containing the HUNYADI JANOS mark (and the cautionary legend) from Saxlehner but nevertheless had imported it into the United States, where it was sold in competition with the plaintiff's product. The action was for a preliminary injunction, and it alleged trademark infringement and unfair competition. The court rejected the complaint with the simple but still hotly disputed statement that because "the defendant is selling the genuine water, . . . the trademark is not infringed."[3]

The court's most often cited passage, however, refers to the indivisibility of world trademark rights. The court stated:

> It was not possible by any contract . . . [for Saxlehner] to create a territorial title to the products of his spring; no such title is known to the law of personal property. No analogy can be drawn from the law of patents, because title to this species of property is purely statutory; and it is by force of arbitrary law alone that the title in the incorporeal property can be subdivided into territorial parts.[4]

This passage is a reference to the so-called "universality" theory of trademarks, a doctrine that today has essentially been abandoned. In its place has arisen a "territorial" approach, which permits the severance and division of geographical trademark rights.

The court's terse dismissal of the complainant's theory was understandable considering the state of the law at the time. Because of the "universality" doctrine, the court treated the plaintiff's rights as a creature of its contract with Saxlehner rather than as a species of property that could not be subdivided. This treatment was undoubtedly motivated equally by the fact that the law of trademarks was not yet well-developed. As a lower court, Judge Wallace rejected the plaintiff's invitation to extend the law and create what in essence was a territorial trademark license. Judge Wallace expressed his frustration, referring to the law as "arbitrary," stating that if a property right existed, the plaintiff's "case would be plain." Without a property right that the law would recognize, plaintiff's attempt to enjoin gray market activities depended on the contract alone, and it could not succeed.

Apollinaris has been criticized by modern courts and commentators principally because of the now discredited "universality" theory of trademarks. In fact the court demonstrated an even more fundamental misconception about trademarks in a modern world. While discussing the purposes of trademark laws, the court opined that "[t]he name has no office except to vouch for the genuineness of the thing which it distinguishes from all counterfeits."[5] This statement is no longer true.

Today, trademarks are recognized as having purposes separate and apart from their principal function as source identifiers. Thus, a second recognized purpose of trademarks is to guarantee to consumers that all products containing a single trademark are consistently of equal quality; a third purpose is to represent the goodwill of a company. Either of these latter two purposes could well justify a prohibition of some gray market trade. But without these twentieth-century concepts, it is slightly unfair to criticize the *Apollinaris* court for its decision.

Indeed, and in spite of the opinion's shortcomings, Judge Wallace was actually quite prescient not only about the injuries that gray market sales can cause authorized dealers but also about the various theories that eventually would be employed to combat the gray market. For instance, Judge Wallace's opinion demonstrates recognition of the free rider concept, indicating that plaintiff was injured because it would have difficulty "hold[ing] out the inducements it formerly could to the agents it has selected to introduce the article to the patronage of the public."[6] But, in the absence of a property right, that injury alone was deemed insufficient to maintain a trademark action.

The court also rejected any inference that defendants had acted in a "dishonest or perfidious" manner: "If the defendant is legally justified in buying where he can and selling as he chooses, it is not material whether he is actuated by a desire to annoy the complainant or to promote his own pecuniary interests."[7] But the court did caution against fraudulent inducements by the defendant, and it did invite a suit against Saxlehner if guilty knowledge of the defendant's intentions existed. The court, however, stated that, absent a false representation, the defendant's mere knowledge of Saxlehner's covenant with the plaintiffs was insufficient to impose on the defendant a duty to abide by the covenant. The contract between plaintiff and Saxlehner therefore would not render the defendant's title imperfect.

The question of title is one that shall recur, as will questions of free-riding, private remedies against diverters, and the development of trademark licensing. But the eventual demise of the "universality" theory was to have the greatest effect on the viability of *Apollinaris* as a foundation for gray market law. Before considering that demise, a brief discussion of two other early gray market cases will demonstrate that the courts of that era were generally unconcerned with allegations of damage from gray market sales.

Russia Cement Co. v. Frauehnar[8] was a case decided by the Second Circuit Court of Appeals, and it addressed issues raised by the importation and sale of gray market glue. The plaintiffs argued that the product they sold in the United States was superior to the product sold in Europe and imported by the defendants. The complaint focused on potential harm to consumers, alleging "a gross fraud on the public." The court, however, was unmoved by such potential injury because the goods were genuine, that is, manufactured by the plaintiff/trademark owner.

> If the public gets an inferior quality of glue when it purchases that [of] defendants it is because the [plaintiff] has seen fit to sell such glue under the same tradename as it has applied to the superior article, and has chosen to reap the profit from the sale to the public of two qualities or grades of the same article under the same tradename.[9]

Absent some other fraud by the defendants, their sale of the trademarked article was not actionable.

Similarly, in *Fred Gretsch Mfg. Co. v. Schoening*,[10] the same court refused to enjoin the sale of gray market violin strings under the trademark "ETERNELLE."[11] Unlike the previous two cases, the *Gretsch* case was brought under Section 27 of the recently enacted Trademark Act of 1905, a statute that prohibited the importation and sale of "merchandise which shall copy or simulate the name of any domestic . . . manufacturer or trader . . . or which shall copy or simulate a trademark registered in accordance with the provisions of this act."[12] The court maintained consistency with its earlier decisions and rationales and refused to hold that the new statute extended any new rights to trademark owners. "The obvious purpose," wrote the court, "is to protect the public and to prevent any one from importing goods identified by their registered trademark which are not genuine."[13] The act therefore did not bar gray market sales.

The demise of *Apollinaris* and the cases that followed it occurred in conjunction with Justice Oliver Wendell Holmes' decision in *Bourjois*. The facts of that case bear some similarities to the facts of *Apollinaris*, but there are some differences. Both cases involved unintended goods obtained because price differentials made their importation and sale lucrative. Significantly, however, and perhaps because of the decisions in the earlier cases, the plaintiff in *Bourjois* had expressly purchased more than just a contract right from the foreign trademark owner. Indeed, the contract between those two entities expressly provided for the sale of "the entire business then and theretofore carried on by [the foreign trademark owner], viz. the entire good will of said business in the United States, and any and all trademarks, tradenames, and trademark rights relating thereto in the United States. . . . "[14]

The two lower courts to decide the case had disagreed over whether issuance of a preliminary injunction was proper. The goods in question were face powder manufactured in France and bearing the trademark "JAVA." The district court found that the differences between the parties' products were slight, but nevertheless enjoined the gray market sales. The court held that neither proof of fraud on the part of the gray market seller nor lost sales by the plaintiff were prerequisites to infringement. "This is but another way of saying that, where a trademark is used in connection with the business of a merchant, and the product sells on the strength of the trademark, and because it is associated in the public mind with the plaintiff's product, such a trademark is entitled to the strongest protection."[15] That statement is the first evidence that the judiciary was, by 1920, prepared to protect a trademark owner's interest in goodwill and that the mark was more than a mere indicator of the product's source.

The court pointed to the plaintiff's investment of a large sum of money for the acquisition of the trademark and its accompanying rights and its expenditure of large sums to advertise and publicize its product. "If, now, the [gray market powder] can lawfully be permitted to compete with plaintiff's [product], it can be readily seen that plaintiff's business may be destroyed, and, in any event, impaired."[16] In his decision, Judge Mayer expressed concern not only with the plaintiff's investment, but also with the incentive U.S. businesses would have to invest in foreign trademarked goods and promote them in the United States. The district court distinguished *Fred Gretsch* (and implicitly *Apollinaris* as well) by finding that the original owner of the marks in *Bourjois* had purchased broad property rights, while the previous cases had involved more limited transactions. The real difference, of course, was that the *Bourjois* court was willing to permit the trademark owner to divide its trademark; the *Apollinaris* court had refused to grant such permission.

The court of appeals rejected the district courts' reasoning. Relying on the strength of its earlier decisions, the court determined that genuine goods cannot infringe even a registered trademark. Judge Hough, however, dissented from the court's opinion, asserting that the decision grants insufficient protection to plaintiff's business and investment. He indicated that at the time it was "not yet settled whether a trademark is to be primarily regarded as protecting the trademark owner's business . . . or protecting the public from imitations."[17] Judge Hough states that while he leaned toward the former purpose, the court leaned too far toward the latter. The defendant's product, he wrote, "has become an infringement because the business of dealing in that article within the United States is the plaintiff's business."[18]

Like Judge Hough, Justice Holmes, writing for a unanimous Supreme Court, favored the more expansive rationale for trademarks. Holmes began by observing that "[a]fter the sale [of their U.S. business to plaintiff] the French manufacturers could not have come to the United States and have used their old marks in competition with the plaintiff."[19] In spite of the fact that the defendants were not in conspiracy with the original owners to violate the plaintiff's rights, he ruled that an injunction was proper.

> [T]he vendors could not convey their goods free from the restriction to which the vendors were subject. Ownership of the goods does not carry the right to sell them with a specific mark. It does not carry the right to sell them at all in a given place. . . . It is said that the trade mark here is that of the French house and truly indicates the origin of the goods. But that is not accurate. It is the trade mark of the plaintiff only in the United States and indicates in law, and, it is found, by public understanding, that the goods come from the plaintiff although not made by it.[20]

Justice Holmes characteristically paints with broad strokes, and several observations can be made about his terse opinion in the case. First, the principle of the "universality" of trademarks is clearly rejected, because the United States courts will treat the U.S. rights as separate from the foreign trademark. Implicit in this separation is the notion that trademark rights are a species of property, which can be bought, sold, licensed and protected in much the same way as patents. Yet Justice Holmes feels the need to rely on contract law as well, holding that "the [foreign manufacturers] could not convey their goods free from the restriction to which the vendors were subject."[21]

The second principle of Holmes' opinion is that the trademark in question served a function beyond that of mere source identifier, that it represented broader concepts of business goodwill. But it is equally important to observe that Holmes was not necessarily prepared to extend this purpose (and thus a complete prohibition of all gray market sales) to all trademarks. That is evident from his emphasis on the foreign manufacturer's sale of the goodwill of its U.S. operations, and the significance of its investment in building that goodwill. The case is thus arguably distinguishable from *Apollinaris* and the cases that follow its reasoning, but that argument has little importance today.

Another distinction that might be drawn from Justice Holmes' opinion, and not dependent upon an expansive interpretation of trademark law, is that the plaintiff in *Bourjois* had gained independent consumer recognition as the sole source (in the United States) of JAVA powder. Justice Holmes emphasized the fact that the plaintiffs repackaged the goods and clearly indicated on its packaging that the goods, although not made by a foreign company, "come from the plaintiff." While the record is silent about whether consumers were actually aware of this, assuming that such recognition in fact existed, a new and independent trademark right (based on source identification) might well arise.

Without regard to the precise interpretation one places on *Bourjois*, the structure of the transaction between the foreign manufacturer and the U.S. trademark owner presents an important factual distinction between *Bourjois* and many modern gray market cases. The plaintiffs in *Bourjois* had evidently purchased their business and its accompanying trademarks during World War I from the Custodian of Alien Property. Many United States citizens had made similar purchases. Some members of the court, and perhaps even Holmes, may have been motivated by this fact and by the perceived need to protect an investment in property purchased under the auspices of the federal government. Regardless of this surmise, it is nevertheless clear that whatever its peculiar facts and whatever interpretation one gives it, *Bourjois* is now considered the starting point for analysis of trademark infringement actions brought against gray market sellers.

Between the time of the court of appeals' decision and the Supreme Court's reversal, however, Congress enacted Section 526 of the Tariff Act of 1922. That statute was intended to undo the court of appeals' decision, and give the U.S. purchaser of trademarks and goodwill a statutory right to exclude all gray market imports of its product. Justice Holmes' opinion made no reference to the statute, a fact that might be deemed unfortunate. Nevertheless, the precise meaning of Section 526 and the obligation of the Customs Service to enforce it in all cases became the subject of extensive litigation in the 1950s and the mid-1980s. These topics are addressed elsewhere in this text.

Two cases closely following *Bourjois* assist in understanding and interpreting the thrust and impact of that decision. In *Prestonettes Inc. v. Coty*,[22] the Supreme Court refused to extend *Bourjois* to situations in which a seller of genuine trademarked goods repacked the goods, affixed new and different labels to them, but described the goods as having been manufactured by a (specific) foreign seller.[23] Such a right to describe one's goods, said the Court, accrues "by virtue of... ownership,"[24] and exists so long as the public is not deceived. Whether *Prestonettes* is properly viewed as a retreat from *Bourjois*, or whether it is truly distinguishable on the basis of its facts, is an issue that has become moot with time.

Indeed, the second case, *Perry v. American Hecolite Denture Corp.*,[25] finds fault with both *Bourjois* and *Prestonettes* for not developing further the concept of independent consumer recognition. In that case, the Eighth Circuit was left to rely on a line of British cases that address that issue, suggesting that "the inquiry be made [into] what, if anything, there was to identify the [plaintiff] with the articles dealt in by him which was used to induce the purchaser to buy them."[26] These cases, said the court, all reached the conclusion that the plaintiffs "sold entirely on the reputation of the [foreign] makers of the goods . . . ,"[27] and that therefore there was no legal protection.

The Eighth Circuit nevertheless found that the necessary recognition existed in the case before it. The plaintiff in *Perry* had

> imported, advertised, demonstrated, . . . processed and put up in . . . distinctive little green boxes, vouched for and replaced [the product] whenever complained against and given the name with the better sound, "Hecolite" [as opposed to the original "Hekolith"], became completely identified in the public mind . . . though it was not the maker nor claimed to be.... It also exercised selection in putting out the [product] . . . and, in addition, it processed the [product].[28]

Based upon these findings, the court ruling stated that not only were the plaintiff's goods recognized by the public as coming from it, but also that the plaintiff's product was superior to that of the gray market seller.[29] The court thus granted plaintiff an accounting to determine the extent of the damages suffered by it as a result of the defendant's gray market activities.

The decision in *Perry* is startlingly similar to that of some 1980s gray market cases, but *Perry* represents the end of the first era of gray market litigation. The Great Depression, World War II, and the rise of antitrust would intervene in the development of gray market trademark principles. Following a brief discussion of these intervening years, the text will return to the question of trademarks and the gray market.

THE AGE OF ANTITRUST: *GUERLAIN* AND THE CUSTOMS SERVICE

As previously demonstrated, Judge Wallace's opinion in *Apollinaris* displayed an uncanny sense of the real issues involved in (but not the right answers to) gray market problems. In response to a suggestion that the plaintiff's contract restrained trade, Judge Wallace wrote that

it is not apparent how the transfer of a part of [Saxlehner's] exclusive right to vend the water by which a territorial division in its enjoyment was created, can be deemed obnoxious to any principle of public policy as tending to create a monopoly or an unlawful restraint of trade.[30]

Nearly seventy years later, the Justice Department would bring precisely such a set of challenges. The complaints named three exclusive U.S. distributors/U.S. trademark owners of high-priced perfumes and colognes, joining them with the foreign manufacturers of their products. The government claimed that this "single international enterprise" monopolized the trade in these products by attempting to exclude gray market imports. District Judge Edelstein, in detailed findings of fact, demonstrated "beyond any gnawing doubt" that "reality" dictated the conclusion that such an enterprise existed.[31]

Judge Edelstein next turned to questions raised by sec. 526 of the Tariff Act and the Supreme Court's decision in *Bourjois*. Judge Edelstein viewed the statute as integrally related to the *Bourjois* decision, which he then determined was factually distinct from the situations facing the court in *Guerlain*. The U.S. corporations in *Guerlain*, rather than emphasizing to consumers that they were the source of GUERLAIN products, traded principally upon the reputation of their foreign suppliers/manufacturers and did nothing to distinguish themselves in the eyes of consumers.

Judge Edelstein was unmotivated by arguments that the inability to exclude gray market trade might injure the defendants' goodwill and thus provide grounds for legal redress. His opinion recites the traditional free rider theory, stating that

> [t]he argument is one for the protection of advertising expenditures and expected profits not necessarily related to good will. . . . The exclusive right to sell in the American market on the part of an international concern exploiting world markets is not an element of good will except so far as it may be made so artificially by import prohibitions.[32]

The opinion then recites verbiage reminiscent of *Apollinaris* about the impossibility of consumer deception or inferior products and states that a gray market seller is neither a " 'pirate' [n]or a 'cheat'." Judge Edelstein is even skeptical about the defendants' motives, stating that gray market activities "bear fruit, in some measure, . . . for the international enterprise reaps some benefit from all sales."[33]

Judge Edelstein's instincts may have been sound, and his distinction between *Bourjois* and *Guerlain* cogent, but his economics was shaky. While the foreign manufacturer does benefit from all sales, it must be recognized that all sellers are not alike and that the manufacturer might have good reason to prefer one over another. As stated in Chapter 1, in the typical gray market case, the foreign manufacturer might prefer a distributor because that distributor promotes or services the product. But another reason might be a desire to unreasonably restrict competition and charge higher-than-normal prices. Judge Edelstein determined that the true motivation for the defendants' conduct rested with the latter objective. He thus devoted the remainder of his opinion to antitrust law, the subject which he was convinced lay at the heart of the case.

The decision in *Guerlain* is principally known for its definition (or misdefinition) of the relevant market. The landmark *Cellophane*[34] opinion was less than a few years old. That case had involved the government's challenge to E.I. DuPont de Nemours & Co., and it alleged monopolization of the trade in the famous wrapping material. The Supreme Court had ruled, five to four, that cellophane existed in a "relevant market" that included other flexible wrapping materials.

The court held that the existence of these "substitutes" for cellophane (termed a "cross-elasticity of demand") inhibited DuPont from acting as a monopolist would, thus negating any inference of monopoly. In support of its "market definition," the majority compared the price, quality, and end uses of cellophane to those of the other products and found "reasonable interchangeability." The question of the appropriate standard for market definition was the subject of a pointed dissenting opinion by Justice William O. Douglas. It was, and still is, a highly difficult matter in virtually all antitrust cases.

To Judge Edelstein, deciding a difficult case of first impression and utilizing a relatively new and complex legal standard, the questions were daunting. After dutifully reviewing the DuPont standard and Brandeis' admonition that one must be guided principally by the facts and the record, he stated:

> This evidence supports the conclusion that the most important element in the appeal of a perfume is a highly exploited trademark. There seems to be agreement that no quality perfume can be successfully marketed without a famous name. It would appear that, to a highly significant degree, it is the name that is bought rather than the perfume itself. This fact gives the market a rigidity not found in the cellophane case. . . . *The kind of cross-elasticity discussed by the Supreme Court in the cellophane case does not exist for perfumes bearing the names and trademarks of the defendants. Objectively, the products may be more than reasonably interchangeable with others. But the lack of objectivity in consumer demand [for perfume] impairs the basis of interchangeability and negates a finding of cross-elasticity.*[35] [emphasis added]

This author does not wish to quibble with those who assert that Judge Edelstein misread the relevant market. That is an argument most often held on the selling floors of major department stores. But it is submitted that the general concern about antitrust as it applies to the gray market is important, and it will be further considered in Chapter 4.

A year and one-half later, the Justice Department moved in the Supreme Court to vacate the judgments in the *Guerlain* litigation and to have the cases dismissed by the district court. The Supreme Court granted the motion without opinion, but Judge Edelstein authored a bitter, two-page decision. The court referred to the recent resolution of a policy dispute within the Executive Branch about the enforcement of sec. 526 of the Tariff Act.

> There is certainly no doubt that the attempt to resolve this issue in antitrust litigation was clumsy, particularly in view of the fact that the government was, through the Collector of Customs, allowing the exclusion that it claimed, through the Antitrust Division to be illegal. Further, there is certainly no doubt that this Court suggested the inappropriateness of this litigation. . . . There is considerable doubt that anything new transpired to cause the singular and abrupt change of heart during the pendency of the appeals. . . . One may be forgiven a degree of perplexity in the circumstances.[36]

Judge Edelstein then dismissed the complaints with prejudice, noting that the defendants will thus be denied their right to appeal, concluding that that is "an opportunity they [were] eager to take advantage of."[37]

The Justice Department had promised a legislative resolution of the sec. 526 issue, but none was forthcoming. The Customs Service amended its regulation later that year so that it extended beyond the limited facts of *Bourjois*, to situations such as those presented in the *Guerlain* litigation. Customs, however, continued selectively to enforce the statute, in some cases in express contradiction to the (new) regulation. This decision was motivated in large part by continued concerns about antitrust. Yet subsequent developments in antitrust and trademark law, as well as in the political arena, have caused the Customs Service recently to relitigate and ultimately to redraft its regulations. These developments in Customs law are treated in depth in Chapter 5.

THE TRADEMARK CONTROVERSY REVISITED: *BHMC* AND *OSAWA*

For reasons that are not fully understood, the gray market controversy lay essentially dormant throughout the 1960s and 1970s. Perhaps the cause was the general state of international trade, or perhaps it was a reaction to the confusion engendered by *Guerlain*. Trademark owners were certainly justified in fearing antitrust prosecution, an attitude which, throughout that time, pervaded large segments of American business. By the end of the 1970s, the vigorous prosecution of antitrust claims and the strict approach to antitrust created by the Warren Court had clearly begun to wane, and a new spate of gray market litigation soon followed.

The paucity of suits to combat gray market sales was, however, not without effect. Indeed, in the 1980s, when the perfume industry again decided to pursue its claim against the Customs Service under sec. 526 to help fight gray market importation, the District Court in Florida in *Parfums Stern v. U.S.*,[38] denied relief on the grounds, inter alia, that the practice of importation without complaint to Customs had gone on too long for the industry to complain.[39] As already stated, this was not the last attempt to use the Tariff Act to fight gray market sales. However, because of a contemporaneous proceeding in federal court in New York, the focus of gray market litigation shifted away from the Tariff Act and back to strict trademark issues.[40]

The names and corporate affiliations involved in that litigation present a tangled web of transactions and interlocking ownership but are not necessarily atypical of multinational enterprise today. Bell & Howell: Mamiya Company (hereinafter referred to as "BHMC") was a Delaware Corporation at one time owned jointly by Bell & Howell Co. and (through several of its subsidiaries) J. Osawa & Co., Ltd. The latter is a Japanese corporation that serves as the exclusive worldwide distributor of MAMIYA cameras. In 1979 Bell & Howell decided to withdraw from the consumer photography business; it thus transferred its interest in BHMC, by then incorporated in Delaware, to the other partners, who, through yet another series of transactions, created Osawa & Co. (USA) Inc., which owned all the stock of BHMC.

There was substantial interlock of both ownership and control between Osawa (Japan) and Mamiya Camera Co., the manufacturer. Both companies also exerted substantial control over Osawa (USA). Osawa (Japan) owned 93 percent of the stock; the remaining 7 percent was owned by Mamiya. The directors of Osawa (Japan) and Mamiya sat on the board of Osawa (USA), but the latter had some independent directors and separate officers and employees. Shortly after the start of the litigation, yet another corporate transaction took place, changing BHMC's name to Osawa & Co. The action thus proceeded under the name of the original plaintiff, and the corporate affiliations were to become important.

Pursuant to oral agreement, BHMC was the exclusive distributor of MAMIYA cameras in the United States. But, as was to become very important, BHMC had also come to own the U.S. trademark rights, a fact registered in the Patent and Trademark Office in Washington and, evidently, with Customs as well. Whether through negligence or intentional selective enforcement of sec. 526 by Customs, large quantities of gray market cameras were being offered for sale in the United States.

In 1981, Masel Supply Corp. purchased in Hong Kong a large supply of MAMIYA cameras and imported them into the United States, where it offered them for sale to (unauthorized) distributors. BHMC obtained a temporary restraining order against their sale, and a hearing was held before Judge Neaher of the Southern District of New York to determine whether a preliminary injunction was proper. The action, brought under the Lanham (Trademark) Act, alleged infringement and unfair competition.

Judge Neaher conceded at the outset of his opinion that there were "only a few . . . landmarks." He referred to *Bourjois* and *Guerlain* and observed that those cases have resulted in a broad divergence of opinion about the legal status of gray market imports. Judge Neaher then set forth the defendant's principal arguments that (1) the rule of *Bourjois* did not apply because of BHMC's corporate interrelationship with the foreign manufacturer, and that (2) an injunction against gray market sales would amount to a violation of the antitrust laws. The plaintiff, of course, took issue with both these arguments, asserting that it was an independent entity entitled to enjoin the sale of confusingly similar goods without fear of antitrust reproach. The plaintiff argued that, like the plaintiff in *Bourjois*, it expended efforts to advertise, warrant, and support sales of MAMIYA cameras, while the defendant's efforts in this regard were essentially nil. Based upon this argument, BHMC contended that it suffered trademark injury because of the defendant's activities.

Judge Neaher granted the injunction. He ruled, essentially without regard to the defendant's activities, that a likelihood of confusion existed between the plaintiff's goods and those of the defendant. The court's analysis began with a summary of general principles of trademark law, focusing on the distinction between the source, quality, and goodwill functions of trademarks. Reviewing some of the applicable precedent, Judge Neaher's opinion concluded that the territoriality principle established in *Bourjois* "readily supports the existence of separate goodwills pertaining to the same trademark."[41]

Thus, according to the decision, if BHMC could be deemed the "owner" of the U.S. trademark in MAMIYA cameras, it was automatically entitled to an injunction to protect the goodwill it had acquired in the name. Judge Neaher thus spent the bulk of his opinion addressing the question of whether BHMC can be deemed an "owner" of trademark rights. He cited a line of cases distinguishing between an ordinary distributor, deemed a mere agent, and an exclusive distributor who has purchased the goods and their accompanying trademark rights. The latter, Judge Neaher stated, is deemed a "special" owner, entitled to register the mark under the trademark statute.

In reviewing the question of ownership and the concomitant right to an injunction, the court considered many of the cases (and events) discussed earlier in this chapter, concluding that *Bourjois* must be read as establishing broad "ownership" rights for the assignee of a foreign manufacturer's U.S. trademark. The rule of *Bourjois*, he stated, was not narrowed, either by the enactment and amendment of sec. 526 or by the decision in *Guerlain*. Indeed, with regard to that latter case, Judge Neaher stated, "[T]here are obvious and substantial flaws in the [*Guerlain*] court's reasoning under sec. 2 in defining the relevant market ... ,"[42] [and] "[u]ndoubtedly, the subsequent vacatur of the *Guerlain* decision undermined its precedential force."[43] It must be observed, however, that regardless of whether Judge Edelstein's conclusions about market definition were correct, Judge Neaher's opinion omitted any detailed consideration of Masel's antitrust claims, again an issue considered in Chapter 4.

Judge Neaher next concluded that certain exceptions to enforcement contained in the Customs Service's regulations on sec. 526 were irrelevant to the case at bar. These exceptions, detailed further in Chapter 5, also concern questions of "ownership," especially as it pertains to the rights of U.S. registrants who are related to the foreign manufacturer. Judge Neaher ruled that the Customs regulations dealt only with rights separately conferred under the Tariff Act, and thus had no application to the trademark infringement case before him. Echoing the language of *Bourjois*, Judge Neaher held that BHMC, as a bona fide assignee and registrant of the mark (as opposed to a "mere shell"), was "the legitimate and actual owner of the business of selling" MAMIYA cameras in the United States. The registration, says Judge Neaher, " 'indicates in law' that the goods come from the plaintiff."[44]

Relying on the potential problems caused by the presence of plaintiff's warranty (and absence of an equivalent, that is, manufacturer's, warranty by defendant), Judge Neaher ruled for the plaintiffs. Judge Neaher additionally ruled that "[n]o proof supports defendant's contention that the public associates the MAMIYA marks with the Japanese manufacturer, even assuming that such proof could alter the legal consequences of the assignment of the marks to the plaintiff."[45]

In these terse statements, Judge Neaher implies two conclusions, the validity of which will be called into question by the Court of Appeals' subsequent decision in the case. First, Judge Neaher's statement implies that the quality of defendant's goods is irrelevant. Second, Judge Neaher states that the United States registration is conclusive proof on the issue of consumer recognition (and thus injury), an assertion arguably supported by a strict reading of *Bourjois*. Even absent that conclusion, Judge Neaher's opinion places the burden of proof of (no) recognition on the defendant, also a dubious proposition in light of *Bourjois* and *Perry*. Of course, at least some of the equities present in *Bourjois* were absent in the case before him, but Judge Neaher was inclined to ignore the differences and treat the cases as similar. Judge Neaher, finally, is unconcerned with the relationship between the United States and foreign entities, concluding that "[t]he business of the plaintiff in this country is different from that of [the foreign entities]. It is the plaintiff's warranty and assurances of quality that are signified by the MAMIYA marks in this country. Defendant's use of those marks carries with it none of these assurances."[46]

The Second Circuit overturned Judge Neaher's decision.[47] Calling for proof of irreparable injury, Judge Pierce, in a brief and basically unenlightening opinion, held that there was insufficient proof of the likelihood of confusion to warrant issuance of a preliminary injunction. The court stated,

On the basis of the present record, irreparable injury may not be present herein since there appears to be little confusion, if any, as to the origin of the goods and no significant likelihood of damage to BHMC's reputation since thus far it has not been shown that Masel's goods, which have a common manufacture with BHMC's goods, are inferior to those sold by BHMC *and* are injuring BHMC's reputation. Further, it does not appear that the lack of warranties accompanying MAMIYA cameras sold by Masel amounts to irreparable injury, since the consumer can be made aware by, among other things, labels on the camera boxes or notices in advertisements as to whether the cameras are sold with or without warranties.[48]

The court's opinion, unfortunately, is not specific as to why Judge Neaher's conclusions about trademark injury were incorrect. Specifically, the court did not confront the issue of whether its doubts about injury resulted from the lack of proof of actual public recognition or from the fact that the defendant's goods were substantially identical to those of the plaintiff. The court's language (use of the conjunction "and") intimates that for the future both issues should be considered elements of any trademark claim against gray market sellers. In *Bell & Howell: Mamiya* the lack of proof about either was of course sufficient to justify reversal, and the court evidently did feel the need to clarify the point. The case was remanded for trial.

The court went on to state that in order for preliminary relief to be granted the plaintiff must show "that 'a significant number of consumers would be likely to be misled,' "[49] and that BHMC had not shown that the sales by Masel are "likely to cause any consumer to be misled about the product he or she purchases."[50] To make matters even more unclear, the court then stated that "[t]he failure of the district court to discuss, and BHMC to prove, the irreparable injury prong of the preliminary injunction test obviates the need to determine whether a substantial likelihood of trademark infringement . . . has been demonstrated."[51] With this statement, the court defers to a later date substantial consideration of the legality of gray market imports.

The remand (actually a separate case) resulted in a change of name for the plaintiff and two new named defendants, eventually producing a decision by Judge Leval in *Osawa & Co. v. B&H Photo*.[52] At one time, the defendants had been authorized dealers of MAMIYA products, but a dispute arose over gray market policies, and termination (and this suit) resulted. Judge Leval's opinion in the case would become the first considered attempt to apply modern trademark law to the gray market scenario.

Judge Leval made extensive findings of fact about the nature of MAMIYA cameras and the efforts of Osawa (USA) to promote, warrant, and service those cameras. Specifically, Judge Leval found that the goods in question were expensive, highly sophisticated, and in need of point-of-sale support, such as the maintenance of an inventory of auxiliary parts and equipment. The court compared the plaintiff's activities with those of the defendants, who were discount dealers, who had developed a substantial mail order and over-the-counter business in gray market goods.

The court stated that the evidence did not fully explain the price disparity between the plaintiff's and defendants' goods. Nevertheless, the evidence did indicate that Osawa expended considerable sums on product promotion and service that the defendants did not undertake. Significant among the promotional expenditures was advertising that stressed product quality, a type of advertising in which the defendants did not engage. Similarly, the court found that the plaintiff (and its authorized distributors) took greater care than the defendants in the areas of inspection, handling, and storage. Furthermore, the court found that the defendants did not maintain an inventory of "related peripheral gadgets," creating inventory costs not borne by them.

But as was the case before Judge Neaher, the matter of warranties became a principal concern of Judge Leval. Not only did the defendants not provide warranty service, but also such service on gray market goods was often provided to consumers by Osawa. Even though Osawa could have refused the service, Osawa felt compelled to provide it because it wished to prevent widespread dissatisfaction with MAMIYA products. Indeed, the court was moved by testimony that the defendants did not tell their customers that the goods were gray market, and that one defendant, B&H Photo, had been guilty of falsely advertising the existence of a manufacturer's warranty. The court referred to the defendants' conduct as manifesting bad faith and even affirmative misrepresentation.

Having made a detailed comparison of the plaintiff's and defendants' business, Judge Leval turned to the question of irreparable injury. Having made the extensive findings, he was quickly able to rattle off a list of free rider injuries, causing actual monetary injuries such as lost sales and increased warranty expense. Judge Leval made explicit reference to such factors as dealer dissatisfaction, warranty service delays, confusion over rebates, and a resulting consumer mistrust of the MAMIYA mark as causing direct injury to Osawa's reputation. The court was simply unpersuaded that anything the defendants actually did or could do to prevent these injuries was sufficient. In view of the circumstances, the court stated that it was convinced that only an injunction could resolve the problem.

In the portion of his opinion denominated "The Merits," Judge Leval began by noting that it was possible to construe the Court of Appeals decision as "express[ing] skepticism as to whether an infringement action can lie against goods genuinely marked abroad."[53] But Judge Leval predicted that "when the issue presents itself for review, such doubts will be resolved [citations omitted]."[54] In his view, and on the facts presented, the Judge found that the plaintiff had a likelihood of success on the merits and that an injunction was thus proper.

Judge Leval, in scholarly fashion, treats the early cases and the rift between "territoriality" and "universality." He explains with cogent examples how a local entity can acquire goodwill separate and apart from the (worldwide) goodwill possessed by the foreign manufacturer or trademark owner. This independent reputation, with both "legal basis [and] / . . . factual significance" is entitled to the protection of the trademark law.

Judge Leval concludes by rectifying confusion in some of the early cases as involving the "exhaustion doctrine," the principle that a (foreign) trademark owner's rights are "exhausted" upon the first sale of the goods and that he thereafter cannot restrict subsequent sale. But this fact did not preclude the possibility that some other entity (i.e., the U.S. trademark owner), could not assert a claim upon the sale in its territory of genuinely marked goods. Of course, that claim had to be grounded in proof of real trademark injury and that in turn required proof of separate local goodwill acquired through the efforts of the local trademark owner.

In view of the expenditures for advertising, and the warranty services provided by Osawa, it was simple for Judge Leval to find that Osawa had developed such independent goodwill. The court highlighted the warranty services, promotional rebates, educational activities, and advertising; and it is thus "not the same trademark either in law or in fact as the MAMIYA trademark at the place of manufacture."[55]

Significantly, Judge Leval refused to narrow the rule of *Bourjois* to its facts, confining it to situations where there is no corporate inter-relationship between foreign manufacturer and U.S. trademark owner. He can "find no basis for this contention either in fact or in logic,"[56] and any attempt to rely on the early cases was deemed erroneous. So too, the defendants' attempt to rely on the Customs regulation which would deny an exclusion order to Osawa was deemed irrelevant to the action for infringement. The court made passing reference to the "curious history of perfume antitrust actions,"[57] stating that it was in general agreement with Judge Neaher's disposal of that case. Judge Leval did, however, credit the possibility that antitrust claims could exist but does not feel called upon to consider them on the motion before him. Before any appeal could be taken, the defendants agreed to cease dealing in gray market MAMIYA cameras, and shortly thereafter, the parties settled their controversy.

Judge Leval's consideration of the issues presented by the gray market is illuminating, but it does not answer all questions. The goods involved in *Osawa* were complex products, requiring high levels of product service and promotion. But a large segment of the gray market involves simpler goods, such as clothing, batteries, toys and, of course, perfume. And not every U.S. trademark owner can boast the careful and extensive marketing efforts of Osawa; indeed, few products require it. And what about the antitrust considerations, and the right to force Customs to make and enforce selective regulations.[58] These are issues that remain unanswered.

In any event, the decision in *Osawa* was clearly a step forward in the legal analysis of gray market trade. The issues were defined, and the older cases put in perspective. But gray market litigation would continue with a fury on a number of fronts. In many respects, the hardest issues were yet to be decided.

NOTES

1. 260 U.S. 689 (1923), *rev'g*, 275 F. 539 (2d Cir. 1921), *rev'g*, 274 F. 856 (S.D.N.Y. 1920).

2. 27 F. 18 (S.D.N.Y. 1886).

3. Id. at 20.

4. Id. at 21.

5. Id. at 20.

6. Id.

7. Id. at 22.

8. 133 F. 518 (2d Cir. 1904). cert. denied 196 U.S. 640 (1905).

9. Id. at 520.

10. 238 F. 780 (2d Cir. 1916).

11. The violin strings were manufactured by C.A. Mueller in Germany. The defendant Schoening had the exclusive agency for the sale of Mueller's strings in the United States. Gretsch bought the genuine strings in Germany and imported them to the United States.

12. Id. at 781.

13. Id. at 782.

14. *A. Bourjois & Co., Inc. v. Katzel,* 274 F. at 857.

15. Id. at 859.

16. Id.

17. 275 F. at 543.

18. Id. at 544.

19. 260 U.S. at 691.

20. Id. at 692.

21. Id.

22. 264 U.S. 359 (1924).

23. Prestonettes, a New York corporation, bought toilet powders and perfumes from Coty, a citizen of France. After repackaging the genuine perfume, Prestonettes relabeled the bottles to state that the contents are Coty's and that they have merely been rebottled in New York. The same was true for the powders. Prestonettes stated clearly on the label that the product was independently compounded from Coty's product.

24. Id. at 368.

25. 78 F.2d 556 (8th Cir. 1935).

26. Id. at 560.

27. Id. at 561.

28. Id.

29. The product in question, originally named "Hekolith," was produced by a German corporation, Heko-Werk Chemische Fabrik A-G. "Hekolith" applied to the plastic material manufactured for making prostheses and artificial dentures for false teeth. While the American Hecolite Corporation had exclusive rights to the sale of this product in the United States, Daniel Perry had imported Hekolith directly from Germany and sold it at a lower price. Perry contended that the Hecolite Corporation sold its product based on the reputation of the German chemists, hence denying the fact that the name "Hecolite" was associated with the Hecolite Corporation and permitting him to sell the identical product.

30. 27 F. at 20.

31. 155 F.Supp. 77 (S.D.N.Y. 1957), *vacated and remanded*, 358 U.S. 915 (1958), *action dismissed*, 172 F.Supp. 107 (S.D.N.Y. 1959). For further discussion and analysis of this case, see chapters 4 and 5, infra.

32. 155 F.Supp. at 82.

33. Id.

34. *United States v. E.I. DuPont de Nemours & Co.*, 351 U.S. 377 (1956). For a detailed discussion, see L. Sullivan, *Handbook of the Law of Antitrust*, 52–58 (1977).

35. 155 F.Supp. at 84–85.

36. 172 F.Supp. at 107–108.

37. Id. at 108.

38. 575 F.Supp. 416 (S.D.Fla. 1983).

39. Parfums Stern, Inc. had exclusive rights to distribute Oscar de la Renta products in the United States. The court's refusal to place an injunction on the gray market importers was based, in part, on reasons other than that detailed in the text. The court also found that the plaintiff had not established a substantial likelihood of success on the merits. Judge Aronovitz distinguished *Bourjois* on the basis of that case's peculiar facts. He also distinguished *Bell & Howell: Mamiya* (discussed infra) as not involving a "single international enterprise." Finally, in the view of Judge Aronovitz, barring gray market goods would do the public a disservice because the products were of

equal quality and were less expensive than the authorized imports. *Parfums Stern* is discussed and analyzed in detail in Chapter 3, under "The Single International Enterprise Disqualification." infra.

40. *Bell & Howell: Mamiya Co. v. Masel Supply Co.*, 548 F.Supp. 1063 (E.D.N.Y. 1982), reversed and remanded, 719 F.2d 42 (2d Cir. 1983).

41. 548 F.Supp. at 1070.

42. Id. at 1077.

43. Id. at 1074.

44. Id. at 1079.

45. Id.

46. Id.

47. 719 F.2d 42.

48. Id. at 46 [emphasis added].

49. Id. at 47.

50. Id.

51. Id.

52. 589 F.Supp. 1163 (S.D.N.Y. 1984).

53. Id. at 1170.

54. Id.

55. Id. at 1174.

56. Id. at 1175.

57. Id. at 1176.

58. The court stated in a footnote that it might have to ultimately reach that issue, as the defendants sought to implead Customs to reverse its exclusion order and plaintiff had crossclaimed to void those regulations. The issue, however, was not before the court on the motion in question.

3

Trademarks, the Gray Market, and the 1980s

In the six years since Judge Leval's landmark decision in *Osawa*,[1] many lower courts have had an opportunity to consider the legal consequences of gray market importation and sale. Many of the cases and decisions have been unremarkable; yet some reveal certain tendencies and trends in the legal analysis of trademark claims against gray marketers. This chapter examines these cases in an effort to scrutinize the current state of the law as well as to project how future cases might be decided.

Judge Leval defined two overriding issues in gray market cases. The first was the inquiry into local goodwill, necessary to determine whether a particular plaintiff possessed a trademark interest worthy of protection. The second issue, less apparent in Judge Leval's decision, is the requirement that for irreparable injury to occur, the plaintiff must show that its (authorized) goods differ in some way from the gray market counterparts. Thus stated, the Leval approach promised to predominate in gray market cases throughout the 1980s.

That was not to be the case, however. The question of corporate structure and foreign parentage of the U.S. trademark owner has become another important theme in gray market–trademark infringement cases. Several cases, most notably in the Third and Ninth Circuits, have cast doubt on whether Judge Leval's approach will in fact take hold. Before considering the cases and the theory they adopt, the text first explores the evolution and elaboration of the Leval approach to gray market goods.

PROVING LOCAL GOODWILL

Only a few cases since *Osawa* have addressed in significant detail the question of local goodwill. Yet in one pre-*Osawa* case, the issue arose in an unusual and slightly different way. That case, *DEP Corp. v. Interstate Cigar Co., Inc.*,[2] was an action for infringement brought by the exclusive U.S. distributor of "PEARS" soap against a gray market importer of the genuine product. The importer had purchased the soap from a European middleman-diverter at prices below those being offered by the plaintiff.

The manufacturer of the soap, A. & F. Pears Ltd., is a British corporation that had licensed Unilever Export Ltd., another British corporation, to be its exclusive (non-Commonwealth) worldwide distributor. Unilever had subcontracted with DEP, the plaintiff, to distribute PEARS soap in the United States. Pears, Ltd. retained ownership of the PEARS registration in the United States, and DEP's contract with Unilever contained the following paragraph:

> You [DEP] shall not during the continuance of this arrangement or thereafter have or claim any right whatsoever, whether of user or otherwise to any such trade marks, trade names or brands used in connection with [the] Products. . . . In the event of any infringement of any such trade marks, trade names or brands coming to your notice, you shall promptly notify us and shall take at our expense such steps as we may require for their protection.[3]

Based upon that language, the district court summarily dismissed the complaint, asserting that DEP lacked standing to bring a trademark action against a seller of genuine goods. The court of appeals affirmed.

The Second Circuit's opinion in *DEP* began with the observation that the Lanham Act provides that only the "registrant," its legal representatives, predecessors, successors, and assigns can maintain a claim under the Act. The above-quoted paragraph, said the court, negates the possibility that DEP was either an assignee or legal representative of the PEARS mark. Furthermore, said the court, an assignment could not exist without a simultaneous transfer of goodwill and a written instrument to satisfy the Lanham Act's Statute of Frauds.

In reaching its conclusion, the court distinguished a pre-Lanham Act case, which arguably created a right to sue, as well as a case similar to that before the court in which the plaintiff was in privity of contract with the trademark owner. While the distinctions drawn between *DEP* and these cases are tenuous, there seems little point in a detailed review; for apparent reasons, the real issues in most gray market cases lie elsewhere.

While the decision in *DEP* is a lesson to distributors' lawyers about contract negotiation and drafting, it is significant also because of its assertion that a distributor who is not a registrant or assignee has limited rights against a gray market competitor. Thus, unless a distributor acquires goodwill and an assignment of rights in the mark, its sole recourse is to complain to the trademark owner, a remedy that may or may not produce the desired result. DEP acquired no trademark rights and thus could not maintain suit in its name. The court suggests that DEP might have a claim for tortious interference with its contractual relations, but the court below made no findings of fact or conclusions of law about that issue.[4]

In *DEP*, the court conceded that the plaintiff had lost sales at the expense of the defendants and that it therefore "has the greatest interest in bringing an infringement action."[5] But the court stated that that fact "hardly creates standing under the Lanham Act."[6] Thus, without a transfer of property rights there can be no infringement suit. Judge Leval, of course, would soon explain that the transfer of rights must not only meet the proper form, but must have substance as well.

There is another noteworthy aspect of the decision in *DEP*. The court makes a curious reference to "palming off" and actions brought for false designations of origin under sec. 43(a) of the Lanham Act of the Act, where a (nonregistrant) competitor is permitted to sue for infringement. These two causes of action generally involve counterfeit goods, a situation obviously not presented in *DEP*. Thus the court, and perhaps the Congress, seem inclined to draw distinctions between counterfeit goods and gray market goods. Indeed, in a footnote, the court notes that it doubts whether genuine goods can infringe a trademark.

The court states that in light of its conclusions about standing, it was unnecessary to decide that issue. That disclaimer notwithstanding, the decision in *DEP* can only be read as raising questions about trademark rights in the gray market context. There are statutory distinctions between sec. 43(a) (false designations of origin) and sec. 32 (infringement), and perhaps the judiciary has been too quick to equate the source identifying function of trademarks with the quality/goodwill function. The former, of course, suffers injury only from counterfeit goods (and not from gray market goods), while the latter interest can be damaged by at least some gray market goods.[7]

It is generally assumed for purposes of this text that whatever the statutory differences between Trademark Act sec. 43(a) and 32, the similarities outweigh the differences. This assumption is proven by the decisions in the vast majority of gray market cases, where both causes of action are alleged and the case is decided on some fundamental point shared by both sections. There are a few judges who expressed different approaches as to the applicability of the individual sections; these judges' opinions are highlighted as they are discussed later in the text.

Whether the Second Circuit in *DEP* might have been inclined, in a proper case, to draw greater distinction between gray market goods and counterfeit goods remains to some extent an open question. But Judge Leval's decision in *Osawa* in part focussed the inquiry elsewhere, and a few cases have followed up on his conclusions about the need for local goodwill. Foremost among these cases was the District Court for New Jersey's decision in *Weil Ceramics v. Dash* (ultimately reversed), and the Third Circuit's subsequent decision in *Premier Dental Products Co. v. Darby Dental Supply, Inc.*[8]

The initial decision in *Weil Ceramics v. Dash*[9] was a decision of Judge Debevoise of the District of New Jersey. The plaintiff, exclusive distributor of LLADRO porcelain figurines in the United States, acquired rights to the LLADRO mark in 1966. At the time, Weil was an independent concern, neither affiliated with nor controlled by the foreign manufacturer and distributor of LLADRO products. After the death of the founder of Weil, and through a complex and sometimes convoluted series of transactions not dissimilar to those presented in *Osawa*, the foreign manufacturer owned all of the stock in Weil. The defendant gray market importers argued that Weil possessed no separate and independent goodwill, and thus could not maintain an action for infringement because "the goodwill behind the LLADRO mark in the United States is identical to the goodwill behind the LLADRO mark in Spain."[10]

Judge Debevoise reviewed the decisions in *Bell & Howell*, *Osawa*, and *Parfums Stern* in detail and then applied the exhaustion doctrine to demonstrate the role of goodwill analysis. Judge Debevoise concluded,

> Based upon my reading of [the] cases, I conclude that the exhaustion doctrine applies when the United States markholder is re-

lated to the foreign markholder and/or manufacturer. However, I also conclude that the exhaustion doctrine does not apply when the United States markholder has developed a 'separate, factually distinct goodwill' in its product. . . . The difference in the goodwill is determined by ascertaining the person who stands behind the product and insures its quality in the United States.[11]

That was the case in *Osawa*, Judge Debevoise wrote, notwithstanding the corporate interrelationship among manufacturer, worldwide distributor, and U.S. markholder. *Parfums Stern*, on the other hand, represented a case at the other extreme, where no separate goodwill existed.[12]

Judge Debevoise offered high praise to Judge Leval's reasoning and seemed to follow it closely in deciding the case before him. He rejected the argument that corporate affiliation and control was determinative of the goodwill question. Indeed he seems to imply that that factor is irrelevant. "What must be determined," [he wrote,] "is whether the United States markholder has developed the goodwill of the product in the United States or whether it has merely relied upon the mark's international goodwill."[13]

Reviewing the evidence before him, Judge Debevoise concluded that separate goodwill had been established. Weil had been the original U.S. importer of LLADRO figurines and had owned the trademark for many years. Weil selects the retailers authorized to sell LLADRO and conducts inspections (of varying degrees) of all products it sells. Finally, Weil warrants each piece against breakage, replacing pieces that were cracked or damaged before being sold. Of course, Weil devotes substantial resources to advertising, produces catalogs, and attends trade shows to promote LLADRO products.

The defendants argued that notwithstanding these efforts, Weil had not demonstrated separate goodwill. They asserted that because Weil does not deal directly with consumers, it cannot claim recognition independent of its parent company. Furthermore, because Weil conducts all its business through independent retailers, "ultimate purchaser[s] would not look to Weil as the party responsible for the quality of merchandise manufactured by [Lladro]."[14]

The court rejected the argument as "facile" and "specious." The court viewed Dash's assertions as amounting to a claim that consumers could not "accurately name" Weil as the source of goods, an irrelevant fact if the public perceives that a single, albeit unknown, entity stands behind the goods. In the eyes of Judge Debevoise, Weil was that entity and was thus entitled to protection.

The facts in *Weil* bear out the notion that the U.S. trademark owner is in fact the entity that stands behind the goods, but that fact alone misses the point of trademark law. The question is not whether Weil in fact stands behind the goods, just as it is not whether consumers know Weil's name. Under the Leval approach, the question should be whether *consumers perceive* that the entity standing behind LLADRO products is separate from the international enterprise that is responsible for their foreign manufacture. Only then could Weil have independent goodwill, and only then could it complain about injury to its U.S. trademark.

On the issue of consumer perceptions, the court made no findings. But the court did find that when consumers have a problem, they normally return the goods to the retailer from whom the goods were bought. The defective piece is then shipped to Weil by the dealer, and Weil credits that dealer's account. These facts support the notion that Weil is truly an unknown entity to consumers; for all they know, the credit might issue from Lladro, or even from the pocket of the retailer with whom they dealt. The court's answer is that "[t]he retailers with whom Weil deals directly are aware that Weil backs the goods,"[15] and that might be enough. But that is not the same as concluding that consumers might be confused as to origin or quality. If they do not know of Weil's existence, how can they claim confusion? On the other hand, dealers cannot claim to be confused as to whether Weil stands behind the goods; either they bought from Weil or they did not. Unfortunately, Judge Debevoise failed to resolve this apparent anomaly in reasoning, but instead found that a likelihood of confusion exists.

Based upon its finding of local goodwill, the court granted Weil's motion and enjoined gray market importation on grounds of trademark infringement.[16] The court rejected the assertion that Dash's goods were identical to Weil's and that Dash took quality control measures at least equal to those of Weil. That aspect of Judge Debevoise's opinion is treated in the next section, where it becomes the subject of a significant dispute at the appellate level.

Premier Dental Products Co. v. Darby is a case not unlike *Perry v. American Hecolite*[17] and is somewhat akin to *Bourjois*.[18] The product involved was a denture material, and the plaintiff, an independent entity, had taken care to acquire the necessary property rights in order to maintain its suit. Indeed, after doing business as an exclusive distributor for ten years, in 1984 the plaintiff acquired all "right, title and interest" in the U.S. trademark "IMPREGUM," recording the assignment with the Trademark Office. The contract between Premier and ESPE, the manufacturer of IMPREGUM, began with this recitation:

> WHEREAS, Premier wishes to obtain title to the registration for "IMPREGUM," including the right to file suit for infringement thereof and ESPE is willing to assign said registration to Premier for that limited purpose. . . . [19]

The agreement then provided that Premier was acquiring not only the trademark and registration but also "the goodwill of the business connected with the use of and symbolized by [IMPREGUM]."[20] Premier's lawyers had obviously read both *DEP* and *Osawa*, and acted accordingly. Shortly thereafter, they sued three gray market importers in federal court, alleging a list of Lanham Act violations.

Darby's principal defense was that the assignment was a sham and that the plaintiff had no real interest in the trademark. Indeed, the assignment recited that it was made for the limited purpose of permitting Premier to sue for infringement in its own name, provided that notice of the suit was given to ESPE. Darby argued further that ESPE retained substantial control over Premier's use of the mark and that ESPE retained the right to demand reassignment on thirty days' notice. Most important, however, Premier exercised no day-to-day quality control over IMPREGUM products. Darby also argued that the district court had found that Premier "had failed to establish that IMPREGUM is associated with [Premier] in the minds of [dentists and dental technicians.]"[21]

The court rejected both arguments. Conceding that the parties' agreement was not dispositive of the issue of ownership of goodwill, the court found that "he who controls the nature and quality of the goods on which the IMPREGUM trademark appears, or whom the public regards as standing behind IMPREGUM, possesses the goodwill in the IMPREGUM trademark."[22] Premier, the exclusive U.S. distributor for ten years, was able to demonstrate substantial investment in promoting IMPREGUM products. That fact led to the district court conclusion that "Premier has come to be . . . 'identified in the trade as the source through which IMPREGUM is obtained' ".[23] In findings reminiscent of *Perry*,[24] the court notes that Premier provided seminars and instruction on the use of its products and that it maintained a toll-free number for those with questions. In the court's eyes, this was enough to establish local goodwill separate from the foreign manufacturer.

The court rejected the argument that the retention of rights by ESPE disqualified Premier from the benefits of trademark ownership.[25] The reversionary right retained by ESPE was deemed irrelevant to Premier's cause of action. The court also declined to examine the details of the day-to-day relationship between manufacturer and distributor, and the question of quality control. Instead, the court took the position that any adverse findings in this area would not disqualify Premier from owning the trademark, and that the issue was thus not material. It was further deemed unimportant that Premier had undertaken its activities and earned its reputation before it took title to the mark. Of course, this latter conclusion belies the need for a formal assignment, and the facts indicate that the transaction was, in any event, directed more toward form than substance.

In order to find local goodwill, the Third Circuit had to resolve a seeming conflict in the district court's findings. As already indicated, at one stage the trial judge found that "consumers" did not associate IMPREGUM with Premier, but, at another stage, that "the trade [identified Premier] as the source through which IMPREGUM is obtained."[26] Rather than remand the case for further findings, the court of appeals interpreted the lower court decision as "conclud[ing] that purchasers of IMPREGUM at all levels understand that it comes from a single source"[27] and that the lower court merely meant that consumers did not know Premier's name. That is a conflict reminiscent of *Weil*, but the Third Circuit seems to have reached a more satisfying resolution in *Premier* because of its finding that the trade recognized the existence of Premier as a source separate from the foreign manufacturer.

The lower court in *Premier* had held that because the defendant's goods were identical to the plaintiff's there was no probability of injury. The Third Circuit, however, seemed to state that that was irrelevant. First, the risk of injury existed because "other 'gray marketers' [might follow] Darby's example,"[28] causing Premier to fall below certain minimums and thus lose its exclusive distribution contract with ESPE. Even if that did not occur, Premier could still be injured:

Purchasers of Premier's IMPREGUM are confident they can obtain the same product, service, and financial guaranties that they have gotten before. The continued availability of IMPREGUM through sources, like Darby, not associated with Premier must inevitably injure Premier's reputation as the exclusive domestic source of IMPREGUM. This would constitute irreparable injury to the value of the mark because consumers would no longer have that same confidence. This is true whether or not the service and financial guaranties are comparable to those offered by Premier. We find this proposition the inevitable corollary of *Bourjois*.[29]

With these two decisions, the Third Circuit seemed to demonstrate a growing hostility to gray market goods, a hostility that goes beyond the balanced reasoning of Judge Leval. "[W]e believe," wrote the court in *Premier*, "that *Bourjois* and Section 526 make it clear that an American distributor's goodwill can be harmed even by the sale of gray market goods that are *identical* to those sold by the distributor."[30] The court thus broke with the Second Circuit, declining to follow the suggestion in *Bell & Howell* that there must be a showing of "inferiority" of the gray market goods. Other courts, however, have relied upon and thus further developed the issue of identity. Those cases are examined in the next section of this chapter.

INFERIORITY VERSUS IDENTITY: INJURY AND THE GRAY MARKET

The Second Circuit's *Bell & Howell* decision expressed doubts about whether gray market goods, by virtue of their character as genuine, could infringe even a U.S. registered trademark. To date, the Second Circuit has yet to provide a definitive answer to this question. But many other courts have considered the issue, and it is without doubt an important aspect of many gray market cases. This section will consider these cases, analyzing their impact and demonstrating the difficulties that gray market trade presents.

In 1924, only a few years after the decision in *Bourjois*, the Supreme Court addressed another case involving the unauthorized sale of genuine trademarked goods. The case was not a gray market case per se, but the decision in *Prestonettes, Inc. v. Coty*[31] has had moderate influence on gray market controversies. The defendants in that case imported, repackaged, and sold genuine perfume and powder in containers bearing labels indicating that the goods involved were genuine Coty products. The defendants sold the perfume in smaller bottles than did Coty, and mixed the powder with a binder so that it could be sold in a compact case. The labels indicated (using Coty's name) that the goods came from the defendants but that they comprised products manufactured abroad by Coty.

The district court had permitted the practice, decreeing that the use of the Coty name must be limited to a legend on the label indicating that the ingredients were Coty products but that Prestonettes was not connected with Coty. The Court of Appeals, fearing that the products involved were delicate, volatile, and easily adulterated, issued a preliminary injunction against any use of the Coty name or trademark, asserting "that the defendant could not put upon the plaintiff the burden of keeping a constant watch"[32] over their quality. In an opinion by Justice Oliver Wendell Holmes, the Supreme Court reversed and reinstated the order of the district court.

There was no doubt that the defendant, having lawfully acquired the goods, could resell them, repackage them, or even change or modify them without legal consequence if it did not mention the trademark of the plaintiff. Rather, the question presented was whether Prestonettes could describe their goods as having originally come from the plaintiff, mentioning plaintiff's name and mark in the process. The Supreme Court ruled that it could indeed do so. Justice Holmes wrote,

> The defendant was exercising the rights of ownership and only telling the truth. . . . [The plaintiff's trademark] does not confer the right to prohibit the use of the word or words. It is not a copyright. . . . A trade mark only gives the right to prohibit the use of it so far as to protect the owner's good will against the sale of another's product as his. . . . When the mark is used in [a] way that does not deceive the public we see no such sanctity in the word as to prevent its being used to tell the truth. It is not taboo.[33] [citations omitted]

Justice Holmes was of course careful to distinguish his opinion in *Bourjois*, a case which he said involved a trademark "indicat[ing] that the goods came from the plaintiff in the United States"[34] Of course, the real key to understanding *Prestonettes* is that the case involved a non-trademark (i.e., descriptive) use of the Coty name, a situation very different from that involved in *Bourjois*. The legend permitted by the district court prescribed that the Coty name be in the same size and style of type as the rest of the legend, so as not to stand out in a way that might deceive purchasers. Then, if the defendant's products were inferior to those of the plaintiff, "the public is adequately informed who [did] the rebottling . . . "[35] In light of that fact, Justice Holmes felt that even if the defendant's product was inferior "it might be a misfortune to the plaintiff, but the plaintiff would have no cause of action."[36]

Some courts, notably the Ninth Circuit in *NEC*,[37] seem to have read *Prestonettes* as limiting the decision in *Bourjois* and creating a right to sell at least certain gray market goods. But most gray market cases involve trademark uses of the mark in question, because the sellers are unwilling to restrict their use of the mark to descriptive phrases. Outright attempts by trademark owners to force "demarking" have met with stiff resistance for obvious reasons. *Prestonettes* is thus of limited precedential value to the proponents of most gray market imports. Historically, however, it was the first case to raise the issue of the right of a seller to describe his goods as coming from another, and thus bears at least some relationship to the continuing gray market controversy.

In part because of the paucity of gray market trademark cases prior to the decision in *Bell & Howell*, most courts never really considered how to deal with the differences between gray market goods and their authorized counterparts. By contrast, courts had great experience dealing with counterfeit goods, where the difference (source) is obviously very great. In the gray market situation, however, the similarities between gray market and authorized goods at first seem greater than the differences. But some cases reveal that upon close inspection, material differences exist.

At a minimum, such differences often dictate a conclusion that gray market trade is injurious to the local mark holder and thus actionable as infringement. The other extreme, however, creates much greater conceptual difficulty. Where it can be proven that gray market goods are for all practical purposes the same as the authorized version, many gray market sellers have argued that no injury to the trademark can occur and that the practice of selling such goods should not be actionable. A handful of courts have had the opportunity to address that subject; these cases form the balance of this section.

Cases in which the differences between gray market and authorized goods are manifest are few in number, but they stand out as a logical starting point for discussion. For instance, in *Selchow & Righter Co. v. Goldex Corp.*,[38] the district court in Florida enjoined importation of Canadian Trivial Pursuit games. When the game first became popular in the United States, plaintiff, the U.S. registrant of the TRIVIAL PURSUIT mark, had difficulty supplying retail outlets with the game. The defendant tried to obtain the Canadian version of the game from Canadian suppliers but was unable to do so because Selchow & Righter held the exclusive U.S. rights. To circumvent this obstacle, the defendant formed a Canadian corporation, purchased a large quantity of Canadian games, and imported them into the United States where they were sold through the mails.

Selchow & Righter sued alleging trademark infringement and received a preliminary injunction. Selchow & Righter's president testified that it suffered injury because Goldex's games do not contain the Selchow & Righter advertising brochure and generated dissatisfaction among Trivial Pursuit distributors in the United States who were unable to obtain the games. But Selchow & Righter's largest complaint stemmed from certain differences between the two versions of the game. Some of the Canadian games sold as TRIVIAL PURSUIT were titled "Sexual Trivia," a topic deemed offensive by Selchow & Righter and not used in its versions of the game.

The court concluded that regardless of the degree of difference between Selchow & Righter's product and that sold by Goldex, trademark infringement existed. Relying on *Osawa*, Judge Paine ruled that the changes made by Selchow & Righter were directed toward promoting and protecting the goodwill in the TRIVIAL PURSUIT mark, and that games manufactured in Canada were barred from importation under the rule of *Bourjois*. The court held that the creator of the game and exclusive distributor in Canada, Horn Abbot, Ltd., had "sold its business and trademarks in this country which relate to TRIVIAL PURSUIT games."[39] The court noted further that Horn Abbot itself was barred from selling in the United States in competition with the plaintiff. The case was thus factually similar to *Bourjois*, justifying the issuance of the injunction.

Another case where different product characteristics motivated the decision was *Original Appalachian Artworks, Inc. v. Granada Electronics, Inc.*[40] That case, a decision of the Second Circuit Court of Appeals, dealt with the importation of another popular toy, the Cabbage Patch Kids doll. The U.S.-intended dolls were manufactured in the United States by Original Appalachian in Georgia and by Coleco

Industries in Connecticut. The Original Appalachian versions are hand-sewn, soft-sculptured dolls, while the Coleco product is molded vinyl. The gray market dolls, manufactured in Spain by Jesmar, S.A., under a territorial license from Original Appalachian, were imported into the United States by the defendant at a time when the goods were in short supply in retail outlets. The words on packages of the Spanish dolls are written principally in Spanish, although the packages contain the "CABBAGE PATCH KIDS" trademark on all panels, as well as "The World of" before the logo. The boxes made no mention of Original Appalachian, except that the bottom of the box contained a copyright notice with Original Appalachian's name.

All Cabbage Patch Kids dolls are sold with "birth certificates" and "adoption papers" to be completed by the "parent," (i.e., the recipient of the doll). The adoption papers are then returned to the manufacturer, who records the adoption in a computer file and sends out a birthday card on the first anniversary of the adoption. Of course, the Spanish version of the dolls contain papers written in Spanish (with Spanish names), to be returned to Jesmar. Original Appalachian and Coleco had been unwilling to honor Jesmar's papers, a fact that the court found resulted in trademark injury to the plaintiffs.

The district court ruled that the birth certificates and adoption papers constituted were "materially different" from those of the English-language dolls. The conclusion was based upon the plaintiff's receipt of letters complaining about deception in the purchase of the Spanish gray market dolls. The court of appeals left that finding undisturbed and granted the injunction against further gray market importation:

> [E]ven though the goods do bear Original Appalachian's trademark and were manufactured under license with [them], they are not "genuine" goods because they differ from the Coleco dolls and were not authorized for sale in the United States.[41]

The court determined that the facts of the case were closest to *Osawa*, stating that the fact that Original Appalachian controlled Jesmar was irrelevant. That of course is the reverse of cases like *Osawa* and *NEC*,[42] where the foreign trademark owner controls the U.S. subsidiary. Granada argued that Original Appalachian cannot be damaged by sales of its own goods and thus could not bar importation of gray market goods. The court rejected that argument, stating that it "has some force where the goods are identical to the domestic goods *and* are intended for sale in the United States"[43] (emphasis added).

The presence of differences in the goods, and thus the lack of identity, distinguished *Bell & Howell* and vitiated Granada's argument. The court viewed *Bell & Howell* as a case that involved only an evidentiary flaw, not as a watershed for proof that identity was dispositive of the injury question. The court also addressed several cases following *Bell & Howell* that actually involved identical goods, drawing from them the second requirement: in order for a defendant to prevail, proof of identity must be accompanied by proof that the goods were "intended for sale in the United States." Among these cases were *DEP*, discussed earlier, *Monte Carlo Shirt, Inc. v. Daewoo Int'l (America) Corp.*,[44] and several cases from the Southern District of New York, *Sasson Jeans, Inc. v. Sasson Jeans, L.A., Inc.*,[45] *Diamond Supply Co. v. Prudential Paper Products Co.*,[46] and *Ballet Makers, Inc. v. United States Shoe Corp.*[47] Of course, in light of the nature of Jesmar's goods, Granada could not prove this element of its defense, and was thus doomed to failure.[48]

As already noted, *DEP* was a case that dealt with standing, but the court, in a footnote, expressed doubts about whether genuine trademarked goods could infringe. *Bell & Howell* preserved the question, and Judge Leval considered it in *Osawa* in the context of cameras, point-of-sale services, and warranties. But the three Southern District cases just mentioned expressly held that the gray market goods in those cases could not infringe. So too, in *Monte Carlo Shirt*, the Ninth Circuit held that the sale of identical goods created no trademark claims.

These four cases are significant, but they do not apply to all gray market scenarios. *Sasson, Ballet Makers,* and *Monte Carlo* all dealt with apparel; and *Diamond Supply* involved stationery. Each is a simple article of commerce, clearly different from sophisticated cameras and arguably different from delicate porcelain figurines. *Monte Carlo,* although decided under California common law, is the leading precedent. The plaintiff was a shirt company that had placed a large order with a foreign supplier. When the documents necessary to clear the shipment through Customs arrived too late for the Christmas season, Monte Carlo rejected the order. Daewoo, the manufacturer, through its U.S. subsidiary, sold the shirts without Monte Carlo's consent to discount retailers, with Monte Carlo labels still attached.

The district court granted Daewoo's motion for summary judgment, and the Ninth Circuit affirmed. The court conceded that there was little established precedent and that "neither [party] has produced persuasive authority pointing either way."[49] The court nevertheless ruled in favor of Daewoo, indicating that the shirts were "genuine," had not been "altered or changed from the date of their manufacture," and that "[t]heir source was Monte Carlo."[50] "[T]he absence of Monte Carlo's authorization of the discount retailers does not alter this [fact],"[51] wrote the court.

> Admittedly the law of trademark has extended well beyond its origins as a remedy for "passing off," but Monte Carlo has not demonstrated that it should reach as far as the facts of this case. Cf. *DEP*, [citation omitted]. The district court was not clearly wrong in granting Daewoo's motion for summary judgment.[52]

The court suggested that perhaps a claim for tortious interference or breach of contract claim might succeed, but, as was the case in *DEP*, those claims were not pursued by Monte Carlo, and thus were not before the Ninth Circuit on appeal.

As already indicated, *Monte Carlo* soon became authority for the proposition that identical goods, albeit sold without authority, could not infringe a trademark. *Sasson* dealt with goods manufactured (but not yet imported) before family discord caused the relationship between various entities in the manufacturing and distribution chain to deteriorate. *Diamond Supply* also dealt with trademarked goods left in the hands of a manufacturer after its relationship with the buyer/trademark owner had terminated. In both cases, the courts relied on the reasoning of *Monte Carlo*, and the fact that the goods being sold were identical to the authorized version.[53]

Of the three Southern District cases, *Ballet Makers* is undoubtedly the most interesting. It concerned goods manufactured by a second licensee of the trademark owner and a complaint brought by the first licensee in an attempt to bar the defendants from carrying out the second license.[54] The court nevertheless treated the case as involving gray market goods, relying on *Monte Carlo* in reaching its decision. Judge Lasker distinguished *Bourjois* and *Weil* because the goods in *Ballet Makers* were manufactured with authority *and* they were intended for sale in the United States. Of course, that was not true of *Bourjois*, *Osawa*, and *Weil*.[55]

By the middle of 1986, these four cases seemed to have all but settled the question of whether identical goods could infringe. Indeed, in yet another case involving similar facts, Judge Glasser of the Southern District also ruled that genuine goods could not infringe. The case, *El Greco Leather Products, Co. v. Shoe World, Inc.*,[56] involved trademark licenses granted to several foreign manufacturers to produce "CANDIES" shoes for the U.S. market. When the licenses were (separately) cancelled with the goods still in the hands of the manufacturers, those firms sold the goods to a U.S. discount retailer (Shoe World). The licensor/trademark owner then brought suit alleging, inter alia, Lanham Act violations.

At trial, there was a substantial question about the quality of the shoes in question. In one instance, the plaintiff contended that the shoes manufactured by Solemio, Ltd. were rejected due to poor quality, but Judge Glasser rejected that assertion as lacking credibility. El Greco's local agent had sent a telex indicating that the reason for cancellation was "late delivery." El Greco claimed that documents existed indicating quality problems, but the documents were never produced. El Greco had also accepted without objection other lots manufactured by the same firm. Finally, defendant's own witness was unable to identify differences between the defendant's shoes and those manufactured by another licensee and sold with authority by the plaintiff. In that case (and in some of the other instances), El Greco also claimed that shoes being sold by the defendant were production overruns, but offered no proof to support its allegations.

Judge Glasser ruled in favor of the defendants. Of course, Judge Glasser reviewed the significance of El Greco's trademark registration, observing that it did not matter that El Greco was not the manufacturer, and equating the mark to "a certification . . . that the shoes so marked are genuine in that they have been determined by plaintiff to possess a certain degree of excellence."[57] After considering some (domestic) terminated-license cases, Judge Glasser turned his attention to the gray market cases, concluding that *Monte Carlo*, *DEP*, and *Diamond Supply* were "[h]elpful to [the] analysis." The court conceded that the facts of *El Greco* differed from the last case cited, in that in *Diamond Supply* the trademark owner expressly stated that it did not care what the defendant did with the goods. Judge Glasser, however, believed that that fact alone did not dictate a different result. In any event, El Greco evidently gave no instructions as to how to dispose of the goods, and the judge found that given the genuine nature of the defendant's goods, no likelihood of confusion existed.

Judge Glasser's opinion expresses an uneasiness with the trademark suit against Shoe World, commenting on the absence of the foreign manufacturer as a defendant. Judge Glasser also distinguished *Osawa*, noting the sophisticated nature of the product involved in that case, the differences between the advertising and ancillary services offered by the authorized and unauthorized sellers, and the importance of the warranties in the camera industry. All of these factors were absent from the case before him, and the injunction was thus denied.

The court of appeals reversed.[58] The panel included Judges Kearse and Pratt, both of whom had participated in the decision in *Bell & Howell*. Writing for a divided court, Judge Pratt framed the issue in terms of whether Shoe World's goods could be classified as "genuine." The key to understanding the term genuine, said the court, lay in

the right to control the quality of the goods manufactured and sold under the holder's trademark. [citation omitted] For this purpose the actual quality of the goods is irrelevant; it is the control of quality that a trademark holder is entitled to maintain.[59]

Judge Pratt focused on El Greco's refusal to issue an inspection certificate, a precondition to Solemio's right to draw against the letter of credit that secured payment. The court concluded that the inspection certificate was an integral part of the plaintiff's quality control mechanism.[60] The court thus rejected Judge Glasser's approach as an "unjustifiably narrow view of the protection afforded trademark holders by the Lanham Act."[61]

Judge Pratt did not place great import in the fact that El Greco did not specifically instruct the foreign manufacturer how to dispose of the goods in the cancelled order. The opinion suggests that Solemio could have sold the goods after "demarking" them, offered the goods to El Greco for inspection and approval, or requested instructions from El Greco about how to dispose of them. On this basis, the court distinguished *Diamond Supply*, leaving that precedent untarnished as it applies to genuine, identical, intended goods. Curiously, the court made no attempt to distinguish *Monte Carlo*, nor did it clarify the meaning of the footnote in *DEP* or the decision in *Bell & Howell*.

The court's language about the right to control has appeal in the context of the product quality–goodwill function of trademarks. This rationale, however, must not be taken too far. For example, no one would seriously assert that a trademark owner's right to control extends past original sale of the product, all the way to retailers and consumers.[62] That concept is often expressed in terms of the "exhaustion" doctrine. And even though a trademark owner (domestic or foreign) might stand behind its product, that is not to say that it does so in all cases. For example, defects or problems that arise because of failures at the retail level might not be rectified by the trademark owner.

That situation is of course different from problems occurring before the trademark owner places the goods in the stream of commerce. In that case, recognition of an absolute right to control is not only justified, it is far more important. As the court points out in *El Greco*, the trademark owner at that point has a duty to protect its mark from substandard products; it would be anomalous if the duty did not carry with it some corresponding right. But as indicated, courts must be careful not to extend the "right to control" rationale to situations where the trademark owner has already approved the goods and permitted them to enter the stream of commerce.[63] That is an entirely different matter from that involved in *El Greco*. To so extend the "right to control" rationale would be tantamount to proscribing all gray market trade.

Thus, in a relatively brief opinion, the *El Greco* court concluded that for unapproved goods manufactured under license, confusion was likely and that an injunction should have been granted. In a separate dissenting opinion, Judge Altimari expressed uneasiness with some of the majority's conclusions. Specifically, he disagreed with the determination that the question of genuineness was one of law rather than fact, and he felt that the court's definition of genuine was "underinclusive." Relying on cases such as *DEP* and *Monte Carlo*, Judge Altimari emphasized Judge Glasser's conclusion that the goods were not inferior; had not been "altered, reconditioned, repackaged or resold [sic]"[64]; and that the goods were manufactured with the authority of the trademark owner who gave no instructions on how to dispose of the rejected shoes.

Judge Altimari then quotes from Justice Holmes' opinion in *Prestonettes* and concludes that no deception took place. He seems to place stock in the fact that the defendant is a retailer who purchased the goods in good faith from the perhaps-delinquent manufacturer. His conclusion might thus be limited to the liability of that particular defendant, and it is somewhat unclear how he would rule if the foreign manufacturer were hailed into court. His conclusions might have been different if El Greco had been more careful about the expressed reasons for the cancellation and about giving instructions on how Solemio should dispose of the goods.

The Second Circuit's decision in *El Greco* seemingly retreats from its apparent position in *DEP* and *Bell & Howell*, and clearly conflicts with the Ninth Circuit's approach to the gray market problem. But the decision in *El Greco* can be interpreted narrowly, confined to cases in which an inspection certificate, required as a condition to sale, was not issued, thus rendering goods "not genuine."[65] In spite of the seemingly broad language about the "right to control," *El Greco* can thus be viewed as another case of unidentical goods, consistent with prior cases and with the subsequent decision in *Original Appalachian Artworks*. The Second Circuit, it must be remembered, stated that cases such as *Sasson* and *Ballet Makers* are best explained by the fact that the goods in those cases were intended for sale in the United States and, by implication, that goods not intended for sale in the United States are de jure not identical. Admittedly, such a rule would exclude from importation and sale nearly all gray market goods, which are usually either different or unintended.[66] But if, as was arguably the case in *NEC*[67], the existent corporate interrelationships can dictate a finding that unintended goods become intended by virtue of the foreign trademark owner's deliberate actions and foreseeable consequences, a conclusion of legality is probably warranted.

As already indicated, Judge Glasser of the Eastern District of New York is one judge unlikely to take the Second Circuit's opinions to the extreme. That fact is proven by his opinion in *Disenos Artisticos E Industriales, S.A. v. Work*,[68] another case involving LLADRO figurines. The plaintiffs in that case are the same corporate entities involved in *Weil*; they brought suit against another gray market importer alleging the same theories and injuries as they had in the earlier litigation against Dash. In a lengthy opinion on cross-motions for summary judgment, Judge Glasser again addressed the issue of infringement by identical trademarked goods.

He first rejected any argument that the plaintiffs, by virtue of the "single enterprise" theory, had implied consent to the importation of unintended goods. He interpreted *Original Appalachian Artworks* as rejecting such a theory when unintended goods are involved, thus limiting the reach of that theory as it was employed in *Parfums Stern*.[69] But Judge Glasser read *El Greco* quite narrowly, emphasizing the "integral" nature of the inspection certificate and stating that the court in that case "declined to decide whether the unauthorized sale of 'genuine' goods could give rise to a likelihood of confusion."[70]

Judge Glasser then read *Original Appalachian Artworks* in a similarly narrow fashion, emphasizing the Second Circuit's conclusion that the goods were materially different *and* were not intended for sale in the United States. Faced with a case where the goods were arguably identical, the court denied both parties' motions, reserving the legal question for decision after trial. Judge Glasser then added more fuel to the fire, stating that the corporate interrelationship among the plaintiff firms created yet another issue for subsequent resolution.[71] Perhaps he will follow the suggestion from *NEC* and *Parfums Stern* that corporate interrelationship can influence the decision about intention.

Judge Cardamone of the Second Circuit also appears to have doubts about barring all unintended, albeit identical, gray market imports. He authored a separate concurring opinion in *Original Appalachian Artworks*, expressing doubt whether the quality control–guarantee function of trademarks is a sufficient ground to issue an injunction against the sale of genuinely marked goods. Rather, he questioned whether the trademark owner should not be held responsible for the original sales (citing *Parfums Stern*) and thus limited to a breach of contract theory against the diverting seller. With respect to *Original Appalachian Artworks*, he would find that parallel importation could not have been prevented except through application of trademark law.[72] And in the end, he too viewed the Spanish Cabbage Patch Kids as materially different, likely to "upset[] the settled expectations of U.S. consumers."[73]

The Second Circuit's refusal to make a blanket statement on the legality of gray market activities, as the Third Circuit seems to have done in *Premier*, is not without appeal. Minding the admonition that "hard cases make bad law," the court has obviously chosen to go slowly. That approach has, however, seemed to produce divergence among the district courts and can thus be criticized. But there are many different gray market scenarios, and a cautious approach is probably justified. Indeed, while the Ninth Circuit's tendency toward the other end of the spectrum has merit in its ease of application, those decisions seem to discount too strongly the injury suffered when gray market activities abound. In the coming years, it is expected that further guidance will be provided by the Second Circuit and that open questions, such as the one in *Disenos*, will be resolved.[74]

One lingering question, however, is the proper gauging of differences between gray market goods and the authorized version. Some obvious cases exist, such as *Selchow & Righter* and *Original Appalachian*, but in most cases the difference is more subtle. The resolution of factual questions aside (e.g., *El Greco*), there remains the problem of articulating a workable legal standard for determining whether differences are material. This author has suggested elsewhere a test based upon Judge Learned Hand's calculus of risk in tort cases. If one multiplies the probability of consumer injury by the gravity of that injury if it were to occur, an appropriate balance is struck. Low-priced gray market goods would be favored, while high-priced products would more likely be barred. Mere differences in calibration or sizing would be immaterial, but the lack of support services for complex goods would be deemed important. The most difficult case might well involve Johnson & Johnson products without the safety seal; in that case, the low probability of harm might be offset by the high gravity of harm if it took place. Resolution of that issue, however, is best left to a jury. With the guidance of the proposed legal test, the jury would have a rational basis for decision.

THE SINGLE INTERNATIONAL ENTERPRISE DISQUALIFICATION

Rather than become involved in controversies over local goodwill and product identity, a growing number of courts have adopted a markedly different approach to the gray market problem. Led by the Ninth Circuit, and recently joined by the Third Circuit, these courts ask a threshold question: Is the U.S. trademark owner a subsidiary controlled by a foreign parent? If the answer is yes, they deny any relief to the U.S. entity. These cases thus constitute the most significant development in gray market trademark law since Judge Leval's decision in *Osawa*.

Parfums Stern v. U.S. Customs Service led the way in pioneering this approach to gray market cases. The litigation was yet another attempt by the perfume industry to combat gray market importation.[75] The District Court in Florida denied a preliminary injunction to the plaintiff because it "is a cog . . . in what appears to be a single international enterprise operating through an amoeba-like structure."[76] The plaintiff was the registrant and authorized manufacturer of Oscar de la Renta fragrance products in various parts of the world including the

United States and France. The company made efforts to limit its distributors to certain territories, but, in spite of those efforts, gray market perfume was being diverted to and imported into the United States.

Judge Aronovitz found that the plaintiff, having invested in advertising and marketing in the United States, "stands behind the product and has thus acquired good will in conducting its business."[77] But the court felt that because the plaintiff was responsible for the initial sales abroad, it was really attempting "to insulate itself from what it placed in motion through its own foreign manufacturing and distribution sources.[78] This "self-help" theme will be seen again in the appeal in *Weil Ceramics v. Dash*. As a second reason for the decision, Judge Aronovitz notes that the plaintiff and its international enterprises benefited from the original sales, a fact that leads him to the conclusion that "there is no evasion of a legal right."[79]

The court's decision clearly manifests overtones of equity jurisdiction, denying trademark relief in spite of the possibility of injury to local reputation. This theme also appeared in *Bell & Howell: Mamiya* and will also play a part in the ultimate decision *Weil*. In any event, the court distinguished *Bourjois* on the ground that that case involved the sale of a business to an independent U.S. company and viewed the *Osawa* facts as distinct because interrelationship and common control in that case were deemed more tenuous.[80] Indeed, the court states that *Guerlain* "is actually closest in terms of factual similarity,"[81] even though the legal theories were different. Without criticizing or defending the decision in that case, Judge Aronovitz denied relief to Parfums Stern.

The Ninth Circuit soon took an approach similar to that of Judge Aronovitz in *NEC v. CAL-Circuit Abco*.[82] NEC-USA is a wholly-owned subsidiary of NEC-Japan, one of the world's largest manufacturers of computer chips. NEC-USA in 1983 received an assignment of the trademark rights in the NEC mark and duly recorded that fact in the patent office. Gray market sellers such as CAL-Circuit Abco were able to obtain genuine NEC chips abroad at prices below those being offered by NEC-USA. NEC-USA sued CAL-Circuit Abco and other defendants for trademark infringement. The district court granted partial summary judgment to NEC, finding that consumers who bought from gray marketers were mistaken in their belief that products were covered by NEC-USA warranties and servicing.

The Ninth Circuit reversed. The court was clearly persuaded that the gray market chips were not of inferior quality, although it did not base its decision on that conclusion. Judge Sneed, writing a unanimous opinion, distinguished *Bourjois*, limiting that case to situations in which the U.S. trademark owner has "real independence from the manufacturer."[83] The notion that *Bourjois* can be distinguished from most gray market situations was novel, and Judge Sneed was well prepared to defend it.

The court interpreted *Bourjois* in two alternate ways, neither of which aided NEC. One view was that *Bourjois* involved an attempt by the foreign manufacturer to "evade" the agreement to sell exclusive trademark rights, "thus depriv[ing] the American mark owner of the entire benefit of its bargain."[84] NEC-USA could not claim that it was deprived of such a benefit because its acquisition of the mark did not flow from a true arm's-length transaction. "Under these circumstances, NEC-Japan would not be 'evading' any terms of its trademark assignment to NEC-USA by selling its computer chips to American distributors abroad. NEC-USA is not losing any benefits for which it bargained and which it might have legitimately expected NEC-Japan not to circumvent."[85]

A second offered reading of *Bourjois* was also of no help to NEC. In that reading, the court viewed *Bourjois* as involving an American company which "had complete control over and responsibility for the quality of goods sold [in the United States] under that mark."[86] NEC, said the court, could not claim that it exercised such control and was thus destined to lose the case. The fact that NEC-USA and NEC-Japan were commonly owned and controlled vitiated any potential for significant confusion. Judge Sneed wrote:

> [T]here is no danger [of NEC-USA] being unable to control the quality of [NEC-Japan's] products. In this situation, we cannot say that Abco is selling goods "of one make under the trade mark of another." [citation omitted] Nor is it inaccurate to say that the "NEC" on Abco's products truly designates the chips as having been manufactured under the control of NEC-Japan, even if the mark has become associated here with NEC-USA. If, as NEC-USA alleges, Abco sales agents mislead their buyers about the availability of NEC-USA servicing, then Abco may be liable in contract or tort, but not in trademark.[87]

The assumption made by Judge Sneed apparently is that the goods were of equal quality when sold by NEC-Japan, whether the sale was made to NEC-USA or to a foreign diverter. Of course, it is possible that the goods were defective when sold or, through mishandling, became defective after NEC parted with title. In either case, however, disappointed consumers would look to NEC for a remedy; not because NEC-USA actually imported and sold the chips but because NEC-Japan manufactured them. NEC-USA may become the responsible party irrespective of whether it was responsible for the defect. Put another way, it would not matter whether a specific defective chip is gray market; the entire NEC network would be viewed as standing behind the goods, and separate goodwill is therefore irrelevant.

In this way, Judge Sneed was thus able to avoid the reasoning of Judge Leval in *Osawa*, and Judge Debevoise in *Weil*. The existence of local goodwill, about which Judge Sneed is skeptical for obvious reasons, would not change the fact that NEC-Japan manufactured the chips, benefitted from their original sale, and could be expected, in whatever corporate form, to stand behind the quality of its products. Indeed, Judge Sneed's real feelings become apparent in the last paragraph of his opinion, where he writes:

> If NEC-Japan chooses to sell abroad at lower prices than those it could obtain for the identical product here, that is its business. In doing so, however, it cannot look to United States trademark law to insulate the American market or to vitiate the effects of international trade. This country's trademark law does not offer NEC-Japan a vehicle for establishing a worldwide discriminatory pricing scheme simply through the expedient of setting up an American subsidiary with nominal title to its mark.[88]

This is not to say that questions of local goodwill have no application in the Ninth Circuit. *Bourjois*-type cases might well exist, and the Ninth Circuit probably would concur in at least some of the rationale of *Premier Dental*. An apparently arm's-length transfer to an independent firm (such as that involved in *Premier*) might be deemed sufficient for the case to fall within the narrowed reasoning of *Bourjois*, notwithstanding the right of reassignment and the limited quality control undertaken by the U.S. trademark owner. But to the extent that the Ninth Circuit concluded that separate goodwill is irrelevant when a single, international enterprise is involved, *NEC* is in direct conflict with the decision in *Osawa*.

The Ninth Circuit's decision in *NEC* thus casts some doubt about the future of the decision in *Osawa*, even if it is viewed as not questioning Judge Leval's reasoning where corporate separateness really exists. *NEC* was therefore an invitation to gray market sellers to continue to raise issues of corporate affiliation. In its appeal of the *Weil*[89] decision, the gray market advocates did just that, with what must be deemed astonishing success.

The appeals court decision in *Weil* is as different from the trial judge's determination as an opinion can possibly be. Judge Leon Higginbotham's opinion is an echo of *NEC*, with new and controversial reasoning employed. The most controversial is Judge Higginbotham's conclusion that the Supreme Court decision in *K-Mart v. Cartier*[90] limits a U.S. trademark owner's rights under the Lanham Act.

K-Mart, which will be discussed at length in Chapter 5, involved no Trademark Act issue whatsoever; it was a decision about whether the Customs Service was required to enforce literally the exclusionary section of the Tariff Act first enacted in 1920 to reverse the lower court decision in *Bourjois*. That statute, of course, has remained on the books long since the time Justice Holmes also reversed the lower court and has been the product of significant legislation, litigation, and agency action since that time. As stated, the litigation, leading up to *K-Mart* did not involve any trademark principles, but this fact did not prevent Judge Higginbotham from extending some of its underpinnings to the trademark area.

Judge Higginbotham held that because Weil was a wholly-owned subsidiary of the manufacturer and foreign trademark holder, it could not complain about gray market sales in the United States. In the most narrow construction of *Bourjois* to date, Judge Higginbotham emphasized the complete independence of the U.S. trademark owner in that case, the arm's length transaction by which Bourjois came to acquire the trademark rights, and the actual quality control that Bourjois had over the product it sold.

> In the present case, no such compelling circumstances exist. Weil is not independent of the foreign manufacturer. Although it was not incorporated by Lladro S.A., it nonetheless benefits from the corporate relationship that exists. Thus, even if Weil loses some share of its United States market to [the defendants], it nonetheless benefits from the profits it received as part of the corporate entity from which [the defendants] purchased the goods abroad.

. . . We do not read the Lanham Act . . . to protect a foreign manufacturer that either owns or is owned by a domestic trademark holder from competition in the sale of its product in the United States by a domestic importer that it has supplied.[91] [footnotes omitted][emphasis added]

The court's conclusion, if uniformly adopted by the circuits, has one clear effect: a foreign manufacturer cannot use U.S. trademark law to protect a U.S. subsidiary from gray market competition. Judge Higginbotham's ironclad rule would prohibit a manufacturer from incorporating or purchasing a U.S. company and then using trademark law to assure that that company will possess exclusivity over the right to distribute its goods. Judge Higginbotham stated that in such a circumstance, the foreign manufacturer–U.S. distributor can, indeed must if it desires to stifle gray market trade, use "self-help" to combat gray market sales. The court lists among the "self-help" mechanisms charging the same price abroad that it charges in the United States or distinguishing the goods sold abroad by "producing or packaging or marking them differently."[92]

Judge Higginbotham's conclusions about self-help are sure to engender debate and violent disagreement from the trademark owners, who feel they cannot practically help themselves. These forces will surely cease on Judge Cardamone's statement in *Original Appalachian*:

It is not clear that [Original Appalachian] could have prevented by contract the importation of these Cabbage Patch dolls by third-party distributors, such as Granada. As a practical matter OAA appears to have tried. Under its license Jesmar agreed not to sell outside its Spanish-licensed territory, and further agreed to sell only to purchasers who also agreed not to sell outside that territory. Without any effective means of further controlling the distribution of its product, for example, by means of an equitable servitude on the dolls, OAA should not be held responsible for the dolls' importation.[93]

Of course, as the passage demonstrates, *Original Appalachian* involved goods manufactured under license. As will be discussed in Chapter 5, importation in such cases is now barred under the Supreme Court's decision in *K-Mart v. Cartier*. But that case did not bar importation in "common control" cases. In those cases, the self-help theme is sure to be repeated.

Arguing the practical difficulties of self-help, trademark owners are then prepared to justify their price differentials with marketing costs and the need to provide special services to U.S. consumers. But Judge Higginbotham's answer is that if a single international enterprise wishes to maintain such a system, it must either suffer the inconvenience of gray market competition or use business (i.e., extra-legal) efforts to combat such competition. Whether contract remedies are practical methods for combatting the gray market is not important in Judge Higginbotham's view because another alternative exists: the firm could always abandon its dual-tiered international pricing strategy.

Judge Higginbotham bolstered his conclusions in *Weil* by embracing *NEC*, and he also distinguishes *Premier* as a *Bourjois*-type case that is different on its facts because of the independence of the U.S. trademark owner. But as already indicated, the opinion takes a controversial theoretical tack, asserting that

> [i]n our view, the Court's conclusion in *Katzel* does not represent the establishment of a broad "territoriality theory" applicable to every instance in which a domestic company acquires the United States trademark for a foreign manufactured good. We read that decision as creating an exception to the general application of trademark law in order protect adequately the interests of domestic trademark holders such as Bourjois.
>
> Our conclusion is consonant with both *K-Mart* and *Katzel* and illustrates the synthesis between those Supreme Court decisions.[94]

Judge Higginbotham relies heavily on Justice Brennan's opinion in *K-Mart*, a split and controversial plurality opinion of the Supreme Court. But in a separate concurring opinion in *Weil*, Judge Becker disagreed that an extension of *K-Mart* was warranted. Judge Becker instead took another approach to the entire problem; that approach is discussed later in this section.

Because of the existence of the *Disenos* litigation, the Third Circuit appears to be on a collision course with the Second Circuit (where *Osawa* remains untouched, and *Original Appalachian* looms) over the single enterprise disqualification and the independent goodwill approaches to gray market infringements. Judge Higginbothan attempted to set the overall tone for the debate, when he wrote:

> we discern two broad policy goals that Congress sought to foster by this legislation: (1) protection against consumer deception ... [and] (2) protection of the trademark holder's investment in goodwill and noteworthiness that has been generated by the holder's advertisements and quality from imitative goods over which the trademark holder has no control of quality. ... [N]either of the goals is undermined by the importation of genuine goods as in this case. Consumers who purchase [gray market] imported LLADRO porcelain get precisely what they believed they were purchasing. For that same reason, Weil's investment in and sponsorship of its trademark is not adversely affected because the goodwill that stands behind its product is not diminished by an association with goods of a lesser quality.[95]

Judge Higginbotham, in making this statement, does not appear to be at odds with the trademark theories espoused by Judge Leval, but the disagreement becomes apparent when he continues:

> The only "injury" that we perceive Weil endures is the uncompensated for benefit that its advertisement and promotion of the trademark confers upon [gray market sellers]. That loss to Weil is not inconsequential or insignificant. The remedy for it, however, is not properly found in the trademark law, particularly not in this case.[96]

The free rider effect that produced the requisite irreparable injury in *Osawa* was thus deemed by Judge Higginbotham irrelevant to trademark law, with horrific consequences to foreign-owned firms like Weil.

By taking views similar to those taken by the Ninth Circuit in *NEC*, Judge Higginbotham has assured the resurrection of the "single international enterprise" theory first seen in *Guerlain*. Judge Edelstein's opinion contained similar language in its discussion of the trademark issues.[97] Perhaps because the opinion in *Guerlain* was so widely discredited for its antitrust reasoning, there is no mention of the case in either *NEC* or *Weil* (although Judge Aronovitz did draw attention to the obvious similarities in *Parfums Stern*). Nevertheless, the single international enterprise disqualification has survived the assault on *Guerlain* and thirty years of legislation and litigation over the gray market. With the assistance of Customs, with the express approval of several circuits, and with the tacit approval of the Supreme Court and congress, that theory now appears to dominate gray market law.

The single international enterprise disqualification is not, however, the only issue on the gray market scene. In *Weil*, Judge Higginbotham also expresses some of his views on the "inferiority/identity" issue. At the heart of all of Judge Higginbotham's decision is his conclusion that the gray market products in *Weil* were identical to the authorized version. This is a conclusion that is highly debatable; Judge Debevoise appeared to draw the opposite conclusion based on the question of quality control; and Judge Becker, in his lengthy separate opinion, actually appeared to disagree with Judge Higginbotham, concluding that there was evidence that the gray market goods in question in fact were inferior.[98] But Judge Higginbotham wrote in a footnote:

> The fact that [the District Court] made no finding that porcelain distributed by [the defendants] and that distributed by Weil are materially different is significant to our disposition of this appeal. Weil has contended on this appeal that the porcelain imported by [the defendants] was of a materially different grade and quality from the porcelain imported by Weil. If true, that fact would provide a stronger argument for Weil's claim of trademark infringement. [citing *Original Appalachian Artworks*] However, we cannot reach that conclusion on the findings of record, and we premise our decision on the assumption that the porcelain imported by [the defendants] was essentially identical to that imported by Weil.[99]

The issue of inferiority/identity was thus preserved for an eventual trial,[100] but under the Higginbotham analysis it does not matter whether Weil possesses independent goodwill.[101] The question remains whether the existence of separate goodwill and a single international enterprise are mutually exclusive conditions. The Third Circuit seems to have come to a collective (though not unified) opinion that *Bourjois/Premier*-type[102] cases present actionable wrongs by gray market sellers regardless of the identity of the gray market goods, but that the existence of a single international enterprise raises questions about "inferiority/identity."[103] Again, that creates a direct collision with *Osawa*, where a significant corporate interrelationship (although not a single international enterprise) also existed between the foreign manufacturer (Mamiya), its exclusive worldwide distributor (Osawa-Japan), and the U.S. trademark owner (Osawa-USA.) Indeed, Judge Higginbotham is unsure how a case that involved more tenuous, but nevertheless significant, corporate control should be decided.

In his separate concurrence, Judge Becker takes a markedly different route to reach the same conclusion about the validity of Weil's lawsuit. Judge Becker viewed *Bourjois* as an example "of a court sitting in equity,"[104] fashioning an appropriate solution to a special problem. Judge Becker, thus, also reads *Bourjois* narrowly, stating that it was "not a blanket change in trademark law."[105] But, he writes that, in spite of this view, "trademarks are still territorial and that the source theory of trademark law is no longer viable. These conclusions lead me to believe, in contrast to the majority that under current trademark law, genuine goods with genuine marks can serve as the basis for an infringement suit. . . . I do not believe, however, that Weil should prevail in this case."[106]

The reasons for Judge Becker's beliefs as to the outcome differ in some respects from those of Judge Higginbotham. Judge Becker's conclusion also relies on self-help mechanisms available to Lladro, S.A., although he identifies a problem (and a solution) different from that identified by his colleague.[107] But Judge Becker draws a conclusion that Judge Higginbotham avoided: "Weil has failed to make an adequate showing of independent good will."[108] In drawing this conclusion, Judge Becker rejects the "single international enterprise disqualification" and endorses the Leval approach to gray market cases.

Indeed, Judge Becker's analysis of territoriality follows somewhat the Leval approach. He states that in the context of international trade, if exhaustion occurred "every time a foreign manufacturer placed its product on the market, . . . then the territoriality theory of trademark rights would lose most of its force and the right to control the trademark of an internationally available good in a given country would not be of much value."[109] But Judge Becker was also hesitant to conclude that the territoriality principle just exalted cannot flow from the limited holding in *Bourjois*, and he thus looks elsewhere for its underpinnings.[110]

Judge Becker finds those underpinnings in his observation that "the Lanham Act is a statute addressing the rights of *domestic* trademark holders *in the United States*. . . . The place to look for the answer to the question whether the United States recognizes the territoriality theory in the context of *international* trademark rights is not domestic trademark law, but rather international law, as expressed in treaties."[111] The Paris Convention for the Protection of Industrial Property, which the United States has adopted, Judge Becker concludes, recognizes that a "mark duly registered in a country of the Union [i.e., a signatory country] shall be regarded as independent of marks registered in other countries of the Union, including the country of origin."[112] Therefore, he concludes, "United States trademark law expressly recognizes trademark rights as territorial."[113] Judge Becker thus views Weil's rights as separate from those of its corporate parent. But that is not enough, because, Judge Becker continues, "[w]hat good these rights do . . . [is] another matter."[114] Presumably only the Lanham Act can answer that question.

Judge Becker then looks to *Premier Dental* for authority that the Lanham Act "potentially covers all genuine goods not just those competing with the goods of an independent domestic company."[115] The discreditation of the source theory and the expansion of infringement rationales to include goodwill, sponsorship, and consistency provided Judge Becker with further authority for that proposition. He thus would hold that "absent other considerations, . . . Weil should be able to sustain a challenge under section 32 [of the Lanham Act] . . . even though the goods which it claims are infringing are genuine goods with genuine marks."[116]

The "other considerations" just mentioned then turn out to preclude Weil from exercising the rights it might otherwise have. Judge Becker's opinion makes reference to a new concept in gray market law: Unity of Interest. This concept, which formed the basis for an important antitrust decision, *Copperweld Corp. v. Independence Tube Corp.*,[117] was extended by Judge Becker to cover trademark law as well. "[T]he unity of interest between a wholly owned subsidiary and its parent," writes Judge Becker, "should be held to exist as a matter of law in the trademark context. Because of their unity of interest, we may attribute those self-help remedies available to the parent to be available a fortiori to the subsidiary."[118]

As alluded to previously, Judge Becker's view of self-help was different from that of Judge Higginbotham. The latter depended upon a belief that Lladro could combat gray market through different pricing policies or through more vigilance in its decisions about with whom to deal. Judge Becker's views on self-help depend upon a different observation, one not made by Judge Higginbotham and one which, because it was the product of an alleged trade secret, was redacted from the trial court's opinion in the case.

In the lower court, the parties stipulated that Lladro manufactures porcelain figurines of varying quality, but imports (through Weil) only premium-grade porcelain into the United States. In Europe, Lladro sells porcelain of both grades. Lladro, however, does not disclose its gradations, so consumers are not even aware that differences exist. The defendants, purchasing in Europe, presumably knew of, but did not (or could not) differentiate among, the various qualities of LLADRO goods; they thus imported what Judge Becker termed "mixed-quality goods."

Judge Becker reasoned that these differences could have been grounds for a finding of infringement, but that that possibility was negated because

> Lladro has full power to use different trademarks for different levels of quality and thereby prevent harm to Weil's reputation. ... [T]he wholly owned subsidiary whose parent sells products on the open market deficient in quality, ... but marked identically, may not prevail on a section 32 claim where the only evidence of likelihood of confusion is the claim that different quality goods are on the market with identical trademarks.[119]

As a result of these facts, Judge Becker concluded that any likelihood of confusion caused by the defendants' importation of mixed-quality goods was attributable to Lladro's (and Weil's) conscious decision to not differentiate publicly the varying levels of quality that exist. Having refused to recognize the different levels of quality, Weil could not prevail. "The source of confusion in this case," wrote Judge Becker, "is not [the defendants], but Weil's parent, Lladro. ... [T]he injury here is self-inflicted."[120]

Having drawn these elaborate conclusions, and having adopted reasoning different from the majority, Judge Becker then makes a quixotic statement:

> [E]ven if Weil/Lladro had not created the opportunity for infringement by marketing two different levels of quality bearing the identical mark, I do not believe Weil could prevail. This is

largely because Weil is a wholly owned subsidiary. Because Weil and Lladro share a unity of interest, I believe that Weil would have an extremely difficult if not impossible time proving a separate and independent goodwill. [citation omitted] Indeed, the evidence it produced before the district court with respect to advertising and inspection of the products is inadequate to create a genuine issue of material fact as to separate and independent goodwill in my view.[121]

Judge Becker, having expressed reasons very different from those of Judge Higginbotham, thus returns to the same point: Weil cannot prevail, because it is owned by Lladro, S.A.

Judge Becker's conclusions are strikingly similar to those involved in an early gray market case: *Russia Cement Co. v Frauenhar*.[122] That case, it might be recalled, involved gray market glue purchased in Europe and imported into the United States. The court found that there were two grades of glue sold by the plaintiff-manufacturer, but both grades were marked identically. The court in that case wrote

If the public gets an inferior quality of glue when it purchases that [of] defendants, it is because the [plaintiff] has seen fit to sell such glue under the same tradename as it has applied to the superior article, and has chosen to reap the profit from the sale of two qualities or grades of the same article under the same tradename.[123]

Russia Cement is not cited by Judge Becker, but it easily could have been. Of course, that case did not involve the single international enterprise issue; nevertheless, whether one adopts the views of Higginbotham or Becker, *Russia Cement* provides an interesting parallel and authority for the proposition that single international enterprise are different from *Bourjois*-type cases.

Indeed, it might be recalled at this juncture that the importation in *Bourjois* offended the senses of both the Court and the Congress because the purchase of the U.S. rights to the mark in question affected other trademark purchases from the Custodian of Alien Property during World War I. Many Americans had made such purchases at least partly under the auspices of the U.S. government. But like the decision in *Russia Cement*, this significant fact also appears lost to history. Nevertheless, when kept in mind, it lends perspective to *Bourjois* and supports the Higginbotham-Sneed approach to gray market importation.

The Supreme Court denied certiorari in *Weil*, suggesting that either it is not upset with the extension of *K-Mart v. Cartier*, or that the controversy over gray market goods is not yet ripe for their attention. In the wake of *Weil* and *NEC*, the legal status of gray market imports remains clouded where foreign corporate control exists. Needless to say, in today's international business climate, that is the status of the bulk of cases. Principally, the question of whether the existence of a single international enterprise precludes a finding of local goodwill remains unresolved, and a continued split among the circuits seems likely. Unfortunately, without Supreme Court involvement, it is unlikely that the lower courts will settle their differences and achieve any significant measure of consistency and uniformity. That involvement may eventually become necessary as *Disenos* makes its way through the courts.

In the meantime, the lack of uniformity obviously invites a significant measure of forum-shopping, always an undesirable result. But together with forum considerations, careful study of the facts of a given case is likely to produce at least some predictability about the outcome. If an independent U.S. entity acquired its rights in an arm's length transaction, advertised, provided warranties and other services, and generally stood behind the product, it will prevail on the single international enterprise question and on the issue of local goodwill (e.g., *Premier Dental*). If, however, the U.S. trademark owner and the foreign manufacturer are part of a single enterprise, at least some courts will disregard the existence of goodwill or at least be incredulous when such assertions are made.

The question of differences between gray market goods and their authorized counterparts lurks prominently in the background, and more elaboration of the contours of this issue will no doubt emerge shortly. But at present, it seems that gray market importers will be successful if they can prove either product identity or the existence of a single international enterprise.

CONCLUSION

The purpose of trademark law is to protect the trademark owner against injury caused by the likelihood of confusion of purchasers. Local goodwill–product identity analysis was intended to balance those interests, and it has now been supplemented by the single international enterprise disqualification. If the goods are inferior (or, by virtue of their character, are materially different from other goods intended for the U.S. market), confusion is likely and importation should be enjoined. If the goods are not different, and nothing in their character makes them unsuitable to the U.S. market, the question of trademark injury is far from clear. As indicated in Judge Leval's scholarly decision, detailed factual findings about the parties, the goods, and consumer expectations are required.

Cases like *Bourjois* are clear-cut, but difficulties abound where the local trademark owner is related to the foreign manufacturer who originally placed the goods into the stream of commerce. At some point, the plaintiff and its related entities must take responsibility for the original sale.[124] As Judge Cardamone astutely reasoned in *Original Appalachian Artworks*, a search for less restrictive alternatives is one place to start. The discussion of "self-help mechanisms" in *Weil* is also of interest, although the question remains about which self-help mechanisms are practical and which are not. A look into real consumer expectations about the entity that stands behind the goods, as the Ninth Circuit undertook in *NEC*, is also a useful approach. Whether one takes the Higginbotham approach to free rider injury or the Leval approach, clear identification of the goals of trademark law and an understanding of the injuries the gray market really causes must be the undisputed starting point for resolving the gray market controversy.

NOTES

1. 589 F. Supp. 1163 (S.D.N.Y. 1984).
2. 622 F.2d 621 (2d Cir. 1980).
3. Id. at 622.
4. The court remanded the case for trial on that issue.
5. 622 F.2d at 624.
6. Id.
7. See the discussion in *Weil Ceramics v. Dash*, infra this chapter, and *Duracell*, Ch. 8, infra, under "The Effect of Laws of Foreign Countries on Gray Market Trade."
8. *Premier Dental Products Co. v. Darby Dental Supply, Inc.* No. 85–1468, slip opinion (E.D.PA. 1986).
9. 618 F. Supp. 700 (D.C.N.J. 1985).
10. Id. at 707.
11. 618 F. Supp. at 710.

12. Judge Debevoise concedes that *Parfums Stern* made no mention of the exhaustion doctrine and the concept of separate goodwill. The details of that case are discussed below.

13. 618 F. Supp. at 711.

14. Id. at 712.

15. Id. at 713.

16. The plaintiffs had asserted claims under sec. 33(b) of the Lanham Act, the portion of the act creating the rule of incontestability and the exclusive right to use a mark that has become incontestable. The court found no private right of action under that section and instead considered the case under sec. 32(1)(a), the traditional infringement section of the Act.

17. 78 F.2d 556 (8th cir. 1935).

18. 260 U.S. 689 (1923).

19. *Premier* at 3.

20. Id. at 4.

21. Id. at 13.

22. Id. at 11.

23. Id.

24. Oddly, the *Perry* case is not cited or relied upon by the court, perhaps indicating a deliberate break with the past.

25. In *Osawa*, Judge Leval noted that a reversionary interest by itself does not preclude a finding of a valid assignment. *Osawa* at 1179.

26. *Premier* at 12.

27. Id. at 14.

28. Id. at 19.

29. Id. at 20–21.

30. Id. at 21.

31. 264 U.S. 359 (1924).

32. Id. at 367.

33. Id. at 368.

34. Id.

35. Id. at 369.

36. Id. at 368.

37. See p. 56 infra.

38. 612 F.Supp. 19 (S.D.Fla. 1985).

39. Id. at 28–29.

40. 816 F.2d 68 (2d Cir.), cert. denied 108 S.Ct. 143 (1987).

41. Id. at 73.

42. See p. 56 infra.

43. 816 F.2d at 73.

44. 707 F.2d 1054 (9th Cir. 1983).

45. 632 F.Supp. 1525 (S.D.N.Y. 1986).

46. 589 F.Supp. 470 (S.D.N.Y. 1984).

47. 633 F.Supp. 1328 (S.D.N.Y. 1986).

48. Note that the court did not consider whether there was a legitimate U.S. market for Spanish Cabbage Patch Kids dolls, a real possibility especially in Hispanic areas. If such sales were to occur, there is a much smaller potential for injury because consumers would not be deceived or disappointed. Granada evidently made no such argument, and the court thus did not consider it.

49. 707 F.2d at 1057.

50. Id. at 1058. The court presumably meant Monte Carlo's agent.

51. Id.

52. Id.

53. One interesting point in *Diamond Supply*, which might well have motivated the court, was the finding that the plaintiff had indicated that it did not care what the defendant did with the goods in its possession.

54. As such, *Ballet Makers* presents some unusual twists to the normal gray market case, raising questions about the rights of a licensee vis-à-vis those of the trademark owner and a subsequent licensee.

55. Unlike *Monte Carlo*, in *Ballet Makers* the plaintiffs had pursued a contract claim, a theory that the court felt was not proper for summary judgment given the record before it. And given the dismissal of the Lanham Act claim, federal jurisdiction was lost against the second licensee, virtually guaranteeing that that issue would never be resolved definitively.

56. 599 F.Supp. 1380 (E.D.N.Y. 1984), rev'd., 806 F.2d 392 (2d Cir. 1986), cert denied, 108 S.Ct 71 (1987).

57. Id. at 1391.

58. 806 F.2d 392 (2d Cir. 1986).

59. Id. at 395.

60. That conclusion, however, is debatable. The refusal to issue the certificate was probably a device employed to deny Solemio the right to be paid under the letter of credit. The conclusion that the inspection certificate was "integral" to the plaintiff's business thus seems to be a way to disagree with Judge Glasser about the lateness-quality claim without having to find that Judge Glasser's conclusion about the reason for cancellation was "clearly erroneous."

61. 806 F.2d at 395.

62. Trademark owners can and often do select retailers who will be authorized to carry their products and those owners sometimes impose limitations or conditions at the retail level.

63. Such reasoning could be used, for example, to sanction trade in domestic distress merchandise, one aspect of the gray market.

64. Id. at 398.

65. Indeed, in light of the Supreme Court decision in *COPIAT*, infra, *El Greco*-type facts are unlikely to arise again.

66. That would appear to be the position of the Third Circuit as evidenced by the decision in *Premier*. The appellate decision *Weil* will presumably clarify any remaining ambiguity in that circuit.

67. See p. 56 infra.

68. 676 F.Supp. 1254 (E.D.N.Y. 1987).

69. It must be noted that consent did not necessarily form the basis of Judge Aronovitz' decision in *Parfums Stern* but that is one tenable explanation for the decision in that case.

70. 676 F. Supp. at 1269.

71. Other significant aspects of Judge Glasser's opinion are discussed in the chapters on antitrust and on copyrights, infra.

72. Judge Cardamone ultimately concludes that such an approach was not practical in *Original Appalachian*, thus comparing that case favorably with the result in *Bourjois*.

73. 816 F.2d at 76. Another example of such differences are goods sized according to the European system and perhaps goods that lack special U.S. packaging (such as Tylenol). In the case of European sizing or instructions not printed in English, however, the use of less restrictive corrective measures might vitiate the injury. See *Bell & Howell*.

74. For the most part, other legal theories related to trademark law have proven largely irrelevant to the gray market context. Claims for unfair competition and trademark dilution have tended to stand or fall with the underlying trademark cause of action. As indicated, several claims of tortious interference with contract have been made, but this author knows of none that have been litigated to conclusion. Other legal theories unrelated to trademark are discussed in some of the chapters that follow.

75. The action was actually brought under the Tariff Act but, because of the issues raised, it is important to the trademark cases.

76. 575 F. Supp. at 418.

77. Id. at 419.

78. Id.

79. Id.

80. Judge Aronovitz handed down his order before the Second Circuit's decision in *Bell & Howell*, and he was thus addressing Judge Neaher's decision in that case. Of course, while the names changed before Judge Leval's decision in *Osawa*, the relationship among Osawa (USA), Osawa (Japan), and Mamiya had not. Judge Aronovitz actually looked only at the relationship between Mamiya and Osawa (USA), which entailed only a 7 percent ownership interest. Of course, the relationship among the three companies is actually far more complicated and probably closer than the 7 percent figure indicates.

81. 575 F. Supp. at 420.

82. 810 F.2d 1506 (9th cir. 1987), cert. denied 108 S.Ct. 152 (1988).

83. Id. at 1509.

84. Id.

85. Id. at 1510.

86. Id. at 1509.

87. Id. at 1510.

88. Id. at 1511.

89. *Weil Ceramics and Glass, Inc. v. Dash*, No. 86–5187, slip opinion (3rd cir. 1989), cert. denied 58 U.S.L.W. 3208 (10/3/89).

90. 56 U.S.L.W. 4478 (May 31, 1988) rev'g, *Coalition to Preserve the Integrity of American Trademarks (COPIAT) v. United States*, 790 F.2d 903, 907 (D.C.Cir. 1986).

91. *Weil* at 11.

92. Id. The court also suggests that Lladro could cease selling to Dash (and its codefendant Jalyn) abroad. That suggestion belies the fact that gray market importers frequently obtain their goods from a source other than the manufacturer (and its subsidiaries). But see [J&J litigation], Ch. 6, infra. But that fact and the middleman's profit serve only to exaggerate the suspicion generated by foreign and domestic price differentials. But see [discussion of antitrust economics] Ch. 4, infra. Judge Becker's concurrence also places great weight on the these "self-help" mechanisms, although the self-help he suggests is different from that suggested by Judge Higginbotham.

93. 816 F.2d at 75 (Cardamone, J., concurring).

94. Id. at 12.

95. Id. at 16.

96. Id. at 17.

97. 155 F.Supp. at 82. Speaking of the free rider effect as possible grounds for trademark relief, Judge Edelstein wrote: "[T]he argument is one for the protection of advertising expenditures and expected profits not necessarily related to good will. . . . The exclusive right to sell in the American market on the part of an international concern exploiting world markets is not an element of good will except so far as it may be made so artificially by import prohibitions." Id. Judge Edelstein, it may be remembered, was reluctant to decide the antitrust issues but was compelled to do so by the government. ("There is certainly no doubt that the attempt to resolve this issue in antitrust litigation was clumsy, . . . ") 172 F.Supp. at 107.

98. Judge Becker also disagreed with much of Higginbotham's reasoning about the single international enterprise. That disagreement is discussed infra.

99. *Weil* at 12.

100. Indeed, Judge Becker, in his separate concurrence, reaches the opposite conclusion about Judge Debevoise's findings about identity.

101. Judge Higginbotham also rejected as "strained" Weil's alternative argument that the importation and sale of genuine LLADRO figurines "copie[d] or simulate[d]" Weil's trademark. The court reiterated its conclusion that *Katzel* did not extend the Trademark Act to all gray market scenarios. The court thus rejected any analogy between gray market and counterfeit goods, see also *DEP*, supra., and again invoked Justice Brennan's reasoning in *K-Mart* as added weight to its argument that no infringement has occurred.

102. It must be remembered that in *Premier*, the Third Circuit said that it did not matter whether the defendants' product was actually different, that the differences in ancillary services sufficed. See also *Osawa*.

103. It must be observed, however, that Judge Higginbotham does not explicitly say that a finding of inferiority would perfect Weil's lawsuit but only that that fact would give them a "stronger argument."

104. *Weil* at 21.

105. Id.

106. Id.

107. See text and notes accompanying 117–118n., infra.

108. *Weil* at 21.

109. Id. at 23. In contrast, it is not clear that Judge Higginbotham extends the exhaustion doctrine to all international sales; rather, his approach bypasses the question because *Weil* involved a single international enterprise.

110. "As I see it, [*Bourjois*] did not create a blanket trademark rule, but rather was a clear exercise of the flexible equitable powers of the Court and an attempt to remedy what was perceived to be unfair in an individual case." Judge Becker does not preclude the possibility that "two affiliated companies [might] become over the years increasingly independent, such that the two entities are essentially independent, [that] there may be good reason for the court to exercise its equitable powers to protect the goodwill and investment in the trademark that the American company has individually developed over the years."

111. *Weil* at 25.

112. Id.

113. Id.

114. Id.

115. Id. at 27.

116. Id. at 28. Judge Becker thus takes issue with majority that sec. 32 does not prohibit the sale of gray market goods, although he seems to agree that sec. 42 does not bar the act of parallel importation. In a footnote, Judge Becker writes,

> I admit that trademark law would be more streamlined if neither section 32 nor section 42 applied to genuine goods. . . . However, there is no internal conflict in finding that an article may be imported, but may [not be sold]. As this concurrence makes clear, cases involving genuine goods, although based on sound trademark principles, must be carefully analyzed to ascertain that the aims of the Lanham Act are being furthered.

117. 467 U.S. 752 (1984).

118. *Weil* at 29.

119. Id. at 31.

120. Id. Judge Becker suggests that Lladro could affix different marks to the different levels of quality and/or inform the public as to the differences.

121. Id. at 31–32.

122. 133 F. 518 (2d Cir. 1904).

123. Id. at 520.

124. To say that the foreign manufacturer has no responsibility is simply incorrect. If the product were defectively manufactured, for example, an injured plaintiff would have recourse against the foreign seller regardless of whether the goods were gray market. Indeed, the wholly owned domestic subsidiary may even be a party through whom jurisdiction can be obtained.

4

Antitrust and the Gray Market: An Issue Lost but Not Forgotten

As was seen in Chapter 2, courts from the beginning understood that gray market cases inevitably involved competition policy. The cases all involved incidents where an unauthorized distributor was able to sell genuine products at prices competitive with those of the exclusive distributor or trademark owner. Judge Wallace, in deciding *Apollinaris*, recognized that gray market competition can harm the distribution system of the local trademark owner because it would have difficulty "hold[ing] out the inducements it formerly could to the agents it has selected to introduce the article to the patronage of the public."

A trademark owner and/or exclusive distributor is expected by its distributors to promote, guarantee, and generally stand behind its product. But the distributors also expect the trademark owner to shield them from price competition, particularly the competition of free-riding gray market sellers. Whenever a distribution relationship exists, questions arise about resale price maintenance and the legal status of non-price distribution restraints.

The antitrust upheaval of the last fifteen years has, of course, changed the way courts look at vertical restraints, and that change has had a significant effect upon the way courts look at the gray market. As might be expected, the easing in antitrust jurisprudence and enforcement has made anti-gray market efforts less dangerous and more likely to succeed than was the case in the days of the Warren Court. Nevertheless, the development of gray market law and the development of antitrust law are inextricably intertwined, and consideration of the former requires an understanding of the latter.

THE HISTORY OF VERTICAL RESTRAINTS IN A NUTSHELL

Contracts in Restraint of Trade

Section 1 of the Sherman Antitrust Act provides that any "contract, combination or conspiracy in restraint of trade" is unlawful. Early in the history of Sherman Act jurisprudence, however, the U.S. Supreme Court ruled that only "unreasonable" restraints fell within the Act's prohibition. However, the Supreme Court has also held that certain agreements, because of their character, are deemed unreasonable per se and thus are automatically illegal. Among restraints that are so characterized are (1) agreements among competitors to fix prices and (2) group boycotts.

A vertical restraint is defined as an agreement between two firms at different levels of the distribution system. Thus a distribution agreement between a manufacturer and a wholesaler or retailer is characterized as vertical. Vertical arrangements take two forms, price and non-price. Each of these forms is treated differently for Sherman Act purposes. Vertical price restraints, frequently known as "resale price maintenance," were held to be unlawful per se in *Dr. Miles Medical Co. v. John D. Park & Sons*. While that decision has been criticized in recent years, and even narrowed somewhat, it remains an important precedent.

In 1967, the Supreme Court also ruled that non-price vertical restraints were unlawful per se. As is the case with *Dr. Miles*, the court's decision in *United States v. Arnold Schwinn Co.* was criticized as founded on faulty economic principles. But unlike *Dr. Miles*, in 1977 the Supreme Court in *Continental T.V. v. GTE Sylvania Inc.* reversed the decision in *Schwinn* and ruled that non-price vertical restraints are not unlawful per se. Rather, the court employed a standard known as the "rule of reason," requiring that before a court condemned a non-price vertical restraint, it had to find that the arrangement in fact had the effect of reducing competition. The court thus ruled that territorial restrictions imposed by a manufacturer or exclusive distributor will be treated under the (more lenient) rule of reason. Thus, restrictions on the territory in which a seller may sell, on the location from which goods could be sold, or even on the customers to whom goods can be sold are not automatically illegal.

In *Sylvania*, the Court identified two types of competition, intrabrand competition and interbrand competition, and ruled that a court must balance reductions in one against improvements in the other in order to come to a conclusion about net competitive effect. Intrabrand competition is the competition between competing sellers of the same manufacturer's product; interbrand competition is competition in the sale of different manufacturers' products. Most non-price vertical restraints have the effect of reducing intrabrand competition by reducing the number of sellers of a specific brand of merchandise or by restricting the location at which those goods may be sold.[1]

Conversely, by reducing intrabrand competition, a manufacturer or exclusive distributor is able to provide incentive (actually, reduce the disincentive) for wholesalers and retailers to undertake point-of-sale advertising and servicing. As stated, the theory is that existence of "free riders" harms the manufacturer's ability to control the distribution of its product, and that restrictions on distribution are both logical and necessary to the efficient sale of those products.

That is not to say that all restrictions imposed by a manufacturer or exclusive distributor on the distribution system are automatically lawful. If a manufacturer or exclusive distributor possesses excessive market power, the negative effect caused by the reduction in intrabrand competition will outweigh any procompetitive effect resulting from greater control over the product's distribution. The principal problem, however, is in defining the relevant market and in identifying how much market power should be deemed excessive.

These are matters for which there is no clear-cut answer. Courts have decided restricted distribution litigation on a case-by-case basis, and there is no simple formula for delineating those situations that offend the Sherman Act and those that do not. It is clear, however, that in order for a distributor to succeed as an antitrust plaintiff, he must first offer proof of a relevant market. That concept is considered in full in the section on monopolization.

Of course, not all products are the same; some, by their nature, require greater point-of-sale service and promotion than do others. Furthermore, not all gray market sellers are free riders. It is thus the thesis of this chapter that courts should take these facts, among other things, into account when considering the antitrust claims of gray market sellers, as well as when analyzing the trademark owners' claims that gray market sales have a negative effect on their distribution system.

Gray market sellers invariably complain that the lawsuits brought against them by trademark owners are motivated by a desire to restrict a distribution system for unlawful purposes or in an unlawful manner. These gray market sellers complain that they are victims of anticompetitive activities and that consumers will suffer needlessly higher prices if the sellers are not allowed to exist. The trademark owners claim that both their means and their purpose are lawful, and invariably the trademark owners have been successful. These decisions will be discussed in the remainder of this chapter.

Dealer Termination

Dealers of goods, at whatever level of the distribution system, are sometimes terminated for a variety of reasons ranging from the lawful to the unlawful. At the former extreme are terminations that result from the refusal or failure to maintain resale prices, and at the other extreme are terminations that are the product of a lawful desire to eliminate free riders. It is not unusual for terminated distributors to seek legal redress for their termination, and the antitrust laws were historically a fruitful source for remedies in this area.

The ascendence of the Burger Court, however, caused this avenue to be reduced substantially. The quantity and quality of evidence required to convince a court that a termination was made in pursuit of an unlawful resale price maintenance scheme has been increased by the Supreme Court in recent years. The current legal standard for proof is that there must be evidence tending to negate the possibility of any lawful purpose (i.e., non-price, justified control over distribution). The court has gone on to hold that evidence of competitor complaints about price-cutting is not conclusive evidence of a desire to maintain an unlawful scheme and that the termination of price cutters motivated by a manufacturer's desire to raise dealer incentive to engage in point-of-sale servicing does not by itself lead to antitrust condemnation.[2]

At least some gray market sellers acquired their status because of an inability to secure authorization to sell the subject goods. A dealer who once did a brisk business in a particular manufacturer's goods may be loathe to give up that trade even after his dealership is officially terminated. The dealer may seek legal redress for the termination, but, as indicated, lawsuits of this nature are unlikely to succeed. These dealers thus turn to gray market sources for their products, resulting in law suits by trademark owners seeking to enjoin such sales. Faced with that prospect, the dealer may consider an antitrust challenge to the original termination. Such challenges are nearly impossible to win; as a result, the antitrust challenge is likely to take a different form. A few such cases exist, such as *Osawa* and *Model Rectifier v. Takachiho*; they will be considered later in this chapter.

Monopolization

Section 2 of the Sherman Act prohibits monopolization and attempts to monopolize. Historically as well as practically, the first is more important than the second, and the discussion herein will primarily concern monopolization. Proof of monopolization requires two elements: monopoly power and unlawful conduct. In order for a court to find that monopoly power exists in a given case, there must be proof of a "relevant market."

The basic conception is twofold: economic power can be evaluated only within the confines of a specific group of products, and a seller's ability to adversely affect competition only exists when there are no "good substitutes" for the product he sells. If substitutes exist, the theory goes, the individual seller cannot control the price at which he sells, because consumers will simply switch if the price being charged is above competitive levels. The seller who is faced with competition from similar products thus cannot act like a monopolist and, thus, cannot monopolize.

Courts thus compute a fraction, or percentage, in order to determine whether monopoly power exists. In the numerator, courts place the alleged monopolist's gross sales, or some other number indicative of the extent of the seller's business. The denominator then consists of the gross sales, or corresponding figure, of the alleged monopolist's product and all good substitutes therefor. If more competing products are included in the denominator, the larger it will be, and the smaller will be the fraction measuring the power of the alleged monopolist.

The difficult question, indeed one which has plagued courts and commentators for nearly forty years, is how to define the "relevant market," the figure that becomes the denominator. In the celebrated *Cellophane*[3] case, the Supreme Court held that the outer boundaries of the relevant market are defined by reference to the concept known as "cross-elasticity of demand." Cross-elasticity of demand is an economic measure of the responsiveness of the demand for one product to price changes in a second product. Where such cross-elasticity exists, products should be deemed substitutes, thus included in the relevant market. Conversely, if cross-elasticity is low or nonexistent, the products in question should not be considered substitutes, and the competing product will not be included in the relevant market.

For a variety of reasons, cross-elasticity of demand is a concept that is of minimal practical utility. First, it is not empirically measurable, and economic data that purports to measure it is susceptible to differing interpretations. Second, if the alleged monopolist in fact possesses and is using the evil power, cross-elasticity will necessarily be high. At a monopolistic price, the seller will have already raised price to a profit maximizing level, that is, the level at which consumers will switch to poor substitutes or simply do without. And because it is impossible to discern whether a given price is at monopolistic levels, there is no way to determine why cross elasticity is high in any given case.

To solve the problem created by the need to define a relevant market, courts have resorted to a functional test involving a concept known as "reasonable interchangeability." Courts thus compare relative prices, end uses, and product features to determine whether consumers would actually switch products in the event that the price of one rises. This too requires some imagination and theorizing, and, as the cases discussed later in this chapter demonstrate, has not been applied without difficulty and controversy.

Once the relevant market is delineated, and the market power fraction computed, courts use the fraction to determine whether monopoly power exists. While other "qualitative" factors are sometimes applied, it is generally held that about 70 percent is the threshold level for a finding of monopoly power. Where monopoly power has been found to exist, the final step is to determine that the monopolist used that power in an unlawful manner, for example, by raising prices or excluding competitors. There have also been allegations of monopolization through copyright and trademark misuse; these allegations are also considered later in this chapter.

Attempt to Monopolize

The cause of action for attempt to monopolize is a seldom successful throw-in to a monopolization claim. Its history dates to a Justice Oliver W. Holmes opinion in which this theory was analogized to the criminal law of attempt. The result was the legal requirement that a plaintiff prove a specific intent to monopolize and a dangerous probability of success. Dangerous probability is another market power concept, requiring proof of a relevant market and a market power fraction approaching, but not quite equal to, monopoly proportions. The impediment to success with an attempt to monopolize claim is the requirement of specific intent; direct proof is almost always impossible to obtain, and circumstantial evidence is, as a general matter, unlikely to persuade a jury that *specific intent* existed. But at least one gray market seller has tried to utilize the theory, so it is another potential counterpunch for a besieged gray market seller.

In recent times antitrust law has not played a major part in the judicial decisions in gray market cases. As will be seen in the next chapter, antitrust law has played its greatest role in the area of Customs Service enforcement of a statute barring gray market goods.

It is nevertheless important to keep antitrust in mind when dealing with the gray market for two reasons. The first is that any attempt by trademark owners to combat gray market sales inherently suppresses intrabrand competition and thus automatically raises antitrust concerns. Furthermore, many trademark owners possess a significant degree of market power or operate in markets that are oligopolistic in structure. Such entities bear a real risk: even a non-price restraint might overstep the boundaries of legality.

The second reason is that history has proven that antitrust law acts in the manner of a pendulum. During the Warren Court era judicial enforcement was at its zenith, but it has waned substantially since that time. It is yet unclear how far the courts will go in relaxing the law, but the magnitude of a treble-damage antitrust judgment undoubtedly serves to deter conduct that is on the margin of the law.

ANTITRUST AND THE GRAY MARKET: THEORIES AND EXPLANATIONS

The gray market can only exist if unauthorized sellers are able to sell at prices below those of their authorized counterparts. That can only take place if their costs are lower. With this parameter, there are two possible explanations for the existence of the gray market.[4] The first is that the gray market exists because manufacturers of trademarked goods are making goods available to foreign distributors at prices lower than those charged to U.S. sellers. That practice, where it exists, is known as economic price discrimination. The second explanation is that the prices charged by the manufacturer are the same worldwide but that the authorized U.S. distributors are charging higher prices to American consumers than their foreign counterparts charge to foreign consumers (and gray market diverters).

By charging higher prices to one set of consumers than to another, a seller can maximize its total revenue and thus gain profits higher than could be obtained if the price differences did not exist. The key to effective discrimination is the ability of a seller to isolate different sets of consumers with different demand curves. Once consumers are isolated, the seller can charge a higher price to the buyer with more inelastic demand and lower prices to more price-sensitive consumers. The seller can thus increase its total revenue at no extra cost, and thus it can increase profits.

In the gray market context, the result of price discrimination is higher prices in the United States than are charged abroad. The question whether that type of discrimination, if accomplished, harms competition in the United States is clearly a matter for the antitrust laws. To accomplish that discrimination, however, the manufacturer/exclusive distributor must curtail gray market activities in order to isolate sellers and consumers in different geographic markets.

The second explanation for the existence of the gray market, equal manufacturer prices but higher U.S. distribution costs for U.S. distributors, possesses subtle but important differences from the first. In this scenario, gray market sellers can be free riders, theoretically injurious to the distribution system. Of course, even as free riders, gray market sellers can benefit competition by infusing into the marketplace competition that would otherwise not exist.

In order for the gray market to exist, however, not every seller in the chain of distribution need be a free rider. To make matters even more complex, it is difficult to identify which entities are actually free-riding and which entities are harmed thereby. Where free-riding is done by gray market dealers operating in the United States, efforts by the exclusive U.S. distributor aimed at curtailing such sales are more likely to be justified as a business necessity, although that justification may not suffice to counteract the loss of competition caused by the elimination of the gray market.

But when the free-riding is done by overseas distributors and diverters, it must be asked why the foreign manufacturer does not combat that free-riding in the foreign market. There are three possible answers. The manufacturer (1) does not care, (2) is unwilling to make the effort, or (3) is unable to do so because foreign law does not permit it. Whatever the reason, whenever foreign free-riding exists, courts should be skeptical about claims that anti-gray market efforts in the United States are business justified.[5] In such a case, the manufacturer is likely to be involved in some form of economic discrimination,[6] and that should not be permitted if the manufacturer is able to combat the problem (free-riding) effectively in the foreign market, rather than using U.S. trademark or customs law to suppress intrabrand competition.

The task of identifying which scenario is present in a given case[7] is accomplished to some degree by the local goodwill–product identity tests developed in the last chapter, and applying such tests should be of use in the antitrust context. Thus, if a trademark plaintiff can prove that it possesses local goodwill and that it stands to be injured by the sale of non-identical gray market goods, it should not matter whether the defendant itself is in fact a free rider. Courts will recognize that the plaintiff can enhance its competitiveness vis-à-vis other brands by curtailing gray market sales, no matter who the free rider is and no matter where the free-riding took place.

In such a case, the plaintiff has a credible claim of business justification. What remains is to balance that claim against the negative competitive impact of eliminating the gray market. Current antitrust dogma indicates that if there is sufficient interbrand competition in the marketplace to assure that consumers are being charged a competitive price, no antitrust concerns are raised. If there is insufficient interbrand competition, for example where the manufacturer/exclusive distributor has a degree of market power, antitrust concerns are present. Where oligopolistic interdependence is suspected, fears should be raised if all similarly situated manufacturers/exclusive distributors engage in the practice of restricting distribution. In such a case, the elimination of gray market sellers (and the intrabrand competition they produce) can permit the raising of prices by all industry participants where conditions are right. As will be explained fully in the next section, in the context of the *Guerlain* case, the existence of inelastic demand for the products in question is the single most important factor in making suppression of gray market competition profitable for the manufacturer or its exclusive U.S. distributor.

Thus, in spite of the possible business justification for the elimination of gray market sellers, it should not be automatically assumed that all anti-gray market activity stems from a desire to eliminate free riders. Aside from questions of monopoly and oligopoly, it must first be observed that not all products are susceptible to free-riding; simple articles of commerce, such as toothbrushes, soap, and apparel, require little if any point-of-sale efforts. When dealing with these products, attempts to curtail gray market activities probably flow from the first offered explanation, rather than the second.

If empirical price and elasticity data were available, it would be possible to separate the first scenario from the second and to understand fully the effects of an elimination of gray market competition. Such data, however, are rarely available. Because of exchange rate fluctuations, allocation of sales and shipping expenses, questions of local tastes and purchasing practices, and even the presence of dual distribution systems, comparative cost data are difficult to derive and analyze. It is thus necessary to analyze the nature of the product involved and whether the elimination of alleged free riders is likely to have procompetitive or anticompetitive effects, before reaching any conclusion about the legality of anti-gray market efforts.

Any decision about whether or not the gray market should be protected is understandably difficult. But understanding the interplay among the competing interests of manufacturers, gray market dealers, and consumers necessitates appreciation of economic principles and antitrust concepts. The following section reviews the court decisions that address these issues and considers the correctness of those decisions in light of current antitrust dogma.

THE DECIDED CASES

When *Apollinaris* was decided in 1896, the antitrust laws were in their infancy. The policies behind those laws were not well understood, and it is therefore logical that antitrust played no real role in the court's decision. To some extent the same is true of the *Bourjois* case.[8] But several years after the Supreme Court's decision in that case, antitrust was to assume a much larger role, not only in American business in general but also in the gray market in particular.

That role began with an attempt by the perfume industry to use trademark and customs law to combat a flood of gray market imports. The response from the executive branch of government was an antitrust prosecution of the leading firms in the industry, alleging monopolization and attempt to monopolize. Three separate but essentially similar civil antitrust actions were brought, naming three American corporations involved in the marketing and sale of perfumes and colognes. Each of the three corporations in the case titled *United States v. Guerlain, Inc.*[9] was closely associated with the foreign manufacturer of the products it sold, having been incorporated solely for the purpose of selling those products and owning the U.S. trademarks under which they were sold. Each U.S. defendant was owned and controlled by its foreign parent and had promised to reassign the marks to the parent if so demanded.

Each of the defendants had filed certificates of trademark registration with the Customs Service and sought to use section 526 of the Tariff Act to have Customs seize all gray market imports at the border.[10] The government contended that utilization of section 526 was improper and in violation of the antitrust laws because the prevention of gray market competition is an attempt to monopolize the trade in that product.

The government's hardest task, of course, was to prove that the trade in each of the defendants' products constituted a relevant market for antitrust purposes. But before Judge Edelstein of the Southern District of New York could reach that issue, he had to first deal with several preliminary issues. He found that the American defendants and their foreign parents were "a single international enterprise." The defendants had tried to assert their independence, but Judge Edelstein found "beyond any gnawing doubt," that the "asserted independence [was] contrived and [that] the 'corporate veil' is easily pierced by the merest glance through the forms of the business organizations to the realities of the relationships [citation omitted]."[11]

The court next found that the right to assert claims under sec. 526 of the Tariff Act was not an absolute one. The court found that the statute in question was enacted solely for the purpose of reversing the Court of Appeals' decision in *Bourjois v. Katzel*, and that the right was thus limited to situations factually similar to that case. The key to *Bourjois*, wrote Judge Edelstein, was the possession of independent local goodwill by the U.S. trademark owner.[12]

The court found that none of the defendants before it possessed such goodwill. Judge Edelstein pointed to the fact that all of the defendants' advertising stressed the foreign manufacture of the products. Any loss that the defendants suffered, wrote the judge, was simply a loss of expected revenue and profit, not an injury to the actual goodwill of the American distributor.[13] The court's refusal to permit the defendants to use sec. 526 was thus characterized not as a deprivation of goodwill but rather as "the denial of a special right . . . [that] Congress [did not intend] to grant [to] an international enterprise."

As will be discussed in the following chapter, Judge Edelstein's views on sec. 526 do not completely coincide with the interpretation the Supreme Court would place on that statute thirty years later. But whether that interpretation would be deemed correct or not, Judge Edelstein in no event was prepared to permit the defendants to invoke rights under the Tariff Act if the exercise of those rights violated the antitrust laws. He refused to read any antitrust exemption into the terms of that statute, requiring any such congressional intent to be clearly expressed in the statute itself. Finding none, Judge Edelstein thus turned his attention to the merits of the government's Sherman Act claims.

The first step for Judge Edelstein was to assess the defendants' market power. That task, in turn, required definition of the relevant market. The landmark *Cellophane* case had recently been decided by the Supreme Court, and Judge Edelstein quoted at length from the majority opinion's reference to reasonable interchangeability, the cross-elasticity of demand, and "objective considerations of utility and price." Judge Edelstein then compared the type of products deemed interchangeable in the *Cellophane* case with that of products involved in *Guerlain* and found them to be different.

Judge Edelstein then began his analysis of the perfume market by observing that there was "undisputed testimony that many purchasers are unable to distinguish between the different scents of various perfumes." The natural conclusion might be that all scents exist in the same relevant market constituting products of similar price and quality. "But this conclusion," wrote the judge, "ignores certain other meaningful evidence . . . that the most important element in the appeal of a perfume is a highly exploited trademark. . . . It would appear that, to a highly significant degree, it is the name that is bought rather than the perfume itself."

From this observation, which is of arguable validity, Judge Edelstein concluded that the perfumes in question did not compete with one another. He hypothesized that a scent sold under an unknown trademark would not compete effectively with an established brand possessing the same fragrance, and that the former thus would have no effect upon the sale of the latter one. "[T]he lack of objectivity in consumer demand impairs the basis of interchangeability and negates a finding of cross-elasticity." That conclusion has been assailed time and again by courts and commentators, and there is good argument that it was altogether erroneous.[14]

Judge Edelstein may have been correct about the competitive impact of an unknown, unexploited brand of perfume, but that is a far cry from a conclusion that established brands have no competitive interaction. But Judge Edelstein is probably correct when he suspects some unusual market characteristics, in this case the inelastic demand (caused by high levels of brand loyalty) of those who purchase perfumes. This inelastic demand by itself does not create the conditions that make monopolization possible, but it can encourage higher prices if conditions are right. A seller faced with an inelastic demand can achieve higher revenues if he is able to raise prices. Higher revenues in such a case will lead to higher profits because marginal (and average) costs will remain constant.

The question then is, under what condition can a seller faced with an inelastic demand raise prices unilaterally? And the answer is: an oligopolistic industry in which all sellers face the same demand and cost inputs. In that situation, where there are few sellers, all faced with an inelastic demand, it is in the interest of all to raise prices above competitive levels. In such a case, all the sellers can raise prices without any significant loss of total sales, producing increased revenues for all participants; conversely, there is no incentive to lower prices because all sellers will inevitably suffer.

The price increases in such cases can arise in one of two ways: through illegal collusion or through the phenomenon known as "interdependence" or "conscious parallelism." The former practice violates sec. 1 of Sherman, but the latter by itself does not because of the statutory requirement of agreement. In *Guerlain*, the fact that the participating sellers made no agreement to raise prices immunized that aspect of the phenomenon from sec. 1 attack, and there was no allegation of conspiracy between the trademark owners and their authorized distributors. But applying modern antitrust principles, the restrictive distribution agreement between manufacturer and distributor might have been attacked as an unreasonable restraint of trade.

In an oligopolistic market, there is, by definition, minimal interbrand competition, and thus a restriction or elimination of intrabrand competition can make interdependence possible. But if intrabrand competition is permitted to exist, interdependence becomes more difficult. Therein lies at least one explanation for a manufacturer's desire to restrict distribution. This scenario (elimination of price-cutting market participants) was likely the case in *Guerlain* and, if pleaded properly by the government, might have resulted in a defensible conviction. Judge Edelstein, however, was unable to articulate it. And because he was faced with a Sherman Act sec. 2 claim only, he was not free to find a sec. 1 violation in the restricted distribution schemes of the manufacturers and their American distributors even if he had been inclined to do so. As was pointed out previously, even under prevailing antitrust doctrine, the reduction in intrabrand competition (caused by the threat of enforcement of the Tariff Act prohibition) was worthy of concern in a market such as that for high-priced perfumes.

Without that supporting logic just articulated, however, Judge Edelstein's conclusion was bound to, and did, draw considerable fire. The perfume industry moved to have the judgment set aside by the Supreme Court, and a negotiated settlement was reached under which the government agreed to the voluntary vacatur of the judgment. Judge Edelstein authored a bitter opinion acquiescing in the settlement,[15] an opinion that was quoted at length in Chapter 2. His time had been wasted, and his obviously anguished decision had seemingly been for naught. But whether Judge Edelstein was right or wrong about his antitrust conclusions, the fact remains that his decision is still discussed, and antitrust law continues to play a part, albeit diminished, in the gray market controversy.

As already indicated, and as will be set forth completely in the following chapter, antitrust law, even after *Guerlain*, continued to play a part in the Customs Service's regulations on enforcing sec. 526. Eventually, antitrust was abandoned as a rationale for Customs' policy, but beginning in the 1980s, when gray market litigation became a growth industry, antitrust issues again arose.

In *Model Rectifier Corp. v. Takachiho International, Inc.*, the Ninth Circuit had occasion to discuss briefly antitrust and the gray market. The plaintiff (MRC) was an importer of model automobile kits, manufactured in Japan by Tamiya Corp., that ran by remote control radio devices. Among the defendants was a gray market importer who had purchased Tamiya goods in the Orient, and the United States retailer of those goods. Less than two years before the suit, the plaintiff had been made the exclusive U.S. distributor of Tamiya products, and a year later it became an assignee of the trademarks.

The plaintiffs contended that they had tried to locate and terminate the source of the gray market goods in Asia but had been unable to do so. MRC alleged that the gray market versions of the Tamiya goods were of inferior quality, having problems with missing or broken parts. The District Court granted a preliminary injunction prohibiting further sale of the goods, and the defendants appealed.

The Ninth Circuit found that the lower court's finding that a likelihood of confusion existed was not clearly erroneous. As authority for its decision, the court cited *Bourjois* and Judge Neaher's decision in *Bell & Howell: Mamiya*. (The Second Circuit's opinion reversing Judge Neaher had not yet been rendered.) The court then went on to consider, albeit briefly, the antitrust claims that were before it. The court's decision is not enlightening, but it is instructive.

The defendants claimed that the trademarks in issue were being employed in violation of sec. 1 and 2 of the Sherman Act. MRC defined the relevant market as including all radio-controlled models and estimated its share of that market as 5 percent to 7 percent. The defendants of course chose a more narrow definition, "model off-road vehicle kits," where the plaintiffs accounted for approximately 98 percent of total U.S. sales. Unfortunately for the defendants, however, there was no proof offered to support their contention, and that failure was fatal. Because the defendants had the burden of proof on that issue, they "failed to make even a colorable showing of an antitrust violation."

In spite of the failure of proof, the Ninth Circuit's brief opinion in *Takachiho* demonstrated a new hostility to antitrust defenses to anti-gray market efforts. "One who opposes enforcement of a trademark on the ground that its use violates antitrust laws has a heavy burden [citation omitted]. The natural monopoly that a trademark owner has over its product does not violate antitrust law unless it is used to gain control of the relevant market." That statement overlooks many of the potential evils of using trademark claims to engage in anticompetitive practices, namely eliminating intrabrand competition. But it does recognize that such effects are possible, and focuses attention where it should be focused: on the dynamics of the relevant market.

In *Osawa v. B & H Photo*, Judge Leval likewise considered in brief fashion some of the antitrust issues presented by the facts before him. And, as was the case in *Takachiho*, the defendants raised antitrust issues but had not developed them sufficiently to place them squarely before the court. As will be seen, that failure was particularly unfortunate in the context of the *Osawa* facts because of the oligopolistic nature of the medium format camera market.

The defendants, in addition to their arguments about the genuineness of their goods and the application of the exhaustion doctrine, contended that granting relief to the plaintiffs would foster "anticompetitive practices, discriminatory pricing and violations of antitrust law and policy."[16] The crux of the defendants' argument was that Osawa-Japan was engaged in a type-1 discrimination scheme, charging higher prices to U.S. distributors than were charged to their foreign counterparts. Judge Leval noted the facts: the gray market sellers were able to sell at lower prices in the United States than could authorized dealers; but price advantage was not necessarily due to an international price discrimination. Indeed, Judge Leval had already found facts that indicated that the defendants were free riders, and that would of course account for the price differences. In the absence of proof "that arbitrary price discrimination was practiced by Osawa-Japan," no antitrust violation was proven.

Judge Leval's conclusion on this matter is certainly defensible in light of the facts. The court, however, went on to hypothesize about what it might do if such proof existed, and postulated that even that evidence might not produce a different result in the trademark action. The court reviewed and considered "the curious history of the perfume antitrust actions." Discussion of *Guerlain* necessitated a review of the Tariff Act provision and accompanying Customs Service regulations, concluding that those regulations "represented an effort on the part of Customs to implement its perception of antitrust policy [citation omitted]." Judge Leval was critical of that "effort," and did not hesitate to condemn it: "[N]othing in the [Tariff Act] suggests that Congress conferred authority on [Customs] to condition [the Tariff Act remedy] on Customs' analysis of antitrust policy. Equally questionable are the wisdom and necessity for such regulations."

Of course, and as will be seen in detail in the following chapter, the Customs regulation was based upon issues of corporate ownership, rather than on industry structure and behavior. "Antitrust questions are far too complex to be reasonably decided by reference to a short questionnaire on corporate ownership," wrote Judge Leval. He points out, correctly, that the Customs regulations take no account of the relevant market definition and market considerations, a fact that Judge Leval stated to be "unsound as antitrust policy and as trademark law."[17]

Judge Leval did concede that "international business complexes might conceivably use trademarks . . . in a manner that violated the antitrust laws." He suggested a plenary action for treble damages or use of the antitrust claim in the action for trademark infringement and indicated in a footnote that those issues might be raised, and be ripe for determination, in later stages of the instant law suit.

Judge Leval indicated that he would consider those antitrust claims, but as already indicated he was skeptical about their validity. The fact the defendants were free riders vitiated any price discrimination claim, and *Osawa* was more likely to be a type-2 gray market scenario than a type-1 case. Curiously, and without necessity, Judge Leval further opined that any reduction in intrabrand competition caused by an injunction against the sale of gray market cameras would be limited because the defendants could still sell their goods if they removed the MAMIYA marks. Judge Leval however ignored the fact that demarking and the inability to advertise and describe their product to consumers would for all practical purposes preclude the defendants from competing effectively in the medium-format camera market. But again, that issue was not really before him, and Judge Leval's comments are mere dicta carrying little precedential weight.

Judge Leval's decision that the antitrust issues were not ripe when placed before him was probably correct. But that fact is unfortunate for observers because the intrabrand–interbrand competition issues discussed earlier in this chapter are raised vividly by the facts of *Osawa*. The plaintiff/exclusive distributor faced with minimal interbrand competition[18] is pitted against the free-riding gray marketeer who was providing arguably necessary intrabrand competition. The case was settled before a trial could be held, so, of course, no final determination of the antitrust issues was ever made.

In spite of the fact that virtually all attempts to bar gray market sales are motivated by a desire to restrict distribution, not all cases raise triable antitrust issues, and antitrust has not played a role in most gray market cases. An antitrust counterclaim, however, was raised in *Original Appalachian Artworks*. The district court dismissed the claim, but on appeal the defendants argued that the "wide disparity in price" between domestic and foreign Cabbage Patch Kids dolls suggested an antitrust violation. The Court of Appeals agreed with the lower court that the claims should be dismissed because the gray market sellers suffered no "antitrust injury that would give it standing to challenge [these] acts. Indeed," said the court, " ... gray market importers ... would have benefitted from [such] anticompetitive conduct."[19] The court further found that there could be no antitrust claim in the fact that a trademark infringement suit was brought because there was no evidence that it was pursued in bad faith.

Antitrust, however, promises to play a large part in the litigation, discussed in another context in Chapter 3, concerning LLADRO porcelain figurines. Judge Debevoise was not asked to consider the antitrust implications of barring gray market sales in *Weil Ceramics v. Dash*, and the Third Circuit did not consider it on appeal. But Judge Glasser, in *Disenos v. Work*,[20] had to decide a motion for summary judgment brought by the plaintiff against an antitrust counterclaim made by the gray market dealers. That motion was granted in part and denied in part, so further litigation on the issue is sure to follow.

The defendants in the case charged both monopolization under sec. 2 of the Sherman Act and a conspiracy in restraint of trade in violation of sec. 1. The key to resolving both antitrust claims, of course, is the definition of the market, a matter that was hotly contested before Judge Glasser, and one that was only partially resolved. The plaintiffs argued in favor of a broad definition, "retail giftware," while the defendant asserted that the proper definition included (1) only LLADRO figurines themselves; alternatively, the defendant argued that the market consisted of (2) Lladro's goods and the products of its principal competitor, Hummel or (3) all porcelain figurines. Either of these three market definitions would provide the defendant with a market definition enabling the defendants to press their antitrust claims credibly, although acceptance by the court of the first two definitions would substantially enhance their chances for success.

Like Judge Leval, Judge Glasser ruled that neither party had conclusively proven a market definition at this preliminary stage of the case. The plaintiffs' suggestion was said to be "overly broad,"[21] because that definition would include such low-price items as mugs, games, and cigarette lighters—products that clearly are not good substitutes for LLADRO products. Aside from price, Judge Glasser cited the "collectibility" of LLADRO as a distinguishing feature, a fact that will undoubtedly play a role in the eventual decision on the merits. But Judge Glasser was equally unpersuaded at this stage by the defendants' suggestions of market definition, stating that "there are at least several types of figurines, including porcelain, crystal, and other materials, and possibly several types of giftware, such as nonfigurine crystal and china, that compete in the same market as LLADRO porcelain figurines." The court thus ruled that the market definition was "an unresolved issue of fact," presumably to be decided at the full trial on the merits.

The court found "no support [in the record] for finding that LLADRO figurines [alone] constitute the relevant market," but found "some support" for a definition including LLADRO and HUMMEL only. But the sales figures before the court were inconclusive for the years in question, leaving Judge Glasser unable to draw any conclusions. The judge did indicate, however, that a market including all porcelain figurines would leave LLADRO with a small share, making proof of substantive antitrust claims difficult. Judge Glasser noted that the burden of proving the market rested with the gray market defendant, of course, but that in the absence of irrefutable proof by the plaintiffs, their motion for summary judgment could not be granted.

The remainder of Judge Glasser's decision addressed these claims and how they would be approached at trial. The court first found that the defendants (who compete with the plaintiffs only at the wholesale level) were unable to prove injury from the alleged horizontal price fixing or resale price maintenance, explaining that if such a scheme existed, the defendants would gain from any attempt to raise prices. As was the case in *Original Appalachian*, if such conduct did take place, the defendants' business would benefit, not suffer, from these higher prices.[22]

Any real harm to the defendant, therefore, could only come from the alleged boycotts and concerted refusals to deal, which, the defendants argued, were part of the overall scheme to control resale prices. That potential injury was sufficient to permit the defendant to proceed with its claims, although the court was careful to point out that at trial the defendant would have to prove an injury to competition, as opposed to an injury to it as a competitor. The latter type of injury is deemed unprotected by the antitrust laws, which were designed with the aim of "protecting *competition*, not *competitors*."[23] In view of its findings about injury, the court then held that because the potential for injury existed and the defendant is the intended target of the plaintiffs' alleged anticompetitive activities, the defendants had standing to assert these antitrust claims. Following these determinations, the court proceeded to the substantive issues raised.

In order to prevail on its sec. 1 claim, the defendants had to prove the existence of a "contract, combination or conspiracy" between the plaintiffs and their authorized distributors. Proof of the existence of a conspiracy amongst the plaintiffs (sans the distributors) simply would not suffice because Lladro, S.A., Disenos, and Weil are all related entities.[24] The defendants thus pointed to a "letter agreement" between Weil and its distributors placing location and customer restrictions on the dealers. One of these restrictions was that the goods sold to the distributors could be sold "only at retail."[25] The defendants argued that these restrictions were placed on the distributors to exclude the defendant and make effective the resale price maintenance scheme. The plaintiffs of course argued that the restrictions were lawful under the *Sylvania* case. The court put that issue aside, but held that the existence of the letter agreement provided the necessary two-party action to meet the requirements of sec. 1 of the Sherman Act.

The court then turned to the question of the appropriate standard to be applied to the agreement just discussed. The defendants argued for per se treatment, but Judge Glasser rejected that argument, holding that the agreement was vertical (even though it was aimed at a competitor of Weil) and that the rule of reason should be applied. That test, in turn, requires market definition and because such proof was lacking, according to Judge Glasser, no further determinations were required. But Judge Glasser did indicate in a footnote that if the market is defined to include other porcelain figurines, the availability of those figurines to the defendants would "weaken, if not destroy, [their argument] that [they] were excluded from the relevant market."[26] That question inevitably leads to the question of whether other competitors engage in a similar practice, a matter whose importance was discussed earlier.

The court also addressed the defendant's sec. 2 claims, discussing the claims of monopolization, attempt to monopolize, and conspiracy to monopolize. Judge Glasser noted again that the absence of conclusive proof of market definition precluded summary judgment on any of the counts charged in the complaint. Judge Glasser declined to address either the issue of monopoly power or dangerous probability of success. But Judge Glasser did address a portion of the defendants' sec. 2 claim, so-called trademark and copyright misuse. The "misuse" characterization, if proven, could result in a sec. 2 violation if the market power prerequisite were proven.[27]

Judge Glasser began by noting that in view of his determination on the market definition issue, he could decline to discuss the misuse theories pending a showing that the requisite market power existed. But the judge addressed these claims anyway, because in his view "some of the allegations are patently unsupportable." The first allegation made by the defendants was that the plaintiffs had "falsely marked

LLADRO products with copyright notices." The court found that even though the plaintiff had forfeited its copyright by omitting notices from some of its early products and by failing to cure that omission,[28] the later affixation of the mark was not done with "willful and fraudulent intent to create the false impression that each and every LLADRO porcelain figurine sold in the United States is subject to a U.S. copyright," as defendants had charged. The plaintiffs, Judge Glasser explained, neither knew nor believed that the copyrights would be subsequently found invalid.

The second allegation concerned "misuse of valid copyrights" by threatening to bring an infringement suit against the defendants. Judge Glasser stated his belief that the plaintiffs' threats were made with the good faith belief that its claims had merits. Only proof that the plaintiffs made their threats and brought litigation in bad faith "would strip the [plaintiffs] of their immunity from suit under the "sham" exception to the *Noerr-Pennington* doctrine.[29] But Judge Glasser found no such proof anywhere in the record.

The third allegation was "misuse of trademark" by using those marks for the sole purpose of stifling competition. Unlike the first two theories of misuse, the court declared that this claim might have merit and raised a triable issue. The court again hid behind the market definition matter, declaring that "[i]f [the defendant] meets its burden on these threshold requirements, it may be able to show that the [plaintiffs] misused the trademark and that this lawsuit falls within the *Noerr-Pennington* sham exception.[30]

Judge Glasser thus concluded a somewhat lengthy analysis of the issues for trial. The entire case almost certainly will turn on the market definition aspect, as properly it should. It will be interesting to see the ultimate resolution of these issues, and there is reason to believe that Judge Glasser will not have the last word.

CONCLUSION

Regardless of how *Disenos* is finally decided, antitrust law and the gray market are inexorably entwined, and one should expect to see even more antitrust claims in the future. Claims by competitors have met with the procedural difficulty of antitrust injury and standing, but the defendants in *Disenos* were able successfully to skirt that issue in some of their claims. Of course, the government (federal or state) could, if it chooses, pursue the claims that competitors cannot. *Guer-*

lain, of course, was just such an attempt; its messy conclusion probably serves as some deterent to future government action. But the era of lax antitrust enforcement appears to be ending, and at this stage it is difficult to predict whether antitrust will make a resurgence in gray market cases.

NOTES

1. Resale price maintenance has a similar effect, eliminating intrabrand price competition. Price restraints, in general, are not relevant to this discussion, and treatment of them is, for the most part, omitted.

2. See *Business Electronics v. Sharp*, 108 S.Ct. 1515 (1988).

3. *United States v. E.I. DuPont de Nemours & Co.*, 351 U.S. 377 (1951).

4. Again, primarily the international gray market is dealt with, and the domestic trade in "distress" goods is not considered directly.

5. Indeed, the manufacturer may be engaged in a form of non-price economic discrimination, encouraging point-of-sale servicing in the United States but discouraging it, or at least being apathetic, in the foreign market. That phenomenon may or may not be justified because of local consumer demand. Whether that practice would be deemed to be unlawful in the United States, however, is dubious. It might raise concerns about the legitimacy of free rider claims in the United States, especially where the exclusive U.S. distributor has market power or operates in an oligopolistic market where all sellers follow the same practice.

6. That is, encouraging the provision of so-called "necessary" point-of-sale services in one market but not in others. That practice would result in higher prices in one market than in another, an indirect form of economic price discrimination.

7. The two are not mutually exclusive.

8. With regard to the Supreme Court decision, Justice Holmes' hostility to antitrust is well-known, evidenced by his famous comment that antitrust is "humbug based on economic ignorance and incompetence."

9. 155 F. Supp. 77 (S.D.N.Y. 1957), vacated and remanded, 358 U.S. 915 (1958), order entered, 172 F.Supp. 107 (S.D.N.Y. 1959).

10. That statute, its history and current legal status, are topics which form the substance of Chapter 5.

11. 155 F.Supp. at 80.

12. Judge Edelstein did not use the term, but his intention to invoke the concept is clear.

13. Judge Edelstein even went on to point out that gray market sellers are neither "pirates [nor] cheats," and that the public "would not be deceived about the authenticity or origin of the product." Id. at 82. Judge Edelstein then, somewhat quixotically, stated that these American entities "could not suffer from the marketing of inferior merchandise," presumably a reference to the distinction between gray market and counterfeit goods. Judge Edelstein's arguments on these points parallel much of the reasoning in *NEC v. Cal-Circuit ABCO*, supra Chapter 3. For instance, he also

observed that the foreign parent gains a benefit from even the gray market sales; a similar observation was made by the court in *NEC*.

14. Judge Edelstein expressed in his opinion and was clearly influenced by evidence that the defendants had a "specific intention to exclude competitors and to control prices." Id. at 85. He observed that such evidence was not present in *Cellophane*, a fact which Judge Edelstein felt gave him the necessary latitude to depart from the strict rule of *Cellophane* and draw a more limited relevant market.

15. 172 F.Supp. 107.

16. 589 F.Supp. at 1176.

17. Id at 1178.

18. There are only five manufacturers of medium-format cameras, and demand among consumers (i.e., professional photographers) is presumably inelastic.

19. *Original Appalachian Artworks v. Granada*, 816 F.2d at 74. A similar conclusion was reached by the Southern District Court in *W. Goebel Porzellanfabrik v. Action Industries*, 589 F.Supp. 763 (S.D.N.Y. 1984).

20. 676 F.Supp. 1384 (S.D.N.Y. 1984).

21. 676 F.Supp. at 1273.

22. The defendants admitted that they never purchased at the full retail price, so they could not be injured in that way either.

23. *Brunswick Corp. v. Pueblo Bowl-O-Mat*, 429 U.S. 477, 488 (1977)(emphasis in original).

24. See *Copperweld Corp. v. Independence Tube Corp.*, 467 U.S. 752 (1984), reversing *Kiefer Stewart, Inc. v. Joseph Seagram & Sons*, 340 U.S. 211 (1951).

25. 676 F.Supp. at 1281.

26. 676 F.Supp. at 1283 n.34.

27. The court noted that there was no allegation that the alleged misuse was the product of an agreement between the plaintiffs and their distributors, and thus there was no need to discuss misuse in the context of sec. 1. Id. at 1285 n.37.

28. See Chapter 6, infra.

29. *Noerr-Pennington* were two cases decided by the Supreme Court in the 1960s that guaranteed the right to sue free from fear that the litigation might be attacked as an attempt to eliminate competition. If the litigation is determined to be a "sham," however, the exemption from antitrust does not apply.

30. 676 F.Supp. at 1287. The defendant had also alleged that by using the trademark in an attempt to block importation of competing LLADRO figurines, the plaintiff had misused its trademark. The court stated that it was unclear as to the specifics of this theory and dismissed it, giving the defendants twenty days to replead it.

Trademarks, the Customs Service, and the Gray Market: The Approach to At-the-Border Restrictions on Gray Market Goods

When the Second Circuit decided *Bourjois* in 1923, Congress did not approve. The case thus became a catalyst for new legislation, which in turn led to new Customs Service regulations and, eventually, much heated debate. That debate became a grand spectacle, culminating in a major Supreme Court decision with great impact on the currents of international trade, the gray market, and corporate composition.

A HISTORY

As seen in Chapter 2, *Bourjois* involved the sale of the entire U.S. business in trademarked face powder from France to A. Bourjois & Co., a New York corporation. Katzel, the defendant, was a New York City retailer who, prior to 1921, had purchased a quantity of the French-packaged JAVA powder, which he then sold at retail and at wholesale. The U.S. District Court enjoined Katzel's distribution of JAVA powder, but the Second Circuit, relying on *Fred Gretsch Mfg. Co. v Schoening* (the ETERNELLE case),[1] reversed on the theory that Katzel had not infringed because his product was "genuine" JAVA face powder.

Setting the Stage

In part because of concern generated by the impact of this decision on purchasers of property from the Alien Property Custodian during

---

This chapter was written by Murray I. Franck, Esquire, New York, New York, a professor of law and practicing attorney, specializing in intellectual property.

World War I, Congress reacted to the court of appeals decision by passing the Genuine Goods Exclusion Act.[2]

The statute has appeared in each subsequent version of the U.S. Tariff Act, including the latest incarnation (1974). Although, through the years, the numbering of sections in the Act has changed, and the section now bears the number 1526, all involved refer to the statute as sec. 526, and this nomenclature is adopted throughout this work. The current statute provides,

> Except as provided in subsection (d) of this section, it shall be unlawful to import into the United States any merchandise of foreign manufacture if such merchandise, or the label, sign, print, package, wrapper, or receptacle, bears a trademark owned by a citizen of, or by a corporation or association created or organized within, the United States, and registered in the Patent and Trademark Office by a person domiciled in the United States, under the provisions of sections 81 to 109 of title 15, and if a copy of the certificate of registration of such trademark is filed with the Secretary of the Treasury, in the manner provided in section 106 of said title 15, unless written consent of the owner of such trademark is produced at the time of making entry.

Some have characterized the original bill as a "midnight amendment" based upon "ten minutes of Senate debate." Whether or not that characterization is accurate, or even relevant, the history of the statute (and its accompanying regulations) is well-documented. This chapter, among other things, presents an eclectic perspective on the history and validity of Customs' enforcement of sec. 526. More detailed versions of this history, as well as other interpretations, can be found throughout the judicial history of sec. 526. One good example was presented by Judge Jane Restani in her opinion in *Vivitar Corp. v. United States*.[3] Judge Restani's version is especially noteworthy because of the attention to detail and clear and concise chronology. While other judges have offered interpretations different from that presented by Judge Restani,[4] in order to avoid needless recitation of that history, Judge Restani's opinion is presented in edited form in Appendix II.

It will become apparent that a "jurisprudence" in this area is lacking. Each case that addresses Customs policy in the gray market arena is revolutionary, rather than evolutionary. The judicial decisions in this area share few premises, and each decision's historical account appears "tailored" to achieve a particular result, without regard to precedent and the need for judicial consistency. Furthermore, as will be demonstrated, much of the debate has focused on whether Customs itself has been consistent in its approach to the statutes, and judges indeed differ widely in their answer to that question alone.

Several months after the enactment of sec. 526, the Supreme Court reversed the Second Circuit in *Bourjois*. That decision, it will be recalled, was based on the "territoriality of trademarks," not upon the newly enacted sec. 526. Nor did Justice Holmes refer to or address the exclusionary impact of sec. 27 of the Trademark Act of 1905 (the predecessor to sec. 42 of the Lanham Act), that is, the bar on importation of goods bearing marks that copy or simulate any trademark registered in the U.S. Justice Oliver W. Holmes opinion instead was based upon traditional trademark infringement caused by the sale of Katzel's goods.

Shortly thereafter, the applicability of sec. 27 to the gray market scenario was considered by the Supreme Court in *A. Bourjois & Co., Inc. v. Aldridge.*[5] The facts in *Aldridge* paralleled those in *Bourjois v. Katzel*, except that the case involved was MANON LESCAUT, another mark purchased by Bourjois N.Y. from Wertheimer, the foreign manufacturer. However, this time Bourjois sued not only the importer, but also the Collector of Customs (Aldridge), under sec. 27 of the Trademark Act. The District Court refused to require Customs to bar the importation of the MANON LESCAUT powder. The Second Circuit certified two questions to the Supreme Court:

1. Is the sale in the United States of Wertheimer's Manon Lescaut powder an infringement of plaintiff's registered trademarks?
2. Is the collector, by section 27 of the Trade-Mark Law, required to exclude from entry genuine MANON LESCAUT powder so as aforesaid made in France?

At the time *Aldridge* arose, Customs had not issued regulations under sec. 27, denying exclusion of parallel imports, and was not actively engaged in preventing the practice. The court, in a memorandum opinion, responded affirmatively to both issues raised by the court of appeals. The first question had already been answered in *Katzel*; and, because the importer infringed, the court held that Customs must, under sec. 27, bar the importation.

Shortly thereafter, Judge Learned Hand was faced with a case that raised a question not addressed in *Aldridge*: the meaning of the newly enacted sec. 526. In *Coty, Inc. v. Le Blume Import Co., Inc.*[6] the plaintiff was a subsidiary of a French corporation that owned the ORIGAN trademark in the United States and France. Coty U.S. had secured a Customs order of exclusion under sec. 526, barring a gray market defendant's importation of genuine ORIGAN perfume. Judge Hand's decision concerned gray market goods that had been repackaged and sold in boxes bearing labels that dismissed any connection between the seller and Coty U.S. With regard to sec. 526, he wrote:

> Section 526 . . . was intended only to supply the casus omissus, supposed [sic] to exist in section 27 of the Act of 1905 . . . because of the decision of the Circuit Court of Appeals in *Bourjois v. Katzel*. . . . Had the Supreme Court reversed that decision [before Congress passed sec. 526, the statute] would not have been enacted at all.

As will be seen, this passage has been used by all sides in the gray market controversy to support the differing points of view.

Section 526 of the Tariff Act was again addressed in *Sturges v. Clarke D. Pease, Inc.*[7] The U.S. rights to the automobile trademark "H-S" were acquired by the defendant who refused to allow plaintiff to import for personal use a second-hand car bearing the "H-S" mark. Justice Augustus Hand rejected the argument that sec. 526 is limited to facts similar to *Bourjois*, stating that

> The object of this drastic statute is to protect the owner of a foreign trademark from competition in respect to goods bearing the mark. . . . Sales of cars bearing the foreign trademark and imported without the consent of [the trademark owner] interfere with its right to control the use of the mark in this country which was the apparent purpose of the congressional legislation.
>
> If they are allowed to import . . . without its consent, [the trademark owner] may certainly lose customers. . . . To obtain such advantages, the local owner of the foreign mark is given control of the importation of all cars bearing [the mark].[8]

Eventually, Congress would pass legislation overturning this case and creating a personal use exemption for gray market imports. But *Sturges* remains important because of its clear statement that Congress meant what it said in the Tariff Act.

In 1936, Customs passed regulations under sec. 526 allowing parallel importation in cases where the U.S. trademark owner and the foreign manufacturer of the goods were owned by the same entity. Some suggest that Customs' action was an attempt to limit the impact of the Supreme Court decision in *Bourjois v. Katzel*; Customs' regulation thus restricted any bar on importation to cases where the owner of the U.S. trademark was independent of the foreign manufacturer.

In 1946 the Lanham Act was enacted. Section 42 of the Act provides (in part)

> Except as provided in subsection (d) of section 526 of the Tariff Act of 1930, no article of imported merchandise which shall copy or simulate the name of the [any] domestic manufacture, or manufacturer, or trader, or of any manufacturer or trader located in any foreign country which, by treaty, convention, or law affords similar privileges to citizens of the United States, or which shall copy of [sic] simulate a trademark registered in accordance with the provisions of this Act or shall bear a name or mark calculated to induce the public to believe that the article is manufactured in the United States, or that it is manufactured in any foreign country or locality other than the country or locality in which it is in fact manufactured, shall be admitted to entry at any customhouse of the United States.

That section in effect recodified sec. 27 of the 1905 Act. Some believe that regardless of whether sec. 526 presents an absolute bar to parallel importation, sec. 27 (as the court explained in *Aldridge*), had no exceptions, that is, that Customs could not limit its scope in the fashion in which Customs limited the scope of sec. 526.

In 1953 Customs' regulation denying exclusion of gray market goods, where the foreign and U.S. trademark registrations were owned by the same company, was expanded beyond unitary ownership to include members of the same corporate family, the so-called "related company" exception to sec. 526 enforcement. The motivation for this change, which amounted to a far more permissive importation policy, undoubtedly was grounded in antitrust policy, a fact reflected in the Justice Department's prosecution of the perfume industry, which is discussed below.

Customs Enforcement and the Perfume Cases

United States v. Guerlain, Inc.[9] involved U.S. distributors of French perfume who had obtained exclusion orders under sec. 526 of the Tariff Act. As was seen in Chapter 2, the Justice Department contended that obtaining the orders constituted monopolization in violation of sec. 2 of the Sherman Act. The district court found the U.S. companies were part of a "single international enterprise" that included the French owners of the U.S. trademarks and, thus, ruled that the exclusion orders should not have been granted.

Aside from his determination under the Sherman Act, Judge Edelstein held that, under *Fred Gretsch*, sec. 27 indeed had exceptions, and that that statute thus did not *mandate* a remedy for the importation by a third party of genuine trademarked goods. Judge Edelstein thus refused to hold that gray market importation was itself a violation of the 1905 Trademark Act, that importation therefore was necessarily a violation of sec. 42 of the newly enacted Lanham Act. Of course, the subsequent history of *Guerlain* raises doubt about the validity of Judge Edelstein's pronouncements on the gray market, and today they have receded well into the background.

Soon after the dismissal of *Guerlain*, Congress entertained legislation to amend sec. 526 to codify Customs' approach to the limitation on exclusion of gray market goods for affiliated companies.[10] That legislation was never enacted. Simultaneously, Customs adopted new regulations dropping the "related company" exception to sec. 526 enforcement.[11] One view is that Customs' change of policy was motivated by the Justice Department's debacle in *Guerlain*. In any event, Customs later asserted that in spite of the changed regulations, no real change in enforcement policy was made, and that Customs continued to deny exclusion in all affiliated company cases. In 1973, Customs again modified its regulations, restoring the "related company" exception, and the regulation remains in place to the present.[12]

The current regulations thus read as follows:

(a)*Copying or simulating marks or names.* Articles of foreign or domestic manufacture bearing a mark or name copying or simulating a recorded trademark or trade name shall be denied entry and are subject to forfeiture as prohibited importations. A "copying or simulating mark" or name is one that so resembles it as to be likely to cause the public to associate the copy, mark, or name.

(b)*Identical trademark.* Foreign-made articles bearing a trademark identical with one owned and recorded by a citizen of the United States or a corporation or association created or organized within the United States are subject to seizure and forfeiture as prohibited importation.

(c)*Restrictions not applicable.* The restrictions set forth in paragraphs (a) and (b) of this section do not apply to imported articles when

(1)Both the foreign and the U.S. trademark . . . are owned by the same person or business entity;

(2)The foreign and domestic trademark . . . owners are parent and subsidiary companies or are otherwise subject to common ownership or control (see sec. 133.2(d) and 133.1(d));

(3)The articles of foreign manufacture bear a recorded trademark . . . applied under authorization of the U.S. owner.

Subsection (c)(1) is often referred to as the "unitary ownership" section, (c)(2) as the "related company" exception, and, (c)(3) as the "authorized use" exception. Paragraphs (c)(1) and (c)(2) are referred to jointly as the "common control" exceptions, and this shorthand will be adopted in this chapter.

In order for a company to attempt to take advantage of sec. 526, the company must deposit with Customs their mark, along with a declaration enumerating the names of all foreign entities permitted to affix that mark to goods. All goods emanating from such enumerated foreign entities are automatically permitted entry regardless of who the importer is. This practice was to become the subject of great dispute.

THE DISPUTE OVER REGULATIONS

In the 1980s, there was a significant amount of litigation over the validity and propriety of Customs' regulations. U.S. trademark owners asserted that the regulations were not in accord with the statutory mandates of sec. 526 and 42. These cases reached their culmination in the Supreme Court's decision in 1988 in *K-Mart v. Cartier*. Before discussing that decision and the details of the litigation that led to it, it is useful to set the tone for these cases by comparing a variety of judicial characterizations of Customs' policy.

One observation, made by Circuit Judge Nies in *Vivitar v. United States* is:

> the regulations are patently less protective of the interests of a U.S. trademark owner than the literal language of the statute.... While reversal of *Katzel* was one purpose of sec. 1526, it was clearly, and we use the word advisedly, not the *sole* purpose.[13]

Other judges viewing the history of sec. 526 enforcement have disagreed over whether Customs' policy has been consistent throughout the statute's history. For example, in *Olympus Corp. v. United States*,[14] Judge Oakes, writing for the majority, maintained that Customs' enforcement since 1951 had indeed been consistent, in spite of the changing regulations. This position was supported by reference to several letters to Congress indicating a consistent policy of withholding the benefits of sec. 526 in cases of common control over the U.S. and foreign users of the mark.

In stark contrast, Judge Ralph Winter, dissenting from Judge Oakes' opinion in *Olympus* and foreshadowing the position of some Supreme Court Justices in *K-Mart*, drew the opposite conclusion. Judge Winter's short but potent opinion asserted that the legislative history of sec. 526 is ambiguous and that the history of Customs' regulations reflects Customs' own confusion over the purpose and validity of the regulation. He noted

> The fact is that the Customs Service has over the years justified this regulation with arguments of opportunity tailored to whatever audience it happened to be addressing at the time. This is hardly unusual administrative behavior, although the degree of vacillation in this case is somewhat exceptional. The fact that courts may indulge in fiction in the area of administrative law more often than in any other field does not mean, however, that we cannot insist upon coherent fiction.[15]

Judge Leval in *Osawa* agreed with Judge Nies that although sec. 526 was indeed enacted to overturn *Katzel*, its provisions are not limited to those narrow facts. He believed that *Aldridge* confirmed this conclusion by excluding genuine goods under sec. 27 (and thus sec. 42) without reference to sec. 526. The implication is that the supposed omission of reference to genuine goods in the original (i.e., 1905) sec. 27 was remedied by both the Supreme Court's decision in *Katzel* and by Congress' enactment of sec. 526. Judge Leval thus contended that sec. 526 is clear and that its benefits do not depend on "subtle variations in [the U.S. registrant's] relationship with the foreign markholder."[16]

Judge Leval notes that the Customs regulations, influenced by the *Guerlain* prosecution, presume antitrust violations without reference to actual market considerations. That, in turn in his view, constitutes both unsound antitrust policy and an incorrect application of trademark law. Simply put, in Judge Leval's view both sec. 526 and, by implication, sec. 42 provide private remedies available against gray market importers which, according to *Aldridge* and *Sturges*, Customs must enforce.

Katzel Revisited and *Guerlain* Resurrected

Prior to discussing the recent litigation leading to *K-Mart v. Cartier*, it is useful to review two recent court decisions that parallel the watershed decisions in *Bourjois* and *Guerlain*. These two cases are important because they demonstrate the continuing validity of the specific holdings of *Bourjois* and *Guerlain* and thus present important benchmarks for the current debate over Customs policy.

Premier Dental Products Co., Inc. v. Darby Dental Supply Co., Inc., discussed at length in Chapter 3, was a case similar to *Bourjois*. The Third Circuit, finding infringement by gray market goods, ordered their exclusion under sec. 526. The action was brought under secs. 32, 42, and 43 of the Lanham Act and under sec. 526 of the Tariff Act. Although the court of appeals agreed with the district court that there was trademark infringement, it apparently based the exclusion solely on sec. 526.

Discussing sec. 526, the court held that the Customs regulations were inapplicable to the facts presented because under trademark law doctrine, Premier was the true owner of the mark, in the fashion that Bourjois was the owner the JAVA mark. It responded to Darby's contention that sec. 526 is inapposite given the "genuineness" of the goods, that is, that they were identical to Premier's and derived from the same source.

The statutory language is broad and unambiguous. It declares illegal the unauthorized importation of any merchandise of foreign manufacture bearing a domestically owned trademark. Moreover, the legislative history amply demonstrates Congress's intent to bar imports even of "genuine" goods, where the importation is not authorized by the domestic trademark owner.... Therefore, we conclude that where a trademark is owned and registered in this country by an exclusive distributor who is independent of the foreign manufacturer and who has separate goodwill in the product, the distributor is entitled under Section 526 to prevent the importation even of genuine merchandise obtained from the same foreign manufacturer.[17]

The second case, *Parfums Stern*[18] is reminiscent of *Guerlain*. Even though the antitrust rationale for that decision is of extremely dubious validity, the perfume industry was still denied exclusion orders for gray market imports. The key to Judge Aronovitz' decision was that the U.S. trademark registrant was a mere "cog" in a "single international enterprise" that maintained full control over the quality and international marketing of the goods and, thus, that the corporate veils of these subsidiaries could be pierced. The thrust of *Parfums Stern*, as demonstrated in Judge Higginbotham's decision in *Weil*, was that "common control" and the fact that all sales, whether authorized or gray market, redounded to the familial purse, indicating that Customs' original, more limited approach (i.e., unitary ownership as opposed to "related companies") at a minimum retains judicial recognition.

The Camera Quadrilogy: Catalysts for *K-Mart v. Cartier*

Until the Supreme Court's decision in *K-Mart*, four cases, all involving the camera industry's attempts to bar gray market trade, were the only instruments for guidance on the proper scope of sec. 526 and sec. 42 and on the validity of the common control exceptions of the Customs regulations.

Two of the cases, *Bell & Howell: Mamiya Co. v. Masel Supply Co. Corp.*, and *Osawa & Co. v. B&H Photo*, turned principally on the interpretation of trademark law, but they also dealt with sec. 526. As was detailed previously in Chapter 2, the first case was a victory for gray market sellers, the second a victory for trademark owners. The first case is significant because the court implied that any private remedy under sec. 526 must be predicated on a finding of irreparable injury. *Osawa* is important because Judge Leval, in deciding the Lanham Act issues, reviewed the history of sec. 526 and its accompanying regulations. He found that although sec. 526 was passed to overturn the circuit court in decision in *Bourjois*, the statute's broad language is not limited to the facts of that case.

Simply put, Judge Leval concluded that the statute means what it says. He relied upon Judge L. Hand's discussion in *Coty, Inc. v. Le Blume Import Co., Inc.*, that "Section 526(a) . . . was intended only to supply the casus omissus supposed to exist in sec. 27 of the Act of 1905." Judge Leval identified Judge Hand's missing element in sec. 27 as "foreign goods with genuine marks imported in derogation of the U.S. mark owner's trademark rights."[19] The hole created by the interpretation of sec. 27 in *Fred Gretsch* was plugged independently by sec. 526 and by the Supreme Court's reversal of *Katzel*. In Judge Leval's view, sec. 27 mandated exclusion of goods that "copy or simulate" regardless of the relationship between the domestic and foreign manufacturer, and irrespective of whether or not the goods are considered genuine. Judge Leval thus implied that *Gretsch* was wrongly decided, that had sec. 27 been properly applied by the circuit court in *Bourjois v. Katzel*, enactment of sec. 526 would not have been required.

In *Vivitar Corp. v. United States*[20] the plaintiff was a California corporation that owned and deposited with Customs the U.S. trademark registrations for VIVITAR. The company sells photographic equipment in the United States and overseas that is made under contract with foreign manufacturers. While its foreign subsidiaries sell VIVITAR products overseas, the U.S. parent is the exclusive domestic distributor. The court stated that it did not know precisely who owned the foreign registrations of the VIVITAR mark. The defendants purchased VIVITAR cameras overseas and marketed them at a substantial discount in the United States. Vivitar sued the Customs Service in the U.S. Court of International Trade (hereinafter referred to as CIT) to invalidate the Customs regulations. Specifically, Vivitar sought to force Customs to bar the importation of all VIVITAR marked goods to which Vivitar had not expressly consented.

The CIT granted summary judgment to the government and upheld Customs' position and the regulations. The court of appeals affirmed. The court, per Judge Nies, however, held that although the regulations are consistent with the statute, they are limited to defining Customs' sua sponte role in administrative enforcement of the statute and that, because sec. 526 provides for a private remedy available to injured parties in federal court, the courts should mandate that Customs bar the importation if Vivitar can establish that the importation infringed its rights.

> When a U.S. trademark owner successfully pursued a claim against a private party, Custom[s] must, of course, give effect to any judicial determination that the owner has a right to bar importation of goods bearing its mark, even though the goods were obtained from or through a foreign related company.[21]

Relying upon Judge Augustus Hand's characterization in *Sturges* of sec. 526 as a "drastic statute," Judge Nies reasoned that a court, in a suit against the importer, could require exclusion because the statute was aimed at giving the U.S. trademark owner the right to control imports of all goods bearing the mark regardless of the relationship between the U.S. trademark owner and the foreign producer. In Judge Nies' view, Customs is permitted to grant a more limited form of remedy by regulation, but it could be required to enforce the statute literally if a court so ordered.

The final case in the camera quadrilogy is *Olympus Corporation v. United States.*[22] Olympus, a wholly owned U.S. subsidiary of the Japanese firm that owns the U.S. trademark OLYMPUS, is the exclusive U.S. distributor of OLYMPUS optical goods. A New York City retailer, 47th Street Photo, purchased OLYMPUS goods abroad at prices that enabled it to sell them at a substantial discount domestically. Again, at issue was the validity of Customs' common control exception to sec. 526. The Second Circuit held that the regulation was valid. The court also found that the plaintiff failed to sustain a sec. 42 trademark infringement claim. Judge Oakes adopted by reference both Judge Restani's explication of the history of sec. 526 and Judge Nies's reiteration of the "checkered" history of the regulations.

However, Judge Oakes emphasized that he disagreed with Judge Nies's belief that the regulations have been inconsistent to the point of not supporting the defendant's reading of the statute. Nevertheless, he agreed with Judge Leval in *Osawa*, that CFR (Code of Federal Regulations) 133.21(c) is unsound from the perspectives of both trademark and antitrust law. From this plinth of splintered wood the court reaches to the legitimating cloud of "congressional acquiescence."

While we find the regulation of questionable wisdom, we believe that congressional acquiescence in the long standing administrative interpretation of the statute legitimates that interpretation as an exercise of Custom's [sic] enforcement of discretion.[23]

The Court then affirmed the dismissal of the sec. 42 trademark infringement claim, reasoning that the statute does not bar the importation of genuine goods but only of goods that "copy or simulate a trademark." Judge Oakes acknowledged the weakness of his position in light of *Aldridge* but concluded that, due to the brevity of the decision and the different facts involved, absent an arm's length sale of U.S. trademark rights, sec. 42 applies only to counterfeit or spurious trademarks that "copy or simulate" genuine trademarks. Although he admitted that his approach results in a fluid definition of "copy or simulate" and that this phrase should have the same meaning in all contexts, he believed in the necessity and acceptability of reinterpretation as a means of dissipating difficulties in statutory interpretation as they arise.

Thus, although the Court bowed to regulations that it characterized as being of "questionable wisdom," it was assertive in its pronouncement that

Customs' interpretation of the statute does not limit the reach of protection of section 526; it only limits Customs' obligation to enforce the section by excluding the goods. The markholder still has rights under the statute: he may pursue private remedies against the importer under section 526(e), notwithstanding Customs' failure to exclude the goods.[24]

Judge Oakes thus appears to agree, however reluctantly, with Judge Nies's invitation to private litigation over the legality of gray market trade. But his decision about the regulation of the statute is clear: Congress, by its inaction, has acquiesced in Customs' interpretation of the statute and its own enforcement history.

As was stated earlier, Judge Winter wrote a vigorous and scathing dissent, disagreeing with Judge Oakes's interpretation of both Customs' practice and the impact of Congress' failure to address the matter. Judge Winter's dissent is an articulate expression of the contrary view that Customs has overstepped its authority in limiting enforcement of sec. 526. That view would soon gain momentum and lead to the Supreme Court's decision in *K-Mart v. Cartier.*

THE *K-MART* DECISION

In 1984, an organization of U.S. trademark owners known as the Coalition to Protect the Integrity of American Trademarks (known by and hereinafter referred to as "COPIAT") sought a Declaratory Judgment that the Customs regulations are invalid because they are inconsistent with sec. 526 of the Tariff Act. COPIAT also sought an injunction against further enforcement of the regulations by the Customs Service. Although the district court upheld the regulations, the Court of Appeals for the District of Columbia found the regulations to be an unreasonable administrative interpretation of the statute.[25] The case was certified to the Supreme Court to resolve the conflict among the circuits, that is, with *Vivitar* and *Olympus*.

The Supreme Court's decision was rendered under the name of a companion case brought by interventors, known as *K-Mart Corp. v. Cartier, Inc.*[26] The Supreme Court's decision resolved many of the outstanding issues about enforcement of sec. 526; however, many fundamental issues remain unresolved. The immediate upshot of the case is that the common control exception to sec. 526 was upheld, but a portion of that regulation that also barred relief in cases where the foreign manufacturer of trademarked goods was licensed or otherwise was "authorized" to use the mark was declared invalid.

The Supreme Court's decision in *K-Mart* is actually a composite of three separate opinions. Justice Kennedy wrote what was to become the majority opinion; Justice Brennan, joined by three other justices, wrote a separate concurrence that would also become a plurality opinion agreeing in part with Justice Kennedy's conclusion. A portion of Justice Brennan's opinion, however, disagreed with that of Justice Kennedy, and in that portion, Justice Brennan is dissenting. Similarly Justice Scalia, joined by three of his colleagues, authored an opinion, part of which becomes a concurrence, and part, a dissent.

Although Justice Kennedy's decision is lucid and succinct, the Brennan/Scalia concurrences and dissents contain much obtuse reasoning, the validity of which is accessible only to a seasoned academic logician and the impact of which is to raise multiple questions for the judiciary and the Bar. While Justice Scalia's arguments appear to test the stronger in logic, both justices are preparing their armor for grave battles over constitutional interpretation that in point of fact have little to do with the gray market. Nevertheless, these two opinions are important expressions of the varying views on sec. 526 enforcement, and much discussion of them is required.

Justice Kennedy, in the manner of a fine teacher and in an effort to elucidate the nature of the gray market problem, utilized models to define three different categories of gray market scenarios. Initially, gray market goods were defined as "a foreign manufactured good, bearing a valid United States trademark, that is imported without the consent of the U.S. trademark holder."

Three scenarios were identified by Justice Kennedy.

Case 1. A company referred to as "the prototypical gray-market victim" is a domestic U.S. firm that has purchased the U.S. trademark, including the rights to use and registration for the assignor/vendor's foreign-made goods. In this scenario, the U.S. purchaser's investment is victimized by intrabrand competition if either his assignor/vendor or a third party imports into the United States the same goods under the same mark. This scenario mirrors *Bourjois* and in fact engendered virtually no dispute.

Case 2. A domestic firm registers a trademark in the United States to cover goods manufactured abroad by a foreign affiliate. Under this scenario, there are three possible arrangements, which the court denominated as follows:

1. Case 2a, the U.S. company is a subsidiary of the foreign firm;
2. Case 2b, the U.S. firm is the parent of its overseas manufacturing subsidiary; and
3. Case 2c, the U.S. firm opens a foreign plant, which is not separately incorporated and the assets of which are owned by the domestic firm.

Case 3. The U.S. proprietor of the U.S. trademark licenses or otherwise authorizes a foreign firm to use the mark, typically in specific markets and on the condition that the goods are not imported into the United States.

Justice Kennedy and his brethren explored the validity of the Customs regulations in the context of these scenarios. In Case 1 situations, the entire court ruled that Customs may (sic) bar gray market importation. But the court split divergently on the other scenarios. One majority, consisting of Justices Kennedy, Brennan, Marshall, Stevens, and White (concurring in part and dissenting in part), held that the common control exception is consistent with sec. 526. In other words, in cases 2a through 2c Customs may allow entry of gray goods, that is, deny the benefit of the statute to the U.S. trademark proprietor. A different majority, namely, Justices Kennedy, Scalia, Blackmun, and O'Connor, and Chief Justice Rehnquist held that the authorized use exception (covering case 3) is inconsistent with the statute, and thus Customs must bar importation in these cases in the absence of the U.S. proprietor's consent.

Regarding "common control" and "case 2" Justice Kennedy reasoned that subsections (c)(1) and (c)(2) of the regulations are permissable constructions designed to resolve real statutory ambiguities. Specifically, the statutory phrase "owned by" in the statute could apply to either of the two entities, the foreign parent or the U.S. subsidiary. It is thus unclear which entity was envisioned by the statute as the "owner" of the U.S. registration. Furthermore, a second statutory ambiguity, the phrase "merchandise of foreign manufacture" sustains the regulations as applied to cases 2b and 2c, in that this language could mean "goods manufactured in a foreign country," "goods manufactured by a foreign company," or "goods manufactured by a foreign company in a foreign country." Given this imprecision, Customs permissibly interpreted the statute to mean that goods manufactured by a foreign subsidiary or division of a U.S. company are not goods of "foreign manufacture" and are thus not excludable.

The limited Kennedy/Scalia majority found subsection (c)(3), the authorized use exception, invalid in that the foregoing statutory ambiguities are "irrelevant."

Under no reasonable construction of statutory language can goods made in a foreign country by an independent foreign manufacturer be removed from the purview of the statute.[27]

Justice Brennan, in his separate opinion, concurred with Justice Kennedy that subsections (c)(1) and (c)(2), the common control exception, are valid, but did so by dint of a different analysis. In Justice Brennan's view, the regulations are valid not as reasonable constructions of statutory ambiguities but because "Congress did not intend to extend sec. 526's protections to affiliates of foreign manufacturers. . . . "[28] In his view, only U.S. companies may invoke sec. 526. In Case 2a situations, a foreign manufacturer who registers a U.S. trademark is not a U.S. domicilliary and thus may not take advantage of the statute.

Under this approach, it is irrelevant that a U.S. subsidiary is the registrant because the foreign parent is the *true* trademark proprietor in that the U.S. company's decisions are controlled by the foreign parent.

In effect, Justice Brennan pierces the corporate veil without inquiring in any particular situation as to whether the companies are truly alter egos. While this may or may not make good sense when limited to a trademark perspective, it may serve as a powerful precedent for the destruction of modern corporate structuring in general. That issue, however, is beyond the immediate scope of this work and will not be addressed further.

Although Justice Brennan accepted the ambiguities pointed up by Justice Kennedy regarding "merchandise of foreign manufacture," he stressed that "cases 2b and 2c" clearly involve "merchandise manufactured in a foreign country" and thus are not protected by what Justice Brennan deems the plain meaning of the statute. For this reason, he would hold that subsections (c)(1) and (c)(2) are valid.

Justice Brennan also discerned another ambiguity amenable to Customs' interpretation, namely, that Congress may have intended to distinguish between cases 1 and 2 based upon what he perceives as the disparate risks involved. Case 1 concerns a supposedly helpless U.S. assignee who has paid real value in an arm's length transaction for both a foreign mark and the business of selling goods under that mark in the United States.

By contrast, case 2 relates to parties who are, by definition, capable of ordering their distribution systems in such a way as to control the flow of gray market goods. These firms are thus capable of dictating their fates by effectively contracting to divide markets, privately policing their distribution system to permit exports consigned only to the U.S. trademark proprietor, or simply by not selling overseas. This trilogy of prophylactic business practices, somewhat embellished, became the "self-help" solution recently adopted by Judge Higginbotham in *Weil*. The implication is that in case 2 all gray market harm is self-inflicted because of a failure to employ these mechanisms and that it is thus unworthy of federal protection.

Furthermore, Justice Brennan reasoned that the legislative history of sec. 526 (as opposed to the plain meaning of the statute) is unclear and that the statute was hastily drawn as a "midnight amendment . . . and allotted a miserly ten minutes of debate, in the context of a debate on a comprehensive revision of tariff (not trademark) law." Nevertheless, he believes that this "sparse legislative history confirms that Congress' sole goal was to overrule Katzel." He characterizes sec. 526 as "protectionist, almost Jingoist" legislation and thus limited to case 1 scenarios.

The remainder of Justice Brennan's opinion, because its conclusion differs from that of Justice Kennedy, becomes a dissent. Justice Brennan would have upheld subsection (c)(3) (authorized use), based upon what he perceived as the previously mentioned statutory ambiguity, extending it to case 3 and that therefore that Customs' interpretation was a reasonable exercise of administrative discretion. Secondly, as in case 2, because self-help is available and harm is, in effect, self-inflicted, no relief should be available. Thirdly, because the Lanham Act permits licensing while retaining the licensor's ownership of the mark if the quality of the goods is licensor controlled, use of the mark on such authorized goods renders them genuine as in Case 2.[29]

Justice Scalia concurred with Justice Kennedy that subsection (c)3, the "authorized use" exception, is invalid. Additionally, he appeared to agree that in case 2a it is sometimes permissible to hold that a U.S. trademark nominally owned by a domestic subsidiary of a foreign company is "owned by" its foreign parent and, thus, that such a U.S. subsidiary cannot claim the benefit of sec. 526. In this case, the U.S. company is nothing more than a shell, set up and designed simply to take advantage of sec. 526.

Justice Scalia, however, dissented with regard to the common control exceptions in cases where the U.S. trademark registrant is not a mere shell. The common control exceptions, he maintained, are in clear conflict with the statutory language. Justice Scalia posited that even if sec. 526 is ambiguous, "the authority to clarify an ambiguity in a statute is not the authority to alter even its unambiguous applications" and that sec. 526(a) unambiguously encompasses most of the situations that the regulations purport to exclude, "specifically cases 2b and 2c."

Justice Scalia reasoned that "words, like syllables, acquire meaning not in isolation but within their context." The statutory distinction, then, is between goods of domestic (U.S.) as opposed to foreign (overseas, abroad) manufacture. In his view, in common understanding "foreign manufacture" means "manufactured abroad," and there is no ambiguity. He thus criticized the majority's reasoning, saying that its views can lead to conclusions such as construing the statement, " 'I have a foreign object in my eye,' as referring perhaps, to something from Italy." One cannot dissect a phrase, he asserted, blaming the majority for making this error, and thus leading, in the example offered, to an absurd conclusion. To support his position, he pointed out that

> A 19th century statute criminalizing the theft of goods is not ambiguous in its application to the theft of microwave ovens simply because the legislators enacting it "were unlikely to have contemplated" those appliances; and a 1922 (or 1930) statute covering a "corporation . . . organized within the United States" unambiguously includes a U.S. corporation that has licensed its trademark abroad, whether or not a U.S. corporation with that characteristic existed at the time.[30]

Justice Scalia further criticized the majority decision for treating goods manufactured on American soil by American companies more favorably than goods manufactured by foreign nationals as a clear violation of basic treaties on international trade.

Regarding subsection (c)(3) and case 3, he believed again that there is no ambiguity and that the statutory language embraces the very situations excluded by the regulation. As already stated, that conclusion becomes part of a plurality, not majority, opinion because it is not joined by Justice Kennedy, who agreed with the result but not with the reasoning.

In response to Justice Brennan's position that an authorized foreign user presents less of a risk to the U.S. trademark proprietor's investment than does the foreign assignor of a U.S. trademark to the U.S. assignee, Justice Scalia argued that "[a]lthough Congress understood that a U.S. trademark owner could authorize the use of its mark abroad, Congress nonetheless chose not to create an exception to sec. 526 for that situation." Furthermore, Justice Scalia reasoned convincingly that the equities in case 1 that motivated congressional protections do not differ significantly from those in case 3. He demonstrated this point with the example of a U.S. trademark owner who assigns to a foreign entity his foreign rights in the same trademark as he uses domestically. Clearly this is an "authorized use" of which Justice Brennan would deny the exclusionary right. In allowing such gray goods entry, the investment at risk is the U.S. registrant's entire goodwill in the mark in the United States (even if the goods are manufactured in the United States), the same risk that required protection in *Katzel*.

In summary, Justice Scalia posited that the authorization of foreign use should not serve to victimize a U.S. trademark proprietor and that it is irrelevant that the U.S. owner can contract to prevent importation since the bulk of gray market imports emanate from third parties not subject to the contract, and perforce not policeable.[31]

While Justice Brennan's dissent characterizes Justice Scalia's position as one of "stolid anachronism," Justice Scalia responds that

In the last analysis it is Justice Brennan's approach that bespeaks "stolid anachronism," because in theory it requires Judges to rewrite the United States Code to accord with the unenacted purposes of Congresses long since called home. (The reality, I fear, may be even worse than the theory. In practice, the rewriting is less likely to accord with the legislative purposes of yesterday than [with] the judicial predilections of today.)[32]

In Justice Scalia's view, the statutory language is clear and encompasses changing commercial relationships, both seen and unforeseen. Congress may amend the statute, but neither the court nor Customs may do so.

While Justice Scalia probably would agree with Judge Restani that " . . . statutory language cannot control if clearly demonstrated Congressional intent requires a different construction,"[33] Justice Scalia would probably say that the operative term is "clearly" and not "tortured logic" or "personal perspective." Rather than misinterpret an ambiguity, he probably would prefer that the Court declare the law "void for vagueness" and hold Congress to its elected job: passing clear and enforceable legislation.

IN THE WAKE OF K-MART

Subsequent to the Supreme Court's decision in K-Mart, only three cases have addressed exclusion based upon sec. 42 and sec. 526. In Yamaha Corp. of America v. ABC Int'l Traders, Corp.,[34] plaintiffs brought suit on the theory that the defendant's importation and sale of YAMAHA brand goods violates, inter alia, these statutory sections. Yamaha Japan, the manufacturer of the goods, is a Japanese corporation that is the sole parent of Yamaha America, a California corporation. The YAMAHA marks were owned by Yamaha Japan until 1986 when they were assigned to Yamaha America. Defendant, without plaintiffs' approval and in direct competition with plaintiff, imported, distributed, advertised, warranted, and provided support services to genuine YAMAHA goods, legally obtained abroad.

The court found that factually not only were the goods genuine but also the marks represented to the public design and manufacture by Yamaha Japan, not Yamaha America. It reasoned that, although sec. 526 prohibits importing or dealing in foreign-made merchandise bearing a mark registered by a U.S. corporation, for fifty years Customs has denied such protection to U.S. subsidiaries of foreign corporations. Relying on *K-Mart*, it found the common control exception in the regulations applicable to the private cause of action. Furthermore, the court justified Customs' interpretation on antitrust grounds reminiscent of *Guerlain*, that is, the need to prevent worldwide price discrimination.

Relying upon *NEC Electronics v. CAL Circuit Abco*,[35] the court held that the Lanham Act does not bar the importation of genuine goods, relying on the "self-inflicted wound" theory, specifically that the foreign manufacturer itself decided to sell to the defendants at a price fostering U.S. discounts. While this approach is an implicit subscription to Justice Brennan's self-help theorem, it more closely parallels the arguments made by Judge Higginbotham in *Weil*. The court thus granted summary judgment to the defendant.

Indeed, *Weil* is the second case, following the Supreme Court's decision, to address the applicability of sec. 526 and sec. 42 in the post–*K-Mart* era. The district court had granted Weil's motion for summary judgment on its sec. 32 infringement claim and, relying upon *Aldridge*, held that plaintiffs provisionally were entitled to an order barring importation of genuine goods under sec. 42 and sec. 526. The district court reasoned that because federal statutes[36] provide that sec. 42 and sec. 526 are inapplicable to importations of genuine goods to the U.S. Virgin Islands, Congress must believe that sec. 42 and sec. 526 bar such importations into the mainland.

On appeal, the decision of the district court was reversed. Judge Higginbotham analyzed *K-Mart* exhaustively. He believed that the Supreme Court was unanimous in holding that the regulations are consistent with sec. 526 where a U.S. subsidiary of the foreign manufacturer of the goods is the trademark proprietor, that is, in case 2a. As demonstrated previously, Judge Scalia had agreed that some 2a cases called for an exception to literal enforcement of sec. 526 (i.e., when the U.S. trademark owner is a mere shell), but he was not prepared to permit importation in *all* 2a cases. Nevertheless, in footnote 5 of the opinion and subsequently, Judge Higginbotham expanded his reading of the "unanimous opinion" to include all "common control" or "case 2" scenarios. That interpretation seemed at the time unjustified, but, in light of the Supreme Court's refusal to review the decision in *Weil*, it may indeed be an accurate reflection of where the law is headed.

The instant case was then deemed to "closely resemble" a "case 2a" scenario and the regulations to unequivocally and absolutely exclude defendant's importations from the ban of sec. 526. Although Weil did not originate as a sham subsidiary established to exploit U.S. law, as an affiliate of Lladro S.A., the Spanish manufacturer, in Judge Higginbotham's view, it enjoys all of the benefits inherent in the case 2a corporate relationship and thus cannot take advantage of the sec. 526 exclusion.[37] Among those benefits are the profits accruing to the Spanish corporations from foreign purchases by gray market sellers. These profits, Judge Higginbotham asserted, made up for lost sales by the U.S. subsidiary.

Furthermore, because of the relationship between Weil and its corporate parents, self-help mechanisms, such as a refusal to sell to the defendant, are available to Weil's corporate family. To Justice Brennan's enumeration of self-help mechanisms, Justice Higginbotham added (1) sales abroad at prices equal to those being offered in the United States, and (2) goods destined for foreign markets marked differently from those intended for sale in the United States.[38]

Judge Higginbotham reasoned that the common denominator of *Katzel* (and presumably *Aldridge*) and *K-Mart* was the nature of the corporate relationships. As stated in Chapter 3, Judge Higginbotham agreed with Justice Brennan, limiting *Katzel* to its facts, that is, domestic markholders "truly independent of the foreign manufacturer" who actually stand to lose the full benefit of their investment if the parallel importation is not barred. Based upon the Weil-Lladro S.A. connection, therefore, the statutory protections also were deemed to be unavailable to Weil.

> We do not read the Lanham Act ... to protect a foreign manufacturer that either owns or is owned by a domestic trademark holder ... from competition in the sale of its product in the United States by a domestic importer that it has supplied.

Clearly, Judge Higginbotham reserved the logical essence of his opinion for footnote 13, where he argued that sec. 526 was enacted solely to overrule the circuit court's decision in *Katzel*, with the intention of closing the gaps in sec. 42 (and its predecessor, sec. 27). Thus, because sec. 526 simply amended the Trademark Act, the latter is controlled by sec. 526 and is not independent of it. Viewed this way, because sec. 526 was the last word from Congress about parallel importation, and because that statute does not mention or except sec. 27, any implied exceptions to enforcement of sec. 526 by implication apply to sec. 27 (and 42) as well. Again, he relied upon Justice Brennan's reasoning and conclusions in *K-Mart*. Judge Higginbotham's reasoning further demonstrates that the "casus omissus" reasoning of Judge L. Hand in *Coty* can be used effectively by both sides in the gray market controversy.

Despite his reasoning limiting the scope of sec. 42, Judge Higginbotham noted that sec. 42 and sec. 27 protection was perhaps expanded by the Supreme Court in *Katzel*. Although *Katzel* was decided subsequent to the enactment of sec. 526, Justice Holmes did not refer to the new statute; as such, it might be argued that sec. 42 is independent of sec. 526, rather than being qualified by it. Nevertheless, Judge Higginbotham again argued that even if that is true, *Katzel*, in his view, is limited to case 1. Thus, sec. 27 (and sec. 42) are similarly limited.

In footnote 14 to his opinion, Judge Higginbotham maintained that when sec. 42 was enacted there existed a long-standing Customs interpretation of sec. 27, namely that the importation of genuine goods with genuine marks did not fall under sec. 27, but rather that that statute applied only to counterfeit marks and that, by enacting sec. 42 without modification of this interpretation, Congress impliedly ratified Customs' interpretation. It is unclear, however, whether Judge Higginbotham's statement about Customs refers to the interpretation of sec. 27 or of sec. 526.

Judge Higginbotham asserted that "the terms 'copy,' 'simulate,' 'counterfeit,' and 'imitate' [in sec. 42] have readily comprehensible ordinary meanings" but he then denied that the terms "copy or simulate" in sec. 42 were meant to be given a "plain meaning." Notwithstanding this conclusion, Judge Higginbotham mentioned the principle that "statutory construction must begin with the language employed by Congress and the assumption that the ordinary meaning of that language accurately expresses the Legislative purpose,"[39] raising an inconsistency within his own opinion. Judge Higginbotham's opinion admitted that his approach results in statutory definitions that are situational rather than constant. At bottom, he held that sec. 42 applies only to counterfeit goods and that importation of genuine goods is not barred by the statute.[40]

Judge Becker's concurring opinion was implicitly more scathing than any imaginable dissent. He believed that because *K-Mart* addressed only sec. 526, Judge Higginbotham was wrong in asserting that *K-Mart* has a bearing on sec. 42. Apparently demurring from Judge Higginbotham's inconsistencies, he reasoned that it is the legislative history of sec. 42, rather than its "plain language," that renders it unavailable to bar parallel importation.

He also maintained that the narrow reading of *Katzel* "is either too broad or too narrow" because this reading would *always* bar importation when the U.S. trademark owner is truly independent but never bar importation in any other circumstance. Such an interpretation, he maintained, is not supported by *K-Mart*, which addressed the power of Customs to interpret the Tariff Act, not the rights of trademark holders under the Lanham Act. Justice Becker instead viewed *Katzel* as "a court sitting in equity, not a blanket change in trademark law" and thus not a case that should affect the breadth of interpretation of sec. 526.

He pointed out that the negative responses to the circuit court's *Katzel* decision by Congress and the Supreme Court are not coextensive or even supplementary but that their respective impact necessarily differs because their authors' respective powers differ. Legislation provides a blanket rule and thus sec. 526 protects a *Katzel*-type party from parallel imports. On the other hand, a judicial decision provides an equitable remedy for specific inequities on a case-by-case basis. The trigger for statutory protection under sec. 526 is the independence of the domestic and foreign entities, and that independence, for judicial intervention, is the presence of inequities. The two should not be confused as Judge Higginbotham seems to have done.

Judge Becker believed that gray market goods can form the basis for an infringement claim and an exclusion order under sec. 42 regardless of the corporate parentage of the U.S. trademark owner. The issue, he believed, was whether the importation should be barred as a matter of equity, as Justice Holmes had done in *Katzel*. He reasoned that in the case before him the equities weighed against Weil. As a wholly owned subsidiary of the foreign complex, it has a unity of interest with Lladro S.A. and access to self-help available to the foreign parent. Furthermore, the infringement was self-inflicted in that the family itself launched the lower quality, infringing genuine goods, into commerce under the identical mark; the Lanham Act (including sec. 42) was not meant to remedy this sort of injury. Based on this reasoning, Judge Becker in reality would limit *Katzel* to its facts.

Lever Brothers Co. v. United States of America[41] tested the validity of the common control exceptions in the face of Lanham Act sec. 42. The case involved the importation of soap intended by Lever Brothers to be sold only in the United Kingdom. The soap had been specially formulated for the United Kingdom and was different from that formulated for sale in the United States. Although the U.S. and U.K. Lever Brothers companies were under common control and the marks were identical, neither company had consented to the importation into the United States of U.K. goods.

Because the companies were under common control, subsection (c)(2) of the Customs regulations applied, and the agency refused to bar importation. The Court pointed to subsection (d), which defines common control as "effective control in policy and operations and . . . not necessarily synonymous with common ownership," indicating that Lever Brothers was unlikely to succeed under sec. 526 in light of *K-Mart*. Judge Williams, however, held that *K-Mart* had upheld the common control regulations only within sec. 526 and had not addressed their validity as applied to sec. 42. Indeed, it might be noted that sec. 42 makes no overt reference to common control or foreign affilation; in fact, it seems to extend exclusionary rights to foreign corporations, and certainly does so when the goods involved are counterfeit.

Relying on what he termed the "trio of face powder cases," (i.e., *Katzel*, *Aldridge*, and *Prestonettes v. Coty*), Judge Williams reasoned that the Supreme Court's understanding was that

> Trademark law was intended to protect a manufacturer's reputation and goodwill and to prevent confusion among consumers [and] enforce trademark territoriality. . . . Where the goods bearing a Foreign trademark valid abroad are physically different from the U.S. trademarked goods, . . . courts have indicated a readiness to find infringement.[42]

Judge Williams thus concluded that because the U.K. goods appeared to be different, the goods should be barred.

As did Justice Scalia in *K-Mart*, Judge Williams found irrelevant Customs' contention that an affiliation between a foreign producer or licensee and domestic mark holder renders the goods genuine. He reasoned that the importation in question was made by unauthorized third parties and, thus, that even if Lever Brothers were a single worldwide entity, in the absence of government assistance — in the form of a Lanham Act injunction or a Customs exclusion order, Lever Brothers would be helpless to prevent third party importation. Again, as though in response to Brennan's and Higginbotham's view that the U.S. trademark owner has the power to avoid the gray market, Judge Williams argues that it is not incumbent upon the plaintiff to use different marks in different markets. Furthermore, he argues, even if gray goods are less expensive to the consumer, that alone does not condone trademark infringement. And by eschewing the necessity of doing so, he rejects Customs' argument that it is administratively inconvenient to assess the loss of goodwill occasioned by an import. Customs need only distinguish between identical and nonidentical goods, not between levels of trademark injury. This argument is a reprise of one made by Judge Winter in his dissent in *Olympus*, where he wrote

> [V]iewing this regulation as an attempt to lighten the Service's administrative burdens is a bootstrap argument. Enforcement of Section 526 as written is simplicity itself. Goods of foreign manufacture bearing a trademark owned by a U.S. citizen or firm must be excluded from the country absent written consent from the owner. Difficulties stemming from variation in grey market relationships or from a supposed need to find a mark's existing domestic good will arise . . . not only after the major legal questions as to the meaning of Section 526 have been resolved.[43]

While some issues remain after *K-Mart*, especially the proper role of sec. 42 of the Lanham Act, some issues were made more clear. Customs may continue its policy of selective enforcement in "common control" situations but may not exercise discretion and refuse to bar licensed or authorized goods. As a result, while cases like *El Greco* and *Original Appalachian* will not arise again, gray market trademark issues will not disappear. Rather, these cases will be resolved by reference to interpretations of *Bourjois*, territoriality, goodwill, and product differences rather than by reference to murky concepts such as congressional acquiescence and legislative history.

CONCLUSION

As demonstrated, there is no consistent jurisprudence in the area of at-the-border restrictions on gray market importation. To begin with, while seeming to address the same harm, the language in sec. 526 and sec. 42 differ. The juxtaposition of sec. 526 and sec. 42, the terms of which make express reference to each other, projects a cavalcade of evil doings and the image of a hero — the Commissioner of Customs — who can prevent the enumerated harms by excluding all gray market goods. Unfortunately, this figure is in practice a phantasm because there is no clear jurisprudence to direct his activities. Indeed, the focus of the issue has changed from what Customs should do to whether what Customs has done is within its lawful power. Furthermore, this debate itself lacks direction, leading to inconsistent cases and inconsistent rules.

As noted throughout this work, the definition of "genuine goods" itself lacks a cohesive jurisprudence. Does "genuine" include CANDY unapproved shoes, Daewoo's shirts that were rejected for late delivery, the Spanish-speaking Cabbage Patch Kids, Jaylin's mixed-quality LLADRO figurines, Lever Brothers United Kingdom's local formulation, and MAMIYA cameras without service and warranties? Can these issues be resolved by a simple checklist about corporate affiliations?

Moreover, the cases lack clear parameters consonant with the various definitions of local goodwill. Can the circuit court's *Weil* decision be reconciled with *Osawa* or even with the dicta in the circuit court's *Vivitar* decision? Can antitrust and equity questions be resolved by reference to "common control"?

Congress abdicated when, with the passage of the Trademark Law Revision Act of 1988, it did not tackle the gray market issue, despite earlier bills in Congress advocating positions on all sides of the controversy. However, it will be interesting to see what impact, if any, the 1988 revisions regarding "related companies" will have. These revisions, which make no reference to the gray market controversy, might some day have some effect. But that effect, if any, remains far in the future, and any projection would be highly speculative.

The judges who have dealt with gray market importation have wrestled, albeit unsuccessfully, with difficult and weighty issues. Should judicial decisions amend the statutes as Brennan and Higginbotham implicitly suggest, or should they merely interpret them as Justice Scalia argues? Is it proper for a judge to choose sides in constitutionally neutral legislative battles, or should judges remain as objective interpreters of legislative action regardless of the perceived wisdom of that action? And, finally, will antitrust law render any decision moot or threaten even the quest for a day in court?

The danger to the rule of law is not so much the correctness of the individual decisions, but rather the (historically proven) approbation of legislative obtuseness and irresponsibility for failing to unify and clarify the law, to say nothing of legal fluidity precluding prediction and planning. Ours is a government of laws, and thus the matter of sua sponte and mandated Customs exclusion demands precise answers. Even if a trademark registrant's rights are violated by a new and precise law, at least he can take cautionary action in planning his trade and manufacturing policies and even seek constitutional relief.

NOTES

1. Supra. Ch. 2.
2. Sec. 1526 of the Tariff Act of 1922 [Pub. L. No. 67-318, 42 Stat. 975] (1922).
3. 593 F.Supp. 420 (CIT 1984), affirmed, 761 F.2d 1552 (Fed.Cir. 1985), cert. den. 106 Sup.Ct. 791 (1986).
4. See, e.g., *K-Mart v. Cartier*, 108 S.Ct. at 1831 (opinion of Justice Scalia).
5. 263 U.S. 675 (1923).
6. 293 F. 344 (2d Cir. 1923).
7. 48 F. 2d 1035 (2d. Cir. 1931).
8. Id. at 1037.
9. 155 F.Supp. 77 (S.D.N.Y. 1957), vacated and remanded 358 U.S. 915 (1958), action dismissed, 172 F.Supp. 107 (S.D.N.Y. 1959).
10. H.R. 7234, 86th Cong., 1st sess. (1959).
11. 19 C.F.R. sec. 1114 and 1115 (1960).
12. 19 C.F.R. sec. 133.21(c)(2) & (d) and sec. 133.12(d) (1973).
13. 761 F.2d 1552, 1557 (Fed. Cir. 1986)(emphasis in original), cert. den. 106 S.Ct 791 (1987).
14. 792 F.2d 315 (2d Cir. 1986).
15. Id. at 322.
16. 589 F. Supp. at 1173.
17. Slip op. at 17.
18. 575 F. Supp. 416 (S.D. Fla, 1983).
19. 539 F. Supp. at 1175.
20. 761 F.2d 1552 (Fed. Cir. 1986).
21. Id. at 1555–56.
22. 792 F.2d 315 (2d Cir. 1986).
23. Id. at 320.
24. Id.

25. *Coalition to Preserve the Integrity of American Trademarks v. United States*, 790 F.2d 903 (D.C.Cir. 1986).

26. 108 S.Ct. 1811.

27. Id. at 1818 (opinion of Justice Kennedy).

28. 108 S.Ct. at 1820.

29. The self-help pillar of Justice Brennan's opinion can be viewed as weak, collapsing on several counts. It assumes an unproven uniform relationship between the U.S. registrant and the foreign affiliate. It ignores the fact that even in *Katzel* situations an assignor may agree never to sell to anyone who does not agree to insure goods not sold in the United States. It ignores the legal and practical inability to police foreign markets in order to prevent third party access to the goods when, as Justice Scalia notes, it is these mavericks or rogues who are the primary importers. Furthermore, Justice Brennan suggests "self-help" only if it is lawful. However, neither he nor anyone else can predict the legality overseas of conditioned sales to third parties. For example, the European Community's policies encourage parallel imports between member states, and our own prohibition of restraints on alienation after a first sale (reflected in the "Exhaustion Doctrine") indicates that legal prohibition of unauthorized sales may not exist. For example, consider the court's statement in *Original Appalachian*.

> It is not clear that OAA could have prevented by contract the importation of these Cabbage Patch dolls by third-party distributors, such as Granada. As a practical matter OAA appears to have tried. Under its license Jesmar agreed not to sell outside its Spanish-licensed territory, and further agreed to sell only to purchasers who also agreed not to sell outside that territory. Without any effective means of further controlling the distribution of its product, for example, by means of an equitable servitude on the dolls, OAA should not be held responsible for the dolls' importation.
>
> 816 F.2d 68, 75 (2d Cir. 1987)(Cardamone, J., concurring).

Furthermore, given his own antitrust record, Justice Brennan might well conclude that such agreements are illegal as applied to the United States.

30. 108 S.Ct at 1834.

31. It is noted that the domestic assignment to a third party of rights in a mark already in use in multiple fields of business, where the assignee gains rights in limited fields, also will not affect trademark rights in the fields retained by the assignor.

32. 108 S.Ct. at 1834–35.

33. 593 F.Supp. at 425.

34. 703 F.Supp. 1398 (C.C.Calif. 1988).

35. 810 F.2d 1506 (9th Cir. 1987).

36. 48 U.S.C. sec. 1643 (1982).

37. Judge Higginbotham also implies that antitrust policy prohibits the opposite view, a position not dissimilar to that taken in *Yamaha*.

38. *Original Appalachian* and *El Greco* were distinguished based upon the alleged genuineness of the gray market goods and upon the differences between the gray market and authorized versions involved in those cases.

39. Citing *Park 'N Fly, Inc. v. Dollar Park and Fly, Inc.* 469 U.S. 189, 194 (1984).

40. In addition to the internal contradictions of his position on sec. 42 enforcement, his logic would permit the importation of goods bearing identical trademarks applied by two different entities if the goods are identical and were produced by the same independent foreign contract manufacturer. Judge Higginbotham also recognized that the gray market activities of the defendant result in unjust enrichment to the gray market seller who takes a free ride on Weil's advertising, promotion, and point-of-sale services. Judge Higginbotham did not explain that unjust enrichment is without a remedy because of Weil's corporate parentage that initiated worldwide use of the same mark.

41. 11 U.S.P.Q. 2d 1117 (D.C.Cir. 1989).

42. 877 F.2d. at 106.

43. 792 F.2d at 322.

The Question of Title: Of Good Faith Purchasers, Stolen Goods, and Voidable Title

In light of the murkiness and protracted nature of trademark claims against gray marketers and in anticipation of the scenario in which sec. 526 enforcement was curtailed, Johnson & Johnson,[1] the multinational manufacturer of consumer products, launched a different and creative attack on gray market trade in its products. Using state law, J&J first charged, as already discussed briefly, that gray market dealers lacked good title to their wares because J&J had been induced by fraud into making the initial sale. The defendant in the case argued that it was innocent of any earlier fraud and that it was therefore protected under Uniform Commercial Code (U.C.C.) Sec. 2–403(1); J&J's response to that argument was that the defendant either knew or should have known of the earlier fraud and, thus, was not protected by the U.C.C.'s provision.

J&J's arguments were eventually rejected by the Third Circuit Court of Appeals,[2] which ruled that remote purchasers had no duty to discover defects in the chain of title, even in the face of suspicion about the bona fides of those higher up in the distribution chain. Faced with this negative result, J&J then changed tack slightly, alleging in *Ortho Pharmaceutical*[3] that the gray market trade (under circumstances similar to the first case) violated the Florida Anti-Fencing Act,[4] which expressly imposes a duty to inquire where the dealer "knows or should know [that the goods were] stolen." Following a trial, the district court awarded J&J nearly one million dollars in damages.[5]

JOHNSON & JOHNSON AND THE GRAY MARKET

Johnson & Johnson, Inc. is a leading manufacturer of pharmaceutical and household products. Among its subsidiaries are Johnson & Johnson, Ltd. (J&J, Ltd.), a corporation organized under the laws of and doing business in Great Britain, and Ortho Pharmaceutical Corporation, a New Jersey corporation. J&J also owns and operates an elaborate network of other foreign and domestic subsidiaries, all of which facilitate the general business operations of the parent. J&J's products are distributed and sold around the world.

In many instances, there are slight variations in nature and packaging as dictated by local needs, but for the most part all of J&J's products are of equal quality worldwide. For example, in order to regain confidence from U.S. consumers after the Tylenol scare, J&J began packaging certain American goods, such as baby products, with a tamper resistant "Quality Seal." J&J products not destined for the U.S. market do not have this seal. In addition, some J&J, Ltd. products are not identical to those sold in the United States. For example, J&J baby powder and baby bath have slightly different formulas to accommodate local tastes. J&J argued that it would be greatly injured if products destined for foreign markets found their way into the United States.[6] J&J seemingly conceded, however, that absent these differences, the authorized and gray market goods in both cases were essentially similar in function, and J&J made no attempt to append a trademark claim to the causes of action discussed in this chapter.

For a variety of reasons, many of which remain undocumented, J&J in the late 1980s became the "victim" of a large volume of gray market sales. Distributors, suppliers, and other middlemen purchased genuine J&J products destined for specific foreign markets and imported them or otherwise contracted to sell them to U.S. wholesalers and retailers at prices below those being offered by J&J for "authorized" products. As can best be discovered, prior to the events about to be related, J&J has not directly brought litigation to enjoin gray market sales of its products.[7]

In 1984 and 1985, J&J, through its various foreign and domestic subsidiaries, made sales allegedly based upon misrepresentations that the goods sold would be resold only in certain foreign markets. The buyer in the litigated case was a firm called DAL International Trading Company owned by the Polish government. DAL allegedly misled J&J into believing that the goods were intended for sale in Poland. While attending a trade fair in Poland, a J&J representative met with DAL's chief buyer of pharmaceutical products and a buyer from Centrum, a Polish retailing chain. At that meeting, the J&J representative requested assurances that goods sold to DAL would not be resold outside of Poland; such assurances were evidently made. Subsequent to that meeting, J&J made a written contract with DAL; that contract, however, contained no mention of the resale restriction.

The goods never entered Poland. At the Germany/Poland border, the trucks were rerouted through Belgium, where they were loaded on ships bound for New Jersey. J&J Ltd. investigators followed the goods to the United States, where at least some of them eventually came into the possession of Quality King, a discount drug chain that sells a significant amount of gray market products. J&J challenged the validity of Quality King's title to the goods, asserting that that title was infected by the previous frauds, and thus was void. J&J therefore claimed that these goods could be replevied, the practice enjoined, and damages for lost profits assessed.

Quality King responded that it was personally innocent of the fraud in its chain of title and thus was protected by prevailing standards of commercial law. J&J responded that even if Quality King were technically innocent, the nature of gray market transactions puts the gray market seller on constructive notice of irregularities, and that, by failing to make detailed inquiry into the bona fides of the suppliers, the gray market seller cannot claim that it obtained indefeasible title.

J&J's suit to enjoin gray market sales was an action for a preliminary injunction brought in the U.S. District Court for New Jersey.[8] Claiming better title to the goods, J&J sued Quality King, as well as DAL. DAL was never served and eventually was dropped from the litigation, perhaps because of foreign relations concerns.[9] Of course, it was not really necessary for J&J to sue DAL; J&J's goal in this litigation was to force U.S. companies to stop engaging in parallel trade, not to recover damages as a result of DAL's alleged fraud. In March 1985, DAL had ordered a large quantity of Reach brand toothbrushes and baby products from J&J, Ltd. J&J asserted, as proof of DAL's intentional fraud, that two days before DAL placed its order, Quality King placed an order for the same quantity of products that DAL ordered from J&J, Ltd.

Before the sale was consummated, J&J executives became concerned about possible diversion of the goods into the gray market and therefore extracted an oral promise from a representative of DAL that the goods would be sold in Poland only.[10] The goods were delivered that summer. Because of the detective work mentioned previously, J&J subsequently learned that some or all of the goods had been diverted to the United States, where they had come into the possession of Quality King. Evidently, a firm called Cubro Trading Company, Ltd. learned of the availability of the J&J products and, through a middleman named Morris Greenfield, sold them to Quality King.[11]

By the time Quality King took delivery, the J&J Ltd. shipping labels had been stripped off most of the shipping cartons, not an uncommon practice in international trade in general and the gray market in particular.[12] The prices at which Quality King received the goods were lower than those for authorized J&J products, and Quality King was thus in a position to distribute them in the United States at prices below those being charged domestically by J&J.[13]

The district court granted the preliminary injunction.[14] Judge Debevoise found that Quality King was not a good faith purchaser within the meaning of U.C.C. sec. 2–403(1) and thus Quality King obtained only DAL's voidable title.[15] Since DAL obtained the goods by fraud, DAL obtained a voidable title, and, under general principles of property law, any subsequent purchasers acquired that voidable title, unless that buyer could establish the requisites of a good faith purchaser. The argument proceeded that J&J Ltd., the victim of DAL's fraud, had better title than Quality King and thus was likely ultimately to prevail on the merits. While the district court found that Quality King had no actual knowledge of the fraud, it found that the transactions in question were conducted under "suspicious circumstances" that "cried out for inquiry."[16] Judge Debevoise wrote that "the entire trade in which Quality King is engaged is conducted in a manner designed to insulate a purchaser of goods from knowledge of potential illegality."[17]

The court of appeals reversed.[18] Judge Sloviter, for a unanimous court, ruled that even if Quality King actually suspected or had reason to suspect that J&J would not have approved the sale, the only relevant question under the U.C.C. is whether Quality King actually knew that the goods had been obtained by fraud, or suspected as much and closed its eyes to the truth. But, said the court, "[t]his is a far different question involving an inquiry as to whether Quality King *knew or had reason to know* that DAL orally represented to J&J Ltd. that it would distribute only in Poland and that this representation was made at a time when DAL had an affirmative intent to do otherwise."[19]

According to Judge Sloviter, fatal to the district court's position was the lack of evidence of the means by which goods normally and legitimately enter gray market channels. Not all gray market goods began their journeys through the distribution system as a result of fraud-in-the-inducement. The presence of price differentials between domestic and foreign markets provides a rational explanation for the existence of the gray market; that explanation has validity even when there is no fraud in the chain of title. "[I]t does not," said the court, "provide a basis for an inference that all those involved in importing less expensive gray goods know or suspect that there is a defect in the title of the goods which they purchase."[20] The fact that the shipping identification was stripped from the cartons, and that Quality King was cautious in its dealings with Cubro similarly raised no inference that Quality King had a duty to inquire about possible frauds further up in the distribution chain.

In anticipation of defeat in Quality King, J&J, along with its Ortho Pharmaceutical subsidiary, brought suit in the U.S. District Court for Southern Florida,[21] repeating its fraud claims, but adding a claim under the Florida Anti-Fencing Act. The defendants in the case were Sona Distributors (then in possession of the goods) and Elmcrest Trading Ltd. (the alleged diverter). Both companies, each having a separate corporate identity, were owned by two brothers, Inder and Kulraj Chawla.[22] The Florida statute expressly places on purchasers a duty to inquire by providing that "[a]ny person who traffics in . . . property that he knows or should know was stolen shall be guilty of a felony."[23] J&J undoubtedly hoped that the "should know" standard would place upon gray market sellers the duty that Judge Sloviter refused to impose.

Ortho Pharmaceutical v. Sona Distributors[24] was tried in December 1986 before Judge Spellman.[25] The court recited the elements of a fraud cause of action and determined that they were present. Judge Spellman also found that the party who committed the fraud (Mr. Lin) did so "under the instruction of [the owner of Sona]."[26] In reviewing the evidence, the court observed that the defendants had engaged in similar schemes in the past and that the defendants admitted that they "knew Mr. Lin obtained these pharmaceuticals against the resale policies of J&J."[27]

Judge Spellman, in a unique and memorable footnote, castigated the defendants for their assertion that they were innocent of the fraud.

No matter how many times this Court reviews the factual essence
of this case, one cannot resist a comparison between the
Defendants' professed ignorance of unlawful conduct, and perhaps the most memorable refrain of *Hogan's Heroes*, a popular
television situation comedy of the 1960's. For those too young to
remember, each episode featured a scene in which Sergeant
Schultz, always unmindful of the clandestine activities of the
irrepressible Colonel Hogan and his men, would be found to
explain away his incompetence to his superior, the irascible
Colonel Klink, by saying "I know n-oth-i-n-g, I see n-oth-i-n-g, I
do n-oth-i-n-g." This dialogue, which each week delighted
television viewers across the country, somehow resurfaced once
again, this time in my courtroom.[28]

Obviously perturbed by what he thought was a baseless argument,
Judge Spellman found a violation of the Act and awarded Ortho over
$325,000 in compensatory damages and $650,000 in punitive damages.
The judge held that because the defendants had engaged in similar
conduct on other occasions, punitive damages were thus appropriate
in order to deter "future abuses."[29]

Aside from the court's ruling that Elmcrest and Sona were a single
entity with direct knowledge of the fraud, the Anti-Fencing Act raises
yet other questions about the meaning of "stolen," as distinguished
from goods sold as a result of mere fraud-in-the-inducement.
Presumably, cases not involving close-connectedness and direct
knowledge (such as *Quality King*) are the norm; in those cases, more
difficult issues must be addressed.

The Act defines stolen as having been subject to a criminal taking.[30]
In the case at bar, the fraud occurred in Hong Kong, and the perpetrator was a citizen of Hong Kong. Under elementary choice of law
principles the question of criminality should be determined under the
laws of Hong Kong, that is, under English law. The English Theft Act
of 1968 casts a wide net and presumably includes as larcenous this type
of fraud.[31] That fact would seem to be enough to invoke the "reason
to know" standard of the Florida statute. Nevertheless, differences do
exist, both internationally and domestically, between traditional
"theft" and such "garden variety" frauds;[32] these differences will be
addressed in the section that follows the next.

A more perplexing question raised by the Act is the application of
the phrase "should know." The statute provides that if the price of the

goods in question is "substantially below the fair market value, unless satisfactorily explained, [there is] an inference that the person in possession knew or should have known that the property had been stolen."[33] The court in *Quality King* found that the mere fact the goods involved were gray market, and thus were cheaper as compared to authorized goods, was insufficient to raise suspicion about the seller's title. That holding, together with the logic inherent in its reasoning, should be sufficient to explain the discrepancy in price and thus either preclude or rebut the statutory inference of knowledge. Absent proof of some sort of grand conspiracy between the diverter and the gray market seller, participation in the gray market should not by itself be held violative of the Florida Anti-Fencing Act.

GOOD FAITH PURCHASERS AND THE GRAY MARKET

In view of the frequency with which the phrase "good faith" is used in commercial law, it is startling that so little has been written defining it.[34] This paucity of discussion is especially true in the context of the "good faith purchaser of goods." Perhaps that is because, like obscenity, the courts will "know it when [they] see it."[35] The lack of large numbers of court decisions, however, only adds to the controversy when difficult fact situations arise. Such is evidently the case with gray market sales.

The Third Circuit's careful consideration of the duty imposed by the U.C.C. is both cogent and, it is submitted, historically correct. The little literature that exists suggests that the U.C.C. adopted a subjective standard of good faith.[36] Evidently borrowing the English "pure heart, empty head" test,[37] the drafters of the U.C.C. defined good faith in terms of "honesty in fact."[38] A merchant, however, is held to the added though more nebulous standard of "the observance of reasonable commercial standards of fair dealing in the trade."[39] That portion of the definition was added at the suggestion of the New York Law Revision Commission "to eliminate the possibility that the definition might be read as imposing on merchants a general standard of due care."[40] The Third Circuit analogized this standard to general concepts of trade practice. Quality King argued that the trade practice in the gray market was not to conduct investigations,[41] and J&J produced no evidence to the contrary.

J&J instead argued that the practice of not investigating the seller's title was designed to insulate buyers from any liability for the fraud.

Furthermore, J&J argued that "those who traffic in stolen goods could confer good title on their customers by proclaiming that they are a 'market' with an 'industry practice' of providing no information about sources."[42] J&J thus tried to assert that the industry practice was not a valid indicator of good faith by intimating that the entire gray market was illegitimate. But the court rejected J&J's argument, holding that absent evidence that industry practice was to investigate, the supplemental merchant standard for good faith "does not aid J&J."[43]

J&J's argument that the U.C.C. imposes a duty to inquire under "suspicious circumstances" thus conflicted with the New York Law Revision Commission's expressed intention. The "duty of special vigilance" imposed by Judge Debevoise, said the court, similarly contravenes that statutory language. Whatever the words of the statute may mean, in Judge Sloviter's view, imposition of a general duty to inquire would stifle the free flow of goods and commerce that the U.C.C.'s drafters sought to promote.[44]

Imposition of a duty to inquire would place on merchants not only a burden that they were not assigned, but also an obligation to determine the level of suspicion that would trigger that duty. To some extent, merchants as well as consumers are always justifiedly suspicious of their immediate sellers. That is especially so in the context of international trade and doubly so when a buyer (such as Quality King) is asked to pay in advance. And while gray market transactions may produce their own forms of suspicion, it is simply unfair to place on buyers any "duty of special vigilance."

When Judge Debevoise wrote of a lack of trust between Quality King and its supplier, he seemingly confused trust in whether delivery would take place with faith in whether the seller had a defective title. Quality King was genuinely concerned with the former, and it not only requested assurances of delivery, but it also evidently took precautions in this regard. Whether or not such precautions were taken, this type of suspicion should not give rise to a broad duty to inquire about frauds in the chain of title because it simply does not speak to that issue.

The distrust and conditions of sale of which Judge Debevoise spoke also led Quality King to take steps to determine that the merchandise was neither stolen nor counterfeit. Purchasing goods of that kind would have grave effect for one in Quality King's position, because even a good faith purchaser would obtain a void title. As will be demonstrated below, any attempt by the trademark owner to obfuscate the difference between gray market goods and stolen goods is misplaced and unsupported by history, economics, and received law.

Having thus eliminated distrust as a rationale for demanding inquiry, J&J is left with only three facts in support of its allegation that gray market sellers such as Quality King acted unreasonably and unfairly in not making a detailed inquiry into the perfection of its supplier's title. The first, and arguably most compelling, fact is that the price paid by Quality King was extremely low. Quality King disputed the conclusion that the price was unusually low, stating that it had obtained similar goods previously at similar prices. Second, Quality King offered explanations for the low prices, among them the possibility that the goods had been dumped[45] by the manufacturer or that the low price was the result of the large quantity purchased.[46] The existence of favorable exchange rates might provide yet another explanation. Finally, it must be observed that lower-than-normal prices abound in the gray market and are by themselves no indication that fraud was at some time present. Indeed, while litigation over the status of gray market goods has abounded in recent years, the J&J litigation is the first reported case involving allegations of fraud. It is thus extremely unfair to charge Quality King with a duty to inquire about fraud merely because it deals in gray market goods.

J&J also alleged that the emasculation of product codes and batch numbers from the shipping cartons was another factor that should result in investigation. But emasculation is a practice that is followed by middlemen around the world, be they authorized or not, to obscure the source of their goods.[47] It is more likely than not to be an attempt to prevent the buyer from bypassing the middleman in the next transaction. J&J also argued that "one phone call to J&J would . . . have [disclosed] the fraud."[48] That is perhaps true, but it would nevertheless be unwise as a general matter to require every buyer to check with every manufacturer whenever product codes have been removed.

In point of fact, J&J did not allege that any one of these factors leads directly to the duty to inquire, but rather that all the factors combined produced a situation that required inquiry.[49] Yet, careful analysis demonstrates that the sale was nothing more than a routine gray market transaction. The district court did not conclude, and the Third Circuit stated, that the record in Quality King "will not support a finding that Quality King suspected fraud."[50]

It must be remembered, as Judge Sloviter observed, that the whole question of fraud revolves not only around the first purchaser's false statements, but also around his intent at the time those statements were made. J&J presented absolutely no evidence, although such evidence could probably have been obtained,[51] of the frequency of fraud-in-the-inducement as it pertains to gray market goods. Instead, J&J continually made reference to stolen or counterfeit goods, the so-called black market, in an attempt to discredit gray market traders.[52] But the fact remains that, in spite of a flurry of litigation by a variety of trademark owners and industry groups, gray market sales remain presumptively lawful.

J&J in essence asserts that all gray market transactions are suspect. The facts of *Quality King* simply would not support that conclusion; they were ambiguous at best. And still J&J sought to impose a broad duty to inquire. What then of cases in which the facts are even more ambiguous or in which the accused buyer does not normally deal in the gray market, but seeks to take advantage of an unusually low price? Is there a duty to inquire under such circumstances? The answer must be no; to hold otherwise would increase transaction costs and retard commerce.[53] The drafters of the Code set out to encourage commerce, and the Third Circuit correctly executed that intention.

This author knows of no new attempts to upset that result directly. The attempt to subvert the rule of *Quality King* (or at least to discover more clear-cut situations) may or may not be successful. In the future, it will probably be difficult for trademark owners to prove close connectedness or direct knowledge. Indeed, the result may simply be further obfuscation of gray market channels.

Nevertheless, the J&J cases will probably prove to be a moderate deterrent to some gray market sellers. If nothing else, the decision in *Ortho* makes clear the danger inherent in committing fraud and then importing the goods for sale in the United States. The result may be a reduction in the occurrence of such frauds, or it may simply result in a separation between diverters and ultimate sellers, and more scenarios like that involved in *Quality King*.

The question remains, however, whether J&J's theories can withstand conceptual analysis and whether the courts, which decided cases brought under them, were ultimately correct. A related question is whether states should enact legislation to prohibit gray market sales of fraud-induced goods or, where such statutes arguably exist (e.g.,

Florida), whether they should be used for this purpose. These questions are the subject of the next section.

OF STOLEN AND FRAUD-INDUCED GOODS

The legal distinction between goods procured by fraud-in-the-inducement and stolen goods has great practical consequences for perpetrators as well as for subsequent purchasers. The perpetrator in the former situation obtains a "voidable title," while the latter individual receives title that is "void."[54] Of no immediate consequence if sued by his victim (as seems to have been the case in *Ortho*), voidable title is clearly the more valuable. That is because subsequent purchasers, in turn, will have very different rights. Under the U.C.C., a good faith purchaser from one with voidable title to goods takes indefeasible title; yet complete pureness and innocence will do nothing to better a title that is void.[55]

These principles are firmly imbedded in our jurisprudence and are seldom questioned. Implicit in the rules are several competing value judgments. The most obvious is that so-called garden-variety fraud is less morally reprehensible than outright stealing,[56] or at least that those who innocently buy from different kinds of criminals deserve different treatment. Perhaps underlying the rule is the notion that fraud is more difficult to establish than is traditional theft, or possibly that it is less capable of discovery by remote purchasers.

Yet, other underpinnings abound. Professor H. Weinberg, who has written virtually the only recent articles on the subject,[57] argues convincingly that economics provides both the source and justification for the law. Professor Weinberg's first article analyzes the effect on supply and demand for stolen goods if an innocent purchaser rule were applied. The effect, he states, would be a stimulation of demand for such merchandise and, thus, an increase in theft-related costs.[58] But, he proceeds

[A] rule protecting legally innocent purchasers of fraudulent (but not stolen) goods could not affect demand to the same degree. While ... purchasers might not know or suspect that the goods are illegitimate in origin, they might not be certain whether they will be protected because the goods were taken through fraud or unprotected because they were taken through theft.[59]

Furthermore, because fraud is generally more preventable than is theft,[60] the original owners in the fraud cases are the class best able to thwart the crime. Weinberg, like Gilmore in his seminal article on good faith purchasers of commercial intangibles, rejects distinctions based upon intent and culpability.[61] "The real issues in voidable title cases," Weinberg concludes, "are a decisional rule's impact on the quantity of illegitimate goods in the market and the identity of the more efficient class of risk preventers and insurers."[62] While granting good title to innocent purchasers of fraud-induced goods might increase both the supply and demand for gray market goods, the manufacturers and trademark owners are clearly the entities in the best position to prevent the frauds.[63]

Additional reasons exist for distinguishing between gray market goods and counterfeit goods. First, because gray market sales follow the traditional fraud-in-the-inducement pattern, they present buyers with fact situations inherently less discoverable and provable than do stolen or counterfeit goods. Second, the purchase of fraud-induced goods in general, and gray market goods in particular, is not covered by any existing legal treaties. In fact, different nations and legal systems take markedly different approaches to the legality of gray market sales.[64] By comparison, most nations punish trademark counterfeiting, as well as traditional theft. It is ill-advised for U.S. law unilaterally to equate these crimes with gray market goods and mere fraud-in-the-inducement.[65]

Whether the justification is historical, moral, or economic, the foregoing demonstrates that the distinction between stolen and fraud-induced has great merit. In the context of the gray market, no reasons have been offered that dictate an approach that equates the two. Indeed, the legal status of gray market goods is subject to substantial judicial, legislative, and scholarly debate. In comparison, the legality of counterfeit goods is much more settled, both domestically and internationally. There is no question that counterfeit goods (i.e., goods with "stolen" trademarks) have no societal or economic benefits, while gray market goods have at least arguable benefits.[66] Furthermore, possession of gray market goods is not criminal under federal trademark law, nor is possession alone a crime in most states; by contrast, possession of counterfeit goods is criminal in most cases.[67]

CONCLUSION

The trend on virtually all fronts is to distinguish between gray market goods and counterfeit goods, at least in some cases. That seems to be the import of current Customs Service practice, and the federal courts, while at times hostile to individual gray market sales, have unanimously refused to condemn gray market goods per se. Some states have enacted legislation to prevent abuses,[68] but to date no jurisdiction, including the federal government, has outlawed the gray market.

J&J's lawsuits seek to do just that: outlaw the gray market. Yet no compelling reason for this has been advanced. Indeed, after failing to achieve the desired result under federal law, J&J turned to state law with the hope of enjoining all gray market sales. By alleging violations of the Anti-Fencing Act J&J asserted not only that gray market sales are akin to traditional theft (which they are not), but also that remote buyers have a higher duty to inquire than has been imposed upon them by a statute enacted by 49 states. In addition to the Third Circuit Court of Appeals' decision in *Quality King*, virtually all the commentators and prior cases are in full accord that the Code does not impose a "duty to inquire" about frauds in the chain of title. It goes without saying that a prime virtue of the U.C.C. is the uniformity of law among the states. Close connectedness and direct knowledge aside, if statutes such as the Florida Anti-Fencing Act are held to reach a result different from that reached under the Code, a measure of uniformity would be lost.

In trying to invoke the Anti-Fencing Act, J&J overlooks all the undisputed reasons for distinguishing between theft and void titles on the one hand, and fraud and voidable titles on the other. On behalf of the trademark owners, J&J seeks yet another forum to halt all sales of gray market goods. The state courts and legislatures should deny this opportunity to the trademark owners. Gray market controversies are best resolved in the federal courts based upon the principles set forth in the first four chapters of this book.[69]

NOTES

1. Johnson & Johnson and its corporate subsidiaries will hereinafter be referred to as "J&J."

2. *Johnson & Johnson Products, Inc. v. Quality King*, 798 F.2d 100 (3rd Cir. 1986).

3. *Ortho Pharmaceutical, Inc. v. Sona Distributors*, 663 F.Supp. 64 (S.D.Fla. 1987).

4. Fla. Stat. Ann. Sec. 812.012 et. seq. (West 1987).

5. The two defendants subsequently filed bankruptcy.

6. Brief of J&J, *Johnson & Johnson v. Quality King*, at 5–6 (hereinafter cited as Brief of J&J).

7. J&J, however, undoubtedly was sympathetic to the litigation begun by *COPIAT* case on behalf of its members. But because of J&J's corporate affiliations, it probably would have lost in any attempt to obtain an exclusion order under sec. 526 of the Tariff Act. Because of that affiliation, J&J probably would have fared poorly under the trademark theories, a fact magnified by similarities in the authorized and gray market products.

8. *Johnson & Johnson v. DAL Int'l Trading Co.*, Civ.No. 85–3966, slip op., August 22, 1985 (D.N.J.). Judge Debevoise, who decided the case, had previous experience with gray market cases, having a week earlier decided *Weil Ceramics*.

9. See J&J, at 4, 7–8.

10. On appeal, Quality King argued that there was at best minimal evidence of fraud by DAL. Quality King asserted that a full trial was necessary to establish that the "assurance" of the DAL representative amounted to a false "representation of fact." Brief of Quality King, at 34–37. The Third Circuit did not reach the issue of whether there was fraud but instead ruled that, even if fraud was present, Quality King was a good-faith purchaser who took good title. 798 F.2d at 103, 106.

11. Cubro Trading Company, Ltd. is a British corporation who acted as a broker of sorts. See J&J, at 8. Greenfield is the proprietor of Tereza Merchandise Incorporated, New York. Tereza regularly acted as an independent distributor of goods purchased overseas from sources other than manufacturers and sold them in the United States in competition with the manufacturers and their regular distributors. J&J, at 16. The final participant in the Quality King purchase is Wendexim, a countertrader who was included in this transaction because DAL did not have western currency, necessitating use of Wendexim to accomplish an intermediate barter trade. 798 F.2d, at 101.

12. *J&J*, supra 144, at 23. The stripping of packaging labels is done ostensibly to protect confidential sources of goods. If purchasers were able to determine where the goods came from they would be able to bypass the middleman in subsequent transactions. J&J argued that these labels were stripped so that no one, including J&J, could trace the goods to discover how and by whom they were diverted. Brief of J&J, at 29. But for the fact that a few of these labels were not removed, through an apparent oversight, J&J probably would not have been able to trace the goods to the DAL transaction. Id., at 10.

13. 798 F.2d at 102. The prices charged to DAL were far lower than the usual prices charged for these products if sold in the United States and even lower than the wholesale prices that would be charged in Great Britain. Id.

14. *DAL*, supra n.65. The opinion is unreported. A copy of the transcript and opinion is on file with the author.

15. Finding that there was a probability of irreparable harm, the court granted a preliminary injunction restraining movement of goods in order to protect J&J's right to replevy the goods if it were to succeed on the merits.

16. *J&J*, at 24.

17. *J&J*, at 22.

18. 798 F.2d at 106.

19. 798 F.2d at 103. Emphasis added.

20. 798 F.2d at 103–104.

21. The action by Ortho Pharmaceutical began before the appeal in the *Quality King* case was decided. In the *Ortho Pharmaceutical* case, J&J had raised the defective title argument as its first cause of action. In view of the negative decision in *Quality King*, J&J has essentially abandoned that theory, relying now on its second cause of action, violation of the Florida Anti-Fencing Act.

22. A motion to dismiss for lack of jurisdiction resulted in a finding that the two corporations "were single entities for all factual and legal purposes." The motion was held to be baseless, and the attorneys were "severely sanctioned." 663 F.Supp. at 67n.2.

23. Fla. Stat. Ann. Sec. 812.012 et. seq. (West 1987).

24. 663 F.Supp. 64 (S.D.Fla. 1987).

25. The defendants in *Ortho* had moved for summary judgment alleging that the Hong Kong dealer, and perhaps even Ortho (a subsidiary of J&J), was a willing participant in the "fraud." Nevertheless, the trial judge denied the motion, holding that there was no credible evidence to support that proposition. A copy of the decision on the motion is on file with the author.

26. The perpetrator of the fraud, Y.L. Lin, so testified. Lin was affiliated with Chung Ching Dispensary, Ltd. and had been a long-time distributor of J&J products. Lin would not have been able to obtain the goods involved because J&J only sold them directly to hospitals and doctors. J&J made the sale in the (evidently false) hope of opening "a new and highly lucrative market." Id. at 65. The evidence thus proved that J&J would not have sold the goods to Lin but for the false representation. It can be argued, perhaps, that officials of J&J were easily fooled; they agreed to leave the English packaging because Lin told them that goods so labeled were more valuable in China. Id.

27. Id. at 66. The court also made reference to a letter received by Sona from one of its distributors suggesting that it would try to ship the contracted goods through Sri Lanka or Mozambique and then to Miami in order to avoid detection. Id.

28. Id. at 66 n.1.

29. Id. at 67–68.

30. Fla. Stat. Ann. Sec. 812.012(6). The Act confers a private right of action. Sec. 812.035.

31. C.60, sec. 1 et seq., as cited in G. Fletcher, *Rethinking Criminal Law* (1978). The House of Lords, interestingly, continues to distinguish frauds of the type involved in gray market cases from other thefts for purposes of determining the validity of title in subsequent purchasers. See, *Saunders v. Anglia Building Soc.*, 3 All E.R. 961 (1970). Florida, as well as most states, also criminalizes to some degree practices that amount to fraud-in-the-inducement. The criminal law of Florida punishes as larcenous any taking "by color of fraudulent or false representations or pretenses." Fla. Stat. Ann. Sec. 812.021 (West 1976).

One need not get bogged down in choice of law questions, however. The proper characterization of the earlier fraud should not be confused with the question of title. The former is determined by the place where the false representation was made, while the latter is almost always determined by the law of the situs of the property (in this case Florida).

32. The term "garden variety" fraud apparently refers to the common nature of the practice. Previous attempts to distinguish this type of fraud from other types of fraud when interpreting vague statutes have generally been unsuccessful. For example, efforts to exclude from liability (under the Racketeer Influenced Corrupt Organizations Act [RICO] those acts characterized as "garden variety" fraud have been rejected. See, e.g., *Banderas v. Banco Central del Ecuador*, 461 So.2d 265 (D.Ct.Fla. 1985)(paraphrasing Justice Cardozo, the court wrote that extending any special immunization to "garden variety" fraud would "spread the study of horticulture to unaccustomed fields.")

33. Fla. Stat. Ann. Sec. 812.022(3). The Act also raises an inference of actual or constructive knowledge if the property was recently stolen. Id., at Sec. 812.022(2). The few reported cases reveal a tendency to give minimal effect to the inference. See, e.g., *R.A.L. v. State*, 402 S.2d 1337 (1981)(juvenile's not unreasonable explanation that he had bought goods at a flea market sufficient to preclude finding of guilt as a matter of law.)

34. E. A. Farnsworth points out that "some fifty out of the four hundred sections of the U.C.C. [mention good faith]." "Farnsworth, Good Faith Performance and Commercial Reasonableness Under the Uniform Commercial Code," 30 *U. Chi. L. Rev.* 666, 667 (1963). The Code's definition of the term is short and not too enlightening. The Official Comments to the U.C.C. shed no light whatsoever. A leading treatise on the law of personal property states that the U.C.C. definition "does not answer all questions" and that the added merchant standard of reasonable commercial standards "can make a difference." That text, however, fails to elaborate on either statement. R. Brown, *The Law of Personal Property*, at 198–199 (Raushenbush ed. 1975). There are very few cases that make an attempt to define the term good faith.

When the U.C.C. was first enacted, several leading scholars wrote articles that attempted a definition but most dealt with good faith in contexts other than that addressed in this chapter. See, e.g., Farnsworth, supra. n.65 (good faith performance); W. Hawkland, "Curing an Improper Tender of Title to Chattels: Past, Present and Commercial Code," 46 *Minn. L. Rev.* 697 (1962)(breach and cure with regard to the warranty of good title); Gilmore, "The Commercial Doctrine of Good Faith Purchase," 63 *Yale L. J.* 1057 (1954) (good-faith purchase of intangibles under Articles 3, 5, and 9); See also Burton, "Good Faith Performance of a Contract Within Article 2 of the Uniform Commercial Code," 67 *Iowa L. Rev.* 1 (1981); Braucher, "The Legislative History of the Uniform Commercial Code," 58 *Colum. L. Rev.* 799, 812–14 (1958) (good faith generally); J. White and R. Summers, *Handbook of the Law Under the Uniform Commercial Code* (1983). The most recent article to address the subject at all is Weinberg, "Markets Overt, Voidable Titles, and Feckless Agents: Judges and Efficiency in the Antebellum Doctrine of Good Faith Purchase," 56 *Tulane L. Rev.* 1 (1981)[Hereinafter cited as Weinberg, Markets]; that article also does not directly address the question of the meaning of good-faith purchaser of goods, although it does delve deeply into the issue of distinguishing (historically and economically, at any rate) frauds that result in voidable titles and frauds that result in void title. If the defrauded owner intended to transfer title (so-called fraud-in-the-inducement), then a good-faith purchaser acquired indefeasible title from the perpetrator. If, on the other hand, the defrauded seller did not intend to transfer title (e.g., if the seller only intended to transfer possession or received no consideration), the converter acquired void title, and a good-faith purchaser was not protected. See, e.g. *Mowrey v. Walsh*, 8 Cow. 238 (N.Y. Sup. Ct. 1828). Weinberg, supra, at 17–31. One reason that there are virtually no cases defining good faith purchaser is that most cases turn on the question of whether the victim intended to transfer title. Most cases seem to involve truly innocent purchasers. See generally cases cited in Weinberg, Markets.

35. *Jacobellis v. Ohio*, 378 U.S. 184, 197 (1963)(Stewart, J., concurring)(referring to the definition of hard-core pornography).

36. See generally, Gilmore, supra. n.66, at 1098; Farnsworth, supra n.65, at 668–670. See also *Breslin v. New Jersey Investors, Inc.*, 361 A.2d 1, 3–4 (N.J. 1976), where a New Jersey court held that good faith in the context of U.C.C. 1–201(19) is "determined by looking to the mind of the particular [buyer]." Accord: *General Investment Corp. v. Agnelli*, 278 A.2d 193 (N.J. 1971). Cf. *Mattek v. Malofsky*, 42 Wisc.2d 16 (1969) (auto dealer held to know of dealer practices in auto registration and title matter).

37. See *Lawson v. Weston*, 170 Eng. Rep. 640 (K.B. 1801).

38. U.C.C. Section 1–201(19).

39. U.C.C. Section 2–103(b).

40. Historical Note, New York Annotations, U.C.C. Sec. 2–103 (McKinney's 1964). The New York case coming closest to elucidating the issue of whether a buyer has a duty to inquire is *Porter v. Wertz*, 53 N.Y.2d 696 (1981). That case, relied upon heavily by J&J, involved "entrusting," a situation not present in gray market cases. The court in *Porter* expressly stopped short of deciding the good-faith issue, disposing of the matter on other grounds. Id. at 708. Based upon *Porter*, the Third Circuit ruled that the law of New York on this issue is "unclear." 798 F.2d at 105. The law of New Jersey, under which *Quality King* was ultimately decided, is similarly unclear. See *O'Keefe v. Snyder*, 416 A.2d 862 (N.J. 1980)(involving stolen artwork).

41. 798 F.2d at 106 n.4.

42. Brief of J&J, at 31.

43. Id.

44. 798 F.2d at 104, 106. An early reference to the way in which the good-faith purchaser rule promotes commerce is found in Blackstone.

[P]roperty may also in some cases be transferred by sale, though the vendor hath none at all in the goods: for it is expedient that the buyer, by taking proper precautions, may at all events be secure in his purchase; otherwise all commerce between man and man soon be at an end.

2 W. Blackstone, *Commentaries* 449–55 (Bell ed. 1771), as cited in Weinberg, Markets, at 3. See generally, Gilmore, at 1057.

45. Id., at 24. Dumping is the practice of selling goods below cost in one market to absorb overhead and keep prices relatively low in some other market. The practice is considered unfair and violative of the General Agreement on Tariffs & Trade, Article VI. There was no hard evidence that that was the case in the J&J litigation, although dumping and price discrimination are among numerous rational explanations for the existence of the gray market. See generally, S. Lipner, *Parallel Imports*, at 572–574.

46. See Brief of Quality King, at 23. J&J asserts that the primary cause of the price difference was the difference in marketing expenses between the United States on the one hand and Poland on the other. Underlying this assertion is the oft-heard argument that gray market sellers are free riders. While that might be the case, that is yet another reason why the legality of gray market sales should be resolved according to principles of trademark and antitrust, not sales law.

47. For example, this is one reason for the development of back-to-back letters of credit, frequently used in international sales. See generally, J. Barton and B. Fisher, *International Trade and Investment: Regulating International Business*, at 45 (1986).

48. Brief of J&J, at 31.

49. Id., at 28. J&J argued, and Judge Debevoise in part rested his decision upon the judgment that Quality King knew that J&J would disapprove of the gray market trade in J&J products. Judge Stapleton mentioned that fact but concluded it was not relevant to the legal issue. 798 F.2d, at 102.

50. 798 F.2d, at 106.

51. As a multinational company, seemingly victimized by the gray market, J&J could have obtained such evidence from other victimized trademark owners. In view of the potential impact that a favorable decision would have had, those other trademark owners would probably have been more than happy to furnish information. It is thus not unreasonable for the court to hold the lack of evidence against J&J.

52. See, e.g., Brief of J&J, at 11, 28–29, 31.

53. See H. Weinberg, "Sales Law, Economics, and the Negotiability of Goods," 9 *J. Legal Stud.* 569, 587–88 [hereinafter cited as Weinberg, Sales Law].

54. See Restatement, Contracts, sec. 475. "Fraud in the inducement exists where the defrauded party understands the identity of the adversary party, the consideration, the subject matter, and the terms of the contract, and he is willing to enter into the contract in question, but his willingness so to enter is caused by a fraudulent misrepresentation of the adversary party as to a material fact." 1 Page on Contracts sec. 87, as cited in *Lovato v. Catron*, 20 N.M. 168 (1915). Included in the term stolen is goods sold as a result of fraud-in-the-factum (i.e., fraud in the execution of a contract, where the seller does not receive the value he bargained for). See generally, J. Calamari & J. Perillo, *The Law of Contract*, 293–294 (1977); E. Farnsworth, *Contracts*, at 235–36 (1982); R. Brown, *The Law of Personal Property*, at 193–201 (Raushenbush ed. 1975). For an outline of the development of law as it applies to good faith purchasers, see n.66, supra. For an article dealing with this problem under Canadian law, see Zysblat, "Sale of Goods – Transfer of Title By Non-Owner," 9 *U.B.C.L. Rev.* 186 (1979).

55. J. Calamari & J. Perillo, *The Law of Contract*, 293–294 (1977); E. Farnsworth, *Contracts*, at 235 (1982).

56. See Weinberg, supra. n.201, at 41. The judgment that fraud of this kind is not as reprehensible as outright theft seems embodied in U.C.C. Sec. 2–403(1)(d), which states that the power to transfer good title to a good-faith purchaser exists even if "the delivery was procured through fraud punishable as larcenous under the criminal law." See also U.C.C. 2–305, which grants to a holder in due course of a negotiable instrument the right to take free of all defenses except, inter alia, "(c) such mis-

representation as has induced the party to sign the instrument with neither knowledge nor reasonable opportunity to obtain knowledge of its character or its essential terms; . . . ." For the English rule, see *Saunders v. Anglia Building Society*, 3 All E.R. at 972 (Opinion of Lord Wilberforce) and at 979 (Opinion of Lord Pearson).

57. See generally, Weinberg, Sales Law, supra. n.53: Weinberg, Markets, supra. n.34. The first article, "Sales Law, Economics and the Negotiability of Goods," analyzes the wisdom of the good-faith purchaser rule and its effect on supply and demand for stolen goods (good-faith purchaser should not take good title) and fraud-induced goods (good-faith purchaser should take good title). See Weinberg, Sales Law, at 586, 588–90. The second article traces the history of these different approaches to different fact situations, concluding that economic values were at least a partial factor in development of these rules in the 19th Century. See Weinberg, Markets, supra. n.34 at 41.

58. Weinberg, Sales Law, at 574–79. The author reasons that if good faith were to render a remote purchaser's title valid, the quantity of stolen goods demanded would increase. Furthermore, he reasons, the economic cost of acquiring questionable goods would decline because the risk of replevin by the original owner would be eliminated. Weinberg reasons that that would attract even more (shady) purchasers, compounding the increase in demand for stolen goods. Id. Similarly, the supply of such goods would rise because of the stimulation of demand and desire of (shady) sellers to enter the market and make a profit. Id., at 579–80.

59. Id., at 587–88. The same is true, perhaps to an even greater degree, for gray market fraud-induced goods, because prevailing on the question of title does not resolve all the issues of legality. Trademark issues will remain, and the good-faith purchaser may nevertheless ultimately lose in its legal dispute with the trademark owner, if a court finds that the gray market sales infringe.

60. Id. at 589. "In the case [of fraud], the owner dealt directly with the wrongdoer. He had the opportunity to . . . not sell the goods." Id. In the context of Quality King, J&J received only oral representations that the goods would not be resold outside of Poland; the contracts of sale, the certificates of dispatch, and the invoices contained no mention of the restrictions.

61. Weinberg, Sales Law, supra. n.53, at 589. Gilmore wrote, "He is protected not because of his praiseworthy character, but to the end that commercial transactions may be engaged in without elaborate investigation of property rights and in reliance on the possession of property by one who offers it for sale." 63 Yale L.J., at 1057.

62. Weinberg, Sales Law, supra. n.53 at 589–90.

63. Weinberg writes that courts in the nineteenth century

appreciated the limited capacity of good faith purchasers for efficiently investigating the quality of their sellers' titles to land and recognized that a rule favoring defrauded owners could inhibit realty transactions. Good faith purchasers' title investigative capacity would have been even more limited for goods sold in a dynamic and impersonal market in which they often would not have dealt face-to-face with the wrongdoer.

Weinberg, Markets, supra. n.34, 30–31.

64. See generally Chapter 8, infra, under "The Effect of Laws of Foreign Countries on Gray Market Trade in the United States."

65. Indeed, export restrictions are generally illegal per se in the European Economic Community. A dispute could thus arise over whether U.S. attempts to restrict parallel trade conflict with the European policy of not restricting it. Strict application of U.S. law might thus violate recognized principles of comity among nations. See generally *Timberlane Lumber Co. v. Bank of America*, 549 F.2d 597 (9th Cir. 1976); *Leasco Data Processing Equipment Corp. v. Maxwell*, 468 F.2d 1326 (2d Cir. 1972).

66. See Chapter 4, supra, and the discussion of intrabrand competition.

67. See The Trademark Counterfeiting Act, 18 U.S.C. sec. 2320 et seq. (1986).

68. See Chapter 8, infra, under "The Effect of Laws of Foreign Countries on Gray Market Trade in the United States."

69. Shakespeare wrote that the theft of one's name (trademark?) was more damaging than the theft of tangible property.

> Who steals my purse, steals trash; . . .
> But he who filches from me my good name
> Robs me of that which not enriches him
> And makes me poor indeed.

Othello, III, iii, 155.

According to Shakespeare, the theft of one's name is among the most reprehensible of crimes. But then again, Shakespeare did not distinguish between the trademark owners' lawyers who now put forth this argument and those of the gray market sellers who oppose it: he would have killed them all. W. Shakespeare, *King Henry VI*, IV, ii, 86 ("The first thing we do, let's kill all the lawyers.")

7

Copyright and the Gray Market: The Trademark Owner's Search for a Winning Theory

Copyright protection is an ancient concept, with roots in pre-Victorian England and a provision in the U.S. Constitution authorizing Congress to grant protection "for limited Times to Authors ... the exclusive Right to their respective Writings."[1] Congress, over the years, has produced several incarnations of the Copyright Act, the most recent enacted in 1976 and taking effect on January 1, 1978.[2] Even though there were no copyright-gray market cases until recently, judicial decisions made as early as 1908 laid the cornerstones for resolving the issues currently being raised.[3]

There are many parallels between trademark law and copyright law, but there are many differences as well. One area of similarity, integrally related to the gray market area, deals with the owner's rights following his initial sale of protected goods to the public. In the trademark arena, the "exhaustion doctrine" limited the rights of trademark owners to control subsequent sales of their goods by unauthorized distributors. A similar concept, known as the "first sale" doctrine, affects the rights of copyright owners in much the same way as the exhaustion doctrine of trademark law. But as has already been demonstrated, the judiciary has created a hole in the exhaustion doctrine and has thus permitted some local trademark owners (i.e., those with independent goodwill) to avoid application of the doctrine and enforce trademark rights against a seller who lawfully purchased from a foreign trademark owner.

The question raised by this chapter is thus whether a similar loophole exists in copyright law's "first sale" doctrine. That doctrine, with roots predating the recent Copyright Act,[4] was codified in sec. 109(a):

> Notwithstanding the provisions of section 106(3), the owner of a particular copy ... lawfully made under this title, or any person authorized by such owner, is entitled, without the authority of the copyright owner, to sell or otherwise dispose of the possession of that copy.

Section 106(3) grants to copyright owners exclusive distribution rights, and, were it not for sec. 109(a), those rights would apparently defeat any gray market seller. But interpretation of sec. 109(a) has not been without controversy, and there are a handful of litigated cases attempting to resolve the question of whether that section protects sales by gray market participants.

Section 602(a), which addresses importation, compounds the difficulty of resolving the sec. 109(a) controversy. Section 602(2) states that

> [i]mportation into the United States, without authority of the owner of copyright under this title, of copies ... of a work that have been acquired outside the United States is an infringement of the exclusive right to distribute copies ... under section 106.

As indicated, courts in recent years have been called upon to determine whether sec. 602(a) bars gray market importation as an infringement of copyright. As will be seen in this chapter, the first few cases favored the copyright owners, but that trend has been reversed, and copyright theories, with one or two exceptions, are unlikely to succeed against gray marketeers.

A COPYRIGHT LAW PRIMER

Copyrights protect "original works of authorship fixed in a tangible medium of expression."[5] That phrase belies a simple but fundamental concept that "the medium is not the message."[6] One must always separate conceptually, for copyright purposes, the protected work from the tangible copy embodying that work. There can be an infinite number of copies of a copyrighted work, but there is only one work. Thus, in a simple application of this concept, the heirs of Mark Twain were unable to gain title to an original manuscript copyrighted by him that appeared, many years later, after being sold by Twain and eventually lost. It is this separation between the work and the copy that underlies the first sale doctrine.

As the definition recited at the outset of this section demonstrates, the threshold requirements for copyright are easily met. The concept "original work of authorship" has received the broadest definition possible, and virtually any uncopied phrase, design, or logo would qualify. Similarly, the "fixation" requirement is easily met; the result is that any book, movie, musical composition, or even trademark will be eligible for copyright protection.

Under sec. 106 of the 1976 Act, the owner of copyright is granted five discreet rights:

1. to make copies,
2. to make derivative works,
3. to distribute the work,
4. to perform the work publicly, and
5. to display pictorial, graphic, and sculptural works.

These rights are then limited by the sections of the Act that follow, including sec. 109(a). Section 501 defines "infringement" in terms of the rights just quoted, and part of the gray market controversy is whether sec. 602 creates any new rights not mentioned in sec. 106.

One important change embodied in the 1976 Act is a reduction in the formalities necessary to qualify for copyright protection. Deposit and Registration with the Copyright Office, formerly prerequisites to protection, were reduced to mere prerequisites for filing suit, permitting protection to attach "from creation"[7] with Deposit and Registration permitted on the eve of suit.[8] But the Act does require the affixation of a copyright notice, although an unintentionally omitted notice can be cured by the use of reasonable efforts. These changes have made copyright protection more broadly available.

COPYRIGHT AND THE GRAY MARKET

The first case[9] challenging gray market imports under the Copyright Act was *Columbia Broadcasting Systems, Inc. v. Scorpio Music Distributors, Inc.*[10] Columbia Broadcasting (hereinafter "CBS") owned the copyright in certain musical compositions that it had licensed to Vicor Music Corporation, a Philippine corporation. Vicor's license was restricted to manufacture and sale in the territory of the Philippines. On November 2, 1981, pursuant to its terms, CBS canceled the license with Vicor. Vicor had sixty days to liquidate its stock and did so by sale to Rainbow Music, Inc., another Philippine corporation. Rainbow, in turn, sold the records to International Traders, Inc., a Nevada corporation, who in turn sold the records to Scorpio. CBS then brought suit against Scorpio, alleging copyright infringement as well as trademark infringement and unfair competition.[11]

The case revolved around an interpretation of sec. 109(a) and 602(a). The court first ruled that it was irrelevant whether Scorpio was actually responsible for the importation, Judge Clifford Scott Green invoking notions of vicarious liability and contributory infringement. It did not matter whether CBS joined International Traders as a defendant, ruled the court, and neither good faith nor lack of knowledge of the illegality was a defense available to Scorpio.[12] To say that Scorpio was not guilty because it was not the importer would permit easy circumvention by successive sales, and, in Judge Green's view, that could not have been Congress' intention.

The key to the case was Scorpio's sec. 109(a) defense, and Judge Green was not prepared to accept it. The court determined that the language of sec. 109(a) applied only to copies manufactured and sold in the United States and not to copies manufactured abroad. Judge Green cited the portion of sec. 109(a) that provides protection to the purchaser of a copy "lawfully made under this section." Judge Green determined that because the Copyright Act does not extend beyond U.S. borders, the copies in question were not "lawfully made under [the Act]," and thus sec. 109(a) did not apply to them.

Judge Green further reasoned that broad construction of sec. 109(a) would render the importation provision of sec. 602(a) "virtually meaningless." In language reminiscent of the trademark cases, the court stated that if gray market importation were permitted, "the copyright owner would be unable to exercise control over copies of the work [manufactured abroad and] which entered the American market in competition with copies lawfully manufactured and distributed under this title."[13]

Judge Green felt that any other construction of the Act would circumvent the intent of Congress to grant importation rights to U.S. copyright owners.[14] The legislative history of these sections of the

Copyright Act have been extensively analyzed elsewhere,[15] and no attempt will be made herein to repeat it. Rather, this text will continue to analyze the judicial decisions interpreting the sections in questions.

The next significant decision in the 109(a)–602(a) controversy was an unpublished opinion in *Cosmair, Inc. v. Dynamite Enterprises, Inc.*[16] The case involved gray market Ralph Lauren toiletries. Cosmair is the exclusive U.S. licensee of the Lauren products. The packaging for each of the products involved contained the "Polo Player Design," a symbol that serves not only as a trademark but has also been registered for copyright. The defendants were the consignees of shipments of gray market Lauren products shipped from abroad. But one significant difference between the goods in *Scorpio* and the goods in *Cosmair* was that the goods in the former case were manufactured abroad while the goods in the latter case were manufactured in the United States, exported, and then reimported by the defendants.

The court reasoned that the original sale of the goods involved in *Cosmair* took place in the United States because they were shipped abroad by the plaintiffs pursuant to a CIF contract. Under the U.C.C. in such a contract, title passed to the buyer when the goods passed the ship's rail, (i.e., at a United States port). The court used that reasoning to sidestep *Scorpio*, although Judge Hoeveler did express "some doubt as to the validity of the reasoning [in that case]."[17]

The court also expressed doubt about the validity of the plaintiffs' copyright in the Polo Player Design. Based on the long-used Polo player trademark, the defendants argued that the failure to affix any copyright notice upon earlier sales placed the design in the public domain. The plaintiffs tried to argue that the original design had been changed, thus rendering it again eligible for copyright. The court, however, was unpersuaded, and, based upon its doubt that the plaintiffs would ultimately succeed on the merits, vacated the temporary restraining order and refused to grant the preliminary injunction.[18]

Hearst Corporation v. Stark[19] involved facts similar to *Scorpio*, although the products involved were books rather than phonorecords. Judge Legge indicated at the outset his belief that the enactment of sec. 602(a) was motivated by a desire on the part of Congress to limit not only piratical copies, but also gray market goods as well. The court was of the opinion that sec. 602(a) created a new right for copyright holders, a right independent of sec. 106, and not limited by the first sale doctrine of 109(a). But the court did not stop there and attempted to further support its opinion with a different fact: the defendants were not importing a single copy, but rather were engaged in wholesale distribution.

In support of this proposition, the court cited the fact that sec. 109(a) was framed in the singular, (i.e., "the owner of a particular copy . . . "). The court offered no further explanation for its decision that sec. 109(a) did not apply to wholesalers because of the volume of their business, although Judge Legge did cite *Scorpio* as proof that courts give a narrow construction to sec. 109(a). Further, Judge Legge rejected *Cosmair*, harmonizing the two earlier cases based upon the situs of manufacture of the goods in question.[20]

Finally, the court rejected the plaintiff's motion for summary judgment that the infringement had been "willful," a finding that would entitle the plaintiffs to statutory damages and, if bad faith were proven, attorneys fees. The court noted that the legal issues raised were essentially of first impression and that it would thus be unfair to grant summary judgment against the defendants on that issue.[21] With the exception of *Cosmair*, which was easily explained away by the time of the *Hearst* decision, copyright claims had scored a measure of success in the fight against gray market imports.

The trend seemed intact when the District Court for New Jersey decided *Sebastian International Corp. v. Consumer Contact (PTY) Ltd.*[22] The case involved gray market hair care products made in the United States, sold to a South African distributor, and reimported into the United States.[23] The plaintiffs moved for a preliminary injunction based upon copyright infringement. The lower court's decision was in line with *Scorpio* and *Hearst*. The defendants first tried to argue that registration certificates had not yet been received and that the designs in question did not qualify for copyright protection. These arguments were unsuccessful, and the court thus turned to the crux of the matter—the 109(a)–602(a) controversy.

The defendants' main argument began with the distinction relied on in *Cosmair*: the goods were manufactured in the United States. The court initially indicated that the reasoning of *Scorpio* and *Cosmair* would seem to support that argument. Judge Barry reviewed the decisions in those cases, but ultimately reached the opposite conclusion. Judge Barry was critical of the distinction drawn in those two cases between goods manufactured in the United States and goods manufactured abroad. The judicial misunderstanding, according to Judge Barry, flowed from several sources, including a misreading of the legislative history and confusion with the Tariff Act. At bottom, the court stated that there is nothing in sec. 602(a) that even mentions place of manufacture, and the "lawfully made" language of sec. 109(a) arose because of a deficiency in the 1909 Act,[24] not because Congress wanted to distinguish between different kinds of gray goods.

The court viewed *Hearst* as a turning point, but Judge Barry express-ly rejected the view that wholesaling multiple copies was not con-templated by Congress as protected by the first sale doctrine, noting that the *Bobbs-Merrill* case involved multiple sales.[25] Instead Judge Barry struck a new chord in the copyright controversy: sec. 109(a) and sec. 602(a) did not conflict at all. Judge Barry reasoned that the distribution right of the Copyright Act had two components — a right to vend and a right to import. These two components were deemed separate and discrete, and only the exclusive right to vend was restricted by the first sale doctrine. That conclusion was drawn from the "right to control the market" theory of intellectual property protection, a theory behind which all authorized sellers seem to try to hide, regardless of the context or legal theory being utilized.

Judge Barry's interpretation of the new Copyright Act is unique. She was unabashed in her belief that copyright law provides the weapon that anti-gray market forces have long sought:

> Surprisingly, American businesses have been slow to recognize the power granted to them to control the importation of gray market copyright works. Indeed, given the confusion in the trademark world, it is unclear why plaintiffs continue to rely on those uncertain rights when the copyright law provides such a formidable shield.[26]

Of course, in making this invitation, Judge Barry overlooked the fact that in spite of four years of litigation of other cases, no judge had yet subscribed to her novel interpretation. Indeed, as she would soon learn, copyright may not be the "formidable shield" that she had believed it to be.

The court of appeals for the Third Circuit reversed.[27] Judge Weis, writing for unanimous panel, began by placing the first sale doctrine in its proper context — an application of the principle that the material copy is distinct from the metaphysical copyrighted work. As stated earlier, understanding that concept is one key to understanding copyright. The question is not one of whether there are two forms of distribution right, but rather is an economic question of the extent of the "right to control" granted to copyright owners. And the Third Circuit did not view that right as being anywhere near as extensive as Judge Barry had.

The primary goal of copyright, said the court, is to encourage creation and dissemination. While that encouragement is accomplished through the rewards that copyright grants, "[u]ltimately, the copyright law regards financial reward to the owner as a secondary consideration."[28] And in words echoing the Ninth Circuit's opinion in *NEC*, Judge Weis quoted from *Burke & Van Heusen v. Arrow Drug, Inc.*[29] that the "ultimate question under the 'first sale' doctrine is whether or not there has been such a disposition of the copyrighted article that it may be fairly said that the copyright proprietor has received his reward for its use."[30]

In the particular context of the sec. 109(a)–602(a) dichotomy, Judge Weis repeated the common, and by now well-documented, proposition that the legislative history was inconclusive. Judge Weis noted the two possible interpretations, but he clearly opted for the latter one. The importation right of sec. 602(a), he wrote, is a subset of the distribution right, and that right is expressly extinguished in sec. 109(a). But the court's opinion was emphatically made fact specific, so that it did not call into the question the propriety of *Scorpio* and *Hearst*.[31]

Instead, the court offered the following:

Although this case turns purely on copyright law, we recognize that the underlying "gray market" or "parallel importing," issues really are dominant. Various economic factors—including the manipulation of global currency standards—encourage transactions in which goods are produced in this country, shipped and sold to foreign concerns, and then returned to the United States for resale at less than the domestic prices.

This practice has led to complaints by manufacturers seeking a fair return on their costs of promotion and servicing of warranties in this country. Equally vocal are consumer advocates asserting the desirability of access to identical goods at lower costs. Because contractual remedies have proved inadequate, see Johnson & Johnson Products v. DAL Int'l Trading Co. [citation omitted], domestic manufacturers now invoke the copyright law to advance their economic interests. This twist has created the anomalous situation in which the dispute at hand superficially targets a product's label, but in reality rages over the product itself. We think that the controversy over "gray market" goods, or "parallel importing," should be resolved directly on its merits by Congress, not by judicial extension of the Copyright Act's limited monopoly.[32]

The Third Circuit's rebuff to Judge Barry's broad interpretation is not surprising, and it is difficult to dispute Judge Weis's insight into the realities of *Sebastian*. The plaintiffs, blocked from a contract action and fearful of a protracted and uncertain trademark litigation, chose a clever legal theory, and it was nearly successful. But Judge Weis's wisdom only takes one so far because, of the cases thus far decided, about half involved real copyright claims rather than disguised trademark complaints.

To observers, it was not surprising that the label cases have all failed, while the literature and music cases have tended to be successful. That fact cannot be explained by copyright law alone because that body of law draws no distinction between the rights granted to different kinds of eligible works. Whether Judge Weis's opinion becomes a watershed for recognizing this distinction or whether it is read to limit in all cases the 602(a) right is yet to be seen. The initial evidence, however, favors the second interpretation.

There have been two significant copyright decisions since *Sebastian*,[33] and they have tended to follow Judge Weis's lead. *Neutrogena Corp. v. U.S.*[34] was a label case where the court was again faced with domestically manufactured goods and ruled against the copyright owner.[35] But *Red Baron-Franklin Park, Inc. v. Taito Corp.*[36] involved gray market video game circuit boards, works that are clearly protected by copyright.[37] The court in *Red Baron* referred to its ruling as a "logical and important extension" of *Sebastian* and expanded sec. 109(a) to include goods manufactured abroad.

In *Red Baron*, Judge Cacheris expressly rejected *Scorpio*, reasoning that the place of manufacture should have no effect on the case's outcome. Adding weight to Judge Weis's arguments, the opinion stated: "This court finds it difficult to accept that Congress would have given foreign corporations greater protection under the copyright laws than it has provided domestic copyright holders." In light of *Sebastian* and the decisions that have followed, the tide seemed to have turned away from successes for copyright litigation against gray market sellers.

But on appeal, the Fourth Circuit reversed.[38] Section 109(a) begins with language making reference to the sec. 106(3) Distribution Right. But there are other rights protected by copyright; an important one is the Performance Right of sec. 106(4). This right guarantees to the copyright owner the right to perform a copyrighted work publicly. On appeal Taito conceded that its distribution right was indeed exhausted upon the first sale; but it also argued that the performance right of subsection 4 is distinct from the distribution right and that the former is not extinguished under the statute.

Judge Winter, writing for the court, agreed. He found that the video games in question were audiovisual works and that activation of the games in an arcade constituted a "public performance." The court then noted that, indeed, sec. 109(a) begins "Notwithstanding the provisions of section 106(3), ..." Judge Winter observed that the argument that the sec. 106(4) performance right was also extinguished by sec. 109(a) had "a certain superficial, logical appeal in this case." He noted that even though it has been held, under the 1909 Act, that the sale of a copy of a motion picture was also a conveyance of performance rights,[39] he declined to extend that holding to this case.

Judge Winter, a well-known strict constructionalist, held that the plain meaning of the statute was clear and that the performance right was not singled out for extinction the way the distribution right was.

> By its very terms, the statute codifying the first sale doctrine . . . is limited in its effects to the *distribution* of the copyrighted work. It prohibits the owner of a copyright in a work who has sold a copy of the work to another from preventing or restricting the transferee from a further sale. . . . Thus, by its terms, sec. 109(a) has no application to the other four rights of a copyright owner, including the right to perform the work publicly.

Judge Winter's decision seems to be supported by an earlier gray market video game circuit board case. In that case, Judge Freeman of the Eastern District of Michigan made a similar observation in another context.

> By distributing, offering for sale, and selling [the gray market version of the game], defendants have induced others to distribute, *operate, or publicly perform the game and have materially contributed to such performances.*[40]

That court's decision in that case was not based on sec. 109(a), but rather on sec. 602(a). Indeed, sec. 109(a) goes completely unmentioned. But the existence of the quoted comment surely lends weight to the argument that copyright law bans gray market importation of video game boards.

The question remains whether the *Red-Baron* decision extends to any other type of copyrighted works. Video game boards consist of copyrightable works in part because of the computer programs they contain. These computer programs generate the images and sounds that, Judge Winter held, comprise the audiovisual works. In some types of computer programs, including certain popular business software, running the program has been argued to similarly create protectable audiovisual works in screen displays and output formats. An inevitable question is whether gray market importation and sale of these types of programs might constitute an infringement of the performance right unprotected by sec. 109(a). One obvious distinction is in the "public" nature of the arcade performance in *Red-Baron*. Business application computer programs are generally not used "publicly," and that is a distinction that should legally separate the video games in *Red-Baron* from most other computer programs.

Musical works, however, are more susceptible to public performance than are business computer programs. And while the copyright law does provide for compulsory licenses of performance rights in musical compositions, that does not change the fact that one infringes if he does not apply for the license. The argument might thus be made that in view of the possibility that a gray market phonorecord (i.e., the tangible copy of a musical work) might be played publicly, the copyright owner's rights under sec. 106(4) require protection. Again, however, one can point to the low probability of that occurring as compared with the likelihood that the video game boards in *Red-Baron* as a reason for limiting the decision in that case to its facts.

Importantly, however, the *Red-Baron* logic cannot possibly apply to copyrighted logos, and it does not apply to books and other purely "literary" works. Thus, copyright law retains only a minor role in the gray market controversy.

CONCLUSION

Judge Weis spoke volumes when he chastised the plaintiffs in *Sebastian* for bringing a trademark case under the guise of copyright. He viewed their attempt as a way to avoid the difficulties of trademark litigation and the failure of the title theory. But there exist real gray market-copyright cases, and the logic of the early decisions has been exposed to solid and persuasive criticism.

Judge Weis's invitation to Congress to address the issue is sound advice but might best be written off as wishful thinking. Copyright law will evidently be considered a bar in the video game–public performance realm but will not be a bar when dealing purely with logos. Nevertheless, cases involving other types of copyrighted works may arise. The goodwill rationales that have dominated the trademark cases are absent from the copyright sphere, where the battleground lies in the proper scope of economic reward the government wishes to grant to authors and creators.

NOTES

1. Art. 1, sec. 8, cl. 8.

2. 17 U.S.C. 101 et seq. (1986). In November 1988, Congress made certain minor changes in the Act, primarily designed to permit the United States to enter into the Berne Copyright Convention. Those changes have no substantial effect on gray market law and are thus not discussed in detail.

3. See *Bobbs-Merrill Co. v. Straus*, 210 U.S. 339 (1908), where the Supreme Court ruled that a copyright owner could not lawfully impose resale restrictions on copyrighted works (books) following their initial sale. See also *Burke & Van Heusen v. Arrow Drug, Inc.* 233 F.Supp. 881 (E.D.Pa. 1963).

4. In recent debates in the House of Representatives, the first sale doctrine was said to have "roots in the English common law rule against restraints on alienation of property." See H.R.Rep. No. 987, 98th Cong., 2d Sess. 2, reprinted in 1984 U.S. Code Cong. & Admin. News 2898, 2899. The Copyright Act of 1909, in force prior to the new 1976 codification, contained in sec. 27, a similar provision restricting a copyright owner's rights upon a product's "first sale."

5. 17 U.S.C. sec. 102.

6. *Apple Computer, Inc. v. Franklin Computer Corp.*, 714 F.2d 1240 (3rd Cir. 1983).

7. 17 U.S.C. 102(a).

8. The Act does limit the remedies available in such a late registration case, barring recovery of "statutory" damages and attorney fees in such a case. 17 U.S.C. 412.

9. But see *Nintendo of America, Inc. v. Elcon Industries, Inc.*, 564 F. Supp. 937 (E.D.Mich. 1982). This early gray market case did not directly address the 109(a)–602(a) controversy.

10. 569 F.Supp. 47 (E.D.Pa. 1983).

11. The latter two counts were withdrawn by CBS. 569 F.Supp. at 47 n.1.

12. Id. at 49.

13. Id. at 49.

14. The judge's statement follows the thrust of some of the trademark cases, although little consideration was given to effectuating control via a better drafted license. Judge Green's decision was affirmed by the Third Circuit without opinion. 738 F.2d 424 (3rd Cir. 1984).

15. See Note, "Parallel Importing Under the Copyright Act of 1976," 17 *N.Y.U.J. Int'l L. & Pol.* 113 (1984), and, Tyson and Parker, "Parallel Importation of Copyrighted Phonorecords," 10 *N.C.J. Int'l L. & Comm. Reg.* 397 (1985). The authors of these articles conduct an extensive analysis of the legislative history, reaching opposite conclusions about sec. 109(a) and the gray market. It is interesting to note, however, that both authors were critical of *Scorpio*.

16. 226 U.S.P.Q. 344 (S.D.Fla. 1985).

17. Judge Hoeveler briefly considered the legislative history of sec. 109(a), concluding that it shielded gray market importation from any copyright claim.

18. The court further noted, in the section of its opinion titled "Public Interest," that the availability of Lauren products at lower prices was a benefit to the public and that injury was unlikely because the goods were genuine and unaltered. The court thus suggests a slight pro-gray market bias absent from other judicial opinions.

19. 639 F.Supp. 970 (N.D.Calif. 1986).

20. The court also considered, and rejected, a First Amendment argument that barring importation would be unconstitutional, reasoning that the Copyright Act, in toto, was an effort to encourage the dissemination of ideas by rewarding authors for their endeavors and that it would be improper to pick it apart in the way suggested by the defendants. Id. at 977–978.

21. The defendants also raised an antitrust issue based upon a consent decree in a tangentially related case. That claim was summarily rejected by the court. Id. at 980–981.

22. 664 F.Supp. 914 (D.N.J. 1987), rev'd 847 F.2d 1093 (3rd Cir. 1988).

23. Plaintiff claimed that the goods came to rest in the hands of Quality King, a large discount drug chain that was a defendant in the case. Quality King has been the subject of other gray market litigation. See Chapter 7, infra. The court issued a temporary restraining order against Quality King based upon the "title" theory discussed in Chapter 7, but it later became apparent that a company named Fabric Ltd., not Quality King, was in possession of the goods. The temporary restraining order was dissolved against Quality King, and a hearing was held to determine whether a "title" claim could be brought against Fabric. The court ruled that Sebastian was unable to prove a probability of success on the merits of that claim. The decision discussed herein considers the Plaintiff's alternate theory: copyright infringement.

24. Section 27 of the old law invoked the first sale doctrine on proof that the copy in question had been "lawfully obtained," leading to the result that the sale of a pirated copy was protected if the buyer purchased from a seller at least one step removed from the original infringer.

25. 664 F.Supp. at 918 n.13.

26. 664 F.Supp. at 922.

27. 847 F.2d 1093 (3rd Cir. 1988).

28. Id. at 1095.

29. 233 F.Supp. 881, at 884 (E.D.Pa. 1964).

30. Id. at 1096–97, citing *Burke & Van Huesen Inc. Arrow Drug, Inc.*, 233 F.Supp. 881, 884 (E.D.Pa. 1964).

31. The court wrote:

In [*Scorpio*] the copies were produced abroad and the sales occurred overseas. The [courts] reasoned that the foreign origin of both manufacture and sale made the first sale doctrine inapplicable. However valid that interpretation of the "lawfully made under this title" language of section 109(a) *— and we specifically do not pass upon it in this case —* it does not affect our decision here. Id. at 1098 (emphasis added).

32. 847 F.2d at 1099.

33. A third decision is *Disenos Artisticos v. Work*, 676 F.Supp. 1254, 1259–1265, discussed at length in Chapters 3 and 4. In addition to the trademark theories, copyright claims were made to combat gray market imports. But Judge Glasser ruled that the failure to cure the omission of copyright notices without reasonable efforts to cure that omission was fatal, and he dismissed the claims. Even though there was thus no decision on the merits of the copyright claim, it is interesting to note that the copyright in LLADRO figurines comes closer to the traditional copyrighted work than do the label cases, and the goods were not domestically made. Presumably, LLADRO figurines will, in the future, bear appropriate copyright notices, and the issue will arise again.

34. No. 2:88–0566–1, Slip op., District Court for South Carolina, April 5, 1988.

35. In another parallel to the trademark cases, it is interesting to note that the court referred to the fact that the goods in question were genuine and that might well preclude a finding that irreparable injury is present. See Chapter 3, infra.

36. No. 88–0156–A, slip op., District Court for the Eastern District of Virginia, August 29, 1988.

37. *Williams Electronics, Inc., v. Artic International, Inc.*, 685 F. 2d 870 (3rd Cir. 1982).

38. *Red-Baron-Franklin Park Inc. v. Taito Corp.*, No. 88–1368, slip op. July 18, 1989.

39. *Universal Film Mfg. v. Copperman*, 218 F. 577 (2d Cir. 1914).

40. *Nintendo of America, Inc. v. Elcon Industries, Inc.*, 564 F.Supp. 937, 942 (E.D.Mich. 1981).

8

State Laws, the International Trade Commission, and Foreign Laws

There is no question that the federal courts, applying the Lanham Act, continue to be principal decisionmakers on the legal viability of the gray market. The role of the Customs Service has been effectively reduced by the Supreme Court decision in *K-Mart v. Cartier*,[1] and even though a few issues remain open, the Court's decision ended many years of battles and debates. The possibility exists that Congress may pass gray market legislation, but, as already indicated, the likelihood of that occurring is minimal. The role of copyright law has been reduced, and while state statutes affecting title might come into play in certain circumstances, cases based on defective title or antifencing statutes are not prevalent.

Because trademark owners are denied their traditional remedies under the Lanham and Tariff Acts and because the copyright window is closed, the inevitable search begins for new weapons to use against gray market sellers. Three areas remain that are pertinent to the gray market. The first area to be discussed in this chapter concerns alternative weapons available under state law. Use of state law to combat gray market sales, especially "anti-dilution" statutes, promises to raise new issues in the gray market context. Other state law theories, including "tortious interference with contractual relations," have appeared in cases from time to time. Finally, some states, notably New York and California, have enacted consumer-protection legislation that affects gray market sellers. These topics are considered in the first section of this chapter.

The second area that requires discussion is sec. 337 of the Tariff Act of 1930, which provides for jurisdiction in the International Trade Commission (hereinafter referred to as "ITC") to combat certain "Unfair Practices in Import Trade," a section that was invoked in 1982 to combat certain gray market imports. The case considering that theory, as well as the prognosis for complaints brought under sec. 337, is the subject of the second section of this chapter. Finally, the third section considers the final principal actor on the gray market scene, the laws of foreign countries as they apply to the gray market (import and export) within the United States.

STATE LAWS

Three areas of state law affect the business and legal status of the gray market. The first is state trademark law, which in some cases differs with federal law because of a cause of action (available in some states) known as "trademark dilution." The second important area of state law is general "unfair competition," a theory which has been used with some, although limited, success in the gray market context. In this area, claims of false advertising (a species of unfair competition) have been used successfully to discipline overreaching by gray market sellers; other theories, (i.e., "tortious interference with contractual relations") have been less successful. The former topic is taken up in this section; for reasons that will become apparent, discussion of the latter is reserved for the final section of this chapter. The third area of state law activity is consumer protection legislation, to date an ineffectual player on the gray market scene but one that nevertheless merits discussion.

Trademark Dilution

Many states have statutes making actionable a practice known as "dilution." The concept is broader than trademark infringement — it is intended to protect a recognized and distinctive trademark from any injury, rather than simply from damage arising from likelihood of confusion. The cause of action has been characterized as a whittling down of the identity or reputation of a tradename or mark. The cause of action has been most effective when the owner of a highly distinctive mark attacks the use of a similar mark in a disparate industry. In such cases, consumers are unlikely to be confused as to source or sponsorship, but a cheapening of the appeal of the plaintiff's mark might result.

A smattering of gray market cases exists in which dilution claims were thrown in atop trademark and Tariff Act claims. In *El Greco*[2] and *Diamond Paper Supply*,[3] for example, claims were made under the New York Antidilution statute.[4] The judges in both cases rejected the claims out of hand. In *El Greco*, the district court judge stated that "plaintiff has offered no proof of dilution,"[5] and in *Diamond* the claim was dismissed "for many of the reasons previously discussed, [especially] . . . likelihood of injury to its business reputation. . . . "[6]

Greater consideration was given to a dilution claim in *Yamaha Corp. of America v. ABC Traders, Corp.*[7] The case involved gray market musical instruments manufactured by Yamaha-Japan. ABC Traders was careful to inform its customers that it was not affiliated with Yamaha-Japan, that it was not sponsored by Yamaha of America, and that it did not offer a Yamaha warranty. The court thus found that no likelihood of dilution was present.

Not a single declaration has been provided to the Court which indicates that consumers who have purchased genuine Yamaha products from ABC were later disappointed to learn that the product was not backed by a Yamaha warranty or authorized Yamaha sales or service personnel. Nor, have any declarations been provided which suggest that consumers value the Yamaha marks because the mark represents certain warranty or consumer education programs. Thus, this Court can assume that the individual who purchases at ABC receives exactly what he or she wants: A genuine product without the Yamaha warranty and other peripheral services that come with the purchase of a Yamaha product through an authorized Yamaha representative. To argue this dilutes the Yamaha trademark is much like saying that the sale of a broken down Chevrolet dilutes the value of the Chevrolet trademark.[8]

The court conceded that the warranty offered by ABC was not identical to that of Yamaha, and that Yamaha-America makes efforts to educate consumers about its goods. The court was nevertheless unmoved by the allegation that ABC's activities "tarnish" the Yamaha mark. In view of the disclaimers made by ABC, the court ruled: "[T]he goods are ABC's and thus any fallout from the lack of quality of these services reflects poorly upon ABC and not Yamaha."[9]

No court to date has ruled that gray market activities result in trademark dilution. The courts that might be inclined to do so are the same courts that found traditional trademark infringement in a given situation. Furthermore, even though courts like the one that decided *Yamaha* might concede that gray market sellers are free riders. Such concessions alone will not be held to be the equivalent of " trademark dilution."

The "dilution" theory was originally created to protect highly distinctive marks from being used (and thus undermined) by firms operating in other industries. By definition, gray market sellers operate in the same industry as do the mark-holders who sue them. Dilution theories are thus logically and historically inapposite to the gray market situation. Simply put, these cases involve potential confusion, not dilution. The mere fact that courts have struggled with the confusion concept in the gray market arena should not invite attempts to skirt the crux of the controversy and divert it into this inappropriate field.

False Advertising

The plaintiff in *Yamaha* also made the claim that ABC engaged in unfair competition by using "deceptive or misleading advertising" in violation of California statutes. Yamaha argued that the use of the Yamaha marks by ABC is likely to cause purchasers to believe that they are buying authorized Yamaha products. The court, however, granted summary judgment to ABC. The court again made reference to ABC's disclaimers, which the court held were sufficient to support its contentions that ABC was not engaged in deceptive advertising. The court also emphasized that Yamaha did not submit any evidence that customers of ABC actually believed they were purchasing authorized Yamaha products. Without such evidence, Yamaha was unable to establish a genuine issue of fact, and its claim was summarily dismissed.

If the *Yamaha* case serves as a lesson on how gray market sellers can avoid liability, *Seiko Time Corp. v. Alexander's, Inc.*[10] is a case showing what gray market sellers should not do. Until 1981, Alexander's, a department store chain with facilities in the northeast, purchased Seiko watches from an authorized distributor. But beginning about that time, Alexander's ceased purchasing the authorized Seiko watches and began purchasing from parallel importers. The watches

Alexander's began to sell in 1981 were genuine Seikos, but they were models not intended for sale in the United States and, as such, were not accompanied by manufacturer's warranties.

Alexander's advertised these watches at substantial discounts from "the manufacturer's suggested list prices." Seiko responded with a full-page advertisement in *The New York Times*, stating that the foreign watches might be damaged or tampered with, were not necessarily "high quality" Seikos, and might not be "a real Seiko at all." Alexander's responded with an advertisement that stated the watches it sold were "the real thing, . . . complete with warranty, [and that] Alexander's is authorized to bring you the best buys possible on Seiko."[11] As a result, Seiko charged Alexander's with deceptive pricing and advertising.

The court held that the Alexander's buyer had extensive experience in comparison shopping for watches, that the watches being sold were of like grade and quality to domestic Seikos, and that they were mechanically equal to those being offered in the United States by Seiko. Nevertheless, the court held that it was false advertising for Alexander's to use the phrase "manufacturer's suggested list price" when the manufacturer was not offering those exact goods for a suggested price "in the same trade area." The fact that independent distributors deemed the goods comparable to watches in the current or past Seiko catalog does not save the advertiser from accusations of deceptive advertising.[12] "An advertiser may advertise his products as 'comparable' or 'similar' to those of another," said the court, "only if both products are of essentially similar quality in those material respects which affect consumer preferences and marketability."[13] Presumably, pricing below a "suggested list price" affects marketability, and it is unlawful to imply that such a price exists if in fact none does.

Alexander's also advertised its watches as warranted by the manufacturer and allowed its sales personnel to inform consumers that the watches being sold were covered by the manufacturer's warranty. The warranty offered by Alexander's in fact came not from Seiko, but rather from the entities from which Alexander's had purchased the watches, and in many cases those warranties were distinctly inferior to the Seiko warranty. Alexander's evidently made little effort to instruct its sales personnel not to make statements that the watches carried a manufacturer's warranty and that a consumer could go to the Seiko Service Center in Manhattan for service, when in fact that alternative was not available to purchasers of gray market watches.

The court held that in view of the misleading warranty information, Seiko was likely to succeed on its false advertising and Lanham Act sec. 43(a) claims. The court felt that consumers were likely to believe that the gray market watches were sponsored by Seiko in the United States.[14] The court noted that although Alexander's had, by the time of the litigation, ceased all the offending practices, it entered an injunction anyway to prevent recurrence. Alexander's was thus enjoined from advertising "suggested list prices" when such prices did not in fact exist and from conveying any impression that gray market Seikos were covered by the manufacturer's warranty.

The thrust of these two cases is that gray market sellers overstep the bounds of legality when they do not clearly and fairly promote their products. They tread a fine line when they advertise gray market goods. Participants in the gray market often wish to take advantage of the domestic and international reputations of the trademarks on the goods they sell, but they must take care not to suggest affiliation with the manufacturer. Gray market products must have the ability to compete on fair and open terms with authorized goods if, ultimately, they are to survive legal challenge. But when gray market sellers try to hide the true nature of their product or act in a deceptive manner about product quality or warranties, claims for false advertising can be formidable weapons.

Consumer Protection Legislation

In 1985, New York State passed the "Warranty Disclosure Act."[15] This act was not intended to curtail gray market industry, but rather to insure that consumers are aware the purchase of gray market goods can have adverse impact upon the applicability of a manufacturer's warranty. The statute required that all sellers of gray market goods post conspicuous signs stating that some products being sold might not be covered by a manufacturer's warranty, might not be eligible for a manufacturer's rebate, or might not come with English-language instructions.

Under the statute, however, a seller is not required to post the sign if its warranty is equal to, or better than, the manufacturer's. Unfortunately, the exception to posting does not address the issue of rebates or instruction manuals, both of which are important to many consumers. Thus, if a seller offers a warranty but does not offer a rebate equal to that offered by a manufacturer for authorized goods, a purchaser expecting the rebate will be disappointed, and that consumer would have no recourse against the seller who posted no sign.

The statute, however well-intentioned, suffers from other problems as well. The terms "knowingly" and "conspicuous" are not clearly defined in the Act, and hence can be interpreted differently by each seller: stores "knowingly" selling gray market goods must post "conspicuous" signs. Furthermore, the statute holds sellers who did not disclose the proper information liable to the consumer for up to twenty days. Warranty problems, however, are not likely to arise within the twenty days, so the remedy provided is unlikely to be of value to a disappointed consumer.

The New York State Attorney General's office has admitted privately that it lacks the resources to police compliance with the law, and the result is a low level of compliance. A tour of gray market retailers in New York further revealed inconspicuous signage that was often not read or understood by the consuming public. Nevertheless, New York State's attempt to increase the flow of information to gray market consumers without barring such sales altogether is laudable.

Following New York State's example, California passed a similar statute, the "Grey Market Consumer Disclosure Act,"[16] in 1986. The California law, however, has far stricter requirements and requires that a greater amount of information be disclosed. For example, the "conspicuous" sign must be posted at the product's point of display rather than at the point of purchase, a provision that will certainly increase the consumer's awareness. Also, a tag must be affixed to each product disclosing the required information. Where applicable, this law also requires that the seller inform the consumer of details, such as the item's incompatibility with U.S. electrical currents or broadcast frequencies, or that replacement parts and compatible accessories may not be available through authorized U.S. distributors.

There is little available information about the impact of these statutes. Even if the impact is minimal, a valuable lesson can be learned: The states recognize the benefits of gray market importation, but they also recognize the problems and are prepared at some level to deal with them. More legislation in this area, whether on the federal or state level, would be welcome, with attention drawn to needed improvements.

In any event, because at least some gray market sales have been held to be lawful, greater attempts should be made by all parties to inform consumers of the problems caused by the purchase of gray market goods.

THE INTERNATIONAL TRADE COMMISSION

The ITC, a U.S. government agency, was created in 1974 and empowered to make recommendations to the president concerning relief to industries injured by practices in international trade deemed "unfair." The ITC is the successor to the United States Tariff Commission, which had a similar though more limited role than does the ITC. The ITC consists of six commissioners, appointed by the president, who have expertise in resolving international trade problems. Petitions may be filed with the ITC, which conducts an investigation and then informs the president of its determination. The president then has the option of granting or denying the relief recommended by the ITC. ITC makes written, reasoned decisions on a legal basis. The president's determination is sometimes accompanied by a brief explanation, but, in any event, it is final and not subject to review.

In 1983, Duracell, Inc., the well-known manufacturer of alkaline batteries, filed a complaint with the ITC alleging injury from the sale of gray market "DURACELL" batteries.[17] The complaint alleged violations of sec. 337 of the Tariff Act of 1974. The ITC then conducted an investigation to determine whether the trade in gray market DURACELL batteries was a violation of sec. 337, and an evidentiary hearing was held.

The complaint named fourteen respondents, but only one participated in the investigation. Three other respondents settled with Duracell; the others were held in default. In the course of the investigation, the respondent who participated (CWE) refused to provide Duracell with documents revealing the name of its supplier and was thus subjected to an evidentiary sanction that its supplier had mishandled the goods in such a way as to cause product deterioration. The sanction was not based upon any proof that the gray market batteries were in fact inferior to the authorized version, but it ultimately had that effect. In any event, the Administrative Law Judge (ALJ) found that sec. 337 had been violated based upon (1) infringement of a registered trademark, (2) misappropriation of trade dress, (3) false designation of origin, and (4) violations of the Fair Packaging and Labeling Act. The ALJ then found that gray market sales have caused "substantial injury to . . . an industry . . . in the United States."[18]

The ITC decided to review the ALJ's determination, and in late 1984 a decision was rendered. A majority of the commissioners voted to uphold the determination of the ALJ and to grant broad relief to Duracell. Two of the five commissioners dissented in part. Before reviewing and analyzing the long and complex decision, it is necessary to consider the relationship of the various parties and certain relevant facts.

"Duracell, Inc." is a Delaware corporation. "Duracell, USA," an unincorporated division of Duracell, Inc., is the domestic manufacturer of U.S.-trademarked DURACELL batteries. These batteries are manufactured in the United States and sold only here. "Duracell International, Inc." is also a Delaware corporation, wholly owned by Duracell, Inc. "N.V. Duracell S.A." (hereinafter "Duracell, Belgium") is a Belgian corporation, wholly owned by Duracell International. Duracell, Belgium manufactures alkaline batteries for sale in Europe (only) under the Belgian trademark registration, owned by Duracell International and licensed by them to Duracell, Belgium. The Belgian batteries are packaged in a variety of European languages (including English); none of these packages states the name or address of the manufacturer. Diverters in Europe purchase the Belgian batteries, reselling them to gray market importers at prices lower than U.S. prices.

The majority opinion begins with a discussion of "General Principles of Trademark Law," focusing on *Bourjois* and *Osawa*. The ITC read *Bourjois* broadly, holding that it embedded the "territoriality" principle into American jurisprudence. The opinion thus states that *Bourjois* "has become generally recognized [as holding that] a trademark is a creature of a country's laws and can stand for different qualities in different national markets."[19] The corollary of this finding is that each country's trademark has a separate legal existence and can symbolize the local goodwill of the owner of a given nation's mark. The ITC observed that its conclusion was supported, inter alia, by the Paris Convention on Trademarks, which sets forth the principle of territoriality in Article 6(3).

The ITC thus concluded that "[w]hen the Belgian DURACELL batteries are imported into the United States, they enter the territory lawfully held by the U.S.-trademarked batteries, and should, therefore, be excluded."[20] The commissioners noted an "aware[ness] of a number of divergent cases," but stated that they were based upon "the theory that the only function of trademark law is to prevent consumer confusion,"[21] in their view, an improper restriction on the purpose of trademark law. Principally, the majority opinion focused on the goodwill function of marks and the possibility of confusion of sponsorship, problems that, it was felt, result from the trade in gray market goods.

The ITC determined that gray market sales divert "a material portion of the profit from those who have earned it (Duracell, Inc.) to those who have not (the importers and the retailers). . . . Respondents are reaping where they have not sown."[22] Of course, it was this precise argument that was rejected by Judge Higginbotham in *Weil*. Judge Higginbotham held that a single international enterprise [such as the Duracell companies] had already received a fair profit upon the initial sale overseas and was not entitled *as a matter of trademark law* to insulate its domestic markets from gray market competition caused by its own dual-tiered international pricing structure. The ITC's answer seems to be that

> Duracell has extensively advertised its batteries in the United States and built up its reputation as a purveyor of quality batteries. Because of this reputation, Duracell is able to sell its batteries at a premium. . . . Thus, the importers and retailers are appropriating the benefits of Duracell's good will for themselves which they have not helped to create. This is the essence of unfair competition and the basis for our finding of trademark infringement.[23]

The above conclusion is said to be based upon "the common law of trademarks." That finding becomes the subject of the dissenting opinion written by the two commissioners. Before exploring that dissent, it is first necessary to consider certain other factors offered by the majority to support its conclusion. First, the majority held that the conflicting Customs Service regulations on the enforcement of sec. 526 of the Tariff Act are not a bar to ITC relief. The commissioners, foreshadowing the arguments made by the court of appeals in *COPIAT*, stated that trademark and antitrust law (the subjects upon which the regulations are based) are not within the expertise of Customs and that other agencies are thus not bound by Customs' rules.

A second rationale offered was that the gray market batteries are a "copy or simulat[ion]" of U.S.-marked DURACELL batteries and thus infringe the rights granted under sec. 42 and sec. 32 of the Lanham Act. The ITC agreed with the Respondents that the *goods* (i.e. the batteries themselves) are "'genuine' goods, and they never cease to be 'genuine' Belgian trademarked goods."[24] But upon importation, the ITC ruled, the trademarks on the batteries become a "copy of the U.S.-registered trademark on the domestic batteries."[25] The ITC wrote

The confusion of the U.S. consumers is not with regard to the "genuineness" of the batteries, ... but as to the efficacy of the goods to fulfill the U.S. consumer's reasonable expectations, one of which surely is that the item being purchased has been given the same care in production and distribution as were the same trademarked previously purchased and used by the consumer with satisfaction.[26]

The majority distinguished *Monte Carlo Shirt v. Daewoo*[27] essentially as a case involving no consumer perception of sponsorship. But that case dealt more with the equality of the gray market and authorized goods; indeed, the Ninth Circuit Court expressly found in that case that consumers deemed the plaintiff to be the source and sponsor of the goods in question. Nevertheless, the ITC found that in *Duracell* consumers do not get what they bargained for—batteries sponsored by Duracell, USA. The opinion observes that the retail price for Belgian batteries is often the same as for U.S.-manufactured ones, indicating that consumers are being confused; why else, asks the ITC, would they pay the same for a foreign, 'un-backed' product as for a domestically sponsored battery. The question is a good one and one to which this text shall return later.

The ITC, however, made no inquiry into the quality of the gray market batteries and expressly stated that its decision was not based upon the ALJ's evidentiary sanction. Instead, it was held that the likelihood of confusion existed regardless of whether the goods were inferior.[28] The majority found a likelihood of confusion as to both source and sponsorship, although it stated that the latter type of confusion was "the most conspicuous."

"Duracell does not sponsor the foreign DURACELL batteries at the point of sale,"[29] wrote the ITC, and that fact was deemed determinative. The ITC was obviously inclined to overlook the fact that the Duracell empire sponsored the goods at the point of shipment. The fact the (gray market) goods were not warranted by Duracell might produce consumer disappointment, they wrote. That conclusion was made without inquiry into whether gray market sellers extend similar warranties or into the number of cases in which warranty claims are actually made. If the product did not function as expected, the consumer "is likely to blame the company whose name is on the package, in this case, Duracell."[30]

Were that to happen as a result of gray market competition, the result would be unfair, wrote the ITC. But the commissioners overlooked two important facts. First, a defect in gray market batteries could indeed be the fault of the foreign link in the Duracell chain, rather than the fault of a gray market participant. In such a case, there is nothing wrong with blaming Duracell; the wide relief granted in this case, however, causes that loss to fall upon those who would now be restricted from the trade in Belgian batteries.

Second, it is possible that defects in domestic DURACELLS are the result of mishandling by an authorized U.S. distributor. In this regard, Duracell undoubtedly does not claim sufficient control over Duracell distributors to prevent this from happening, although Duracell evidently makes an effort to insure against overextension of shelf life of domestic DURACELLs. Nevertheless, Duracell's warranty extends only to the purchase price and damaged equipment, not to a consumer's disappointment (or even economic loss) incurred when a DURACELL battery fails "in a pinch." The effect of the warranty might thus be overstated, but the respondents were unable to so convince either the ALJ or the ITC.

But it is still not clear that a purchaser of a defective gray market battery will stop buying DURACELL altogether even if the warranty is not honored.[31] That consumer may only cease to buy gray market batteries, precisely the type of decision that consumers make every day as they play a part in the creation of an efficient free market. As Judge Higginbotham observed in *Weil*, if a U.S. trademark owner like Duracell has real fears in this area, those fears can be laid to rest through business solutions rather than through litigious alternatives.

The commissioners made reference to a survey offered into evidence by Duracell that showed a large percentage of consumers said they did not notice where the batteries they were purchasing were made, even when the batteries had foreign-language packaging. A majority of the consumers surveyed indicated that they would not buy foreign-made batteries after they were told that these batteries "were not authorized by the U.S. Duracell company and that no control over the shipping, storage, and handling"[32] was exercised by Duracell. The ITC cited that as "convincing evidence" that consumers do care whether or not Duracell authorizes the batteries at the point of sale.

Of course that conclusion overlooks the implication of the disclaimer upon which the question was based. Most consumers do not appreciate the distinction between gray market goods and counterfeit goods, and the question does not indicate whether the consumers who responded had thought that the survey was asking about counterfeit batteries. Also, because gray market goods, and presumably at least some Duracell batteries,[33] are sold in the United States at prices lower than their authorized counterparts, the survey, indeed the ITC's entire opinion, ignores the role that relative prices play in a consumer's decision and in the overall evaluation of the economic benefits of gray market competition.

The use of surveys in trademark cases is a common practice. But one must always be careful of surveys because the wording of questions and the way they are asked often influence the outcome. It is thus submitted that a survey of the kind relied upon by the ITC in *Duracell* should not be favored. Indeed, it might be better to ask whether there is actual proof of dissatisfied customers, a question suggested by the Second Circuit Court in *Bell & Howell: Mamiya*[34] and asked directly by the Judge in *Yamaha*.[35]

The ITC also found that the gray market DURACELLs were a misappropriation of trade dress, a common law trademark concept, and a "false designation of origin," a violation of sec. 43(a) of the Lanham Act. On the latter point, the majority rejected any attempt to invoke the single international enterprise theory, stating that the statutory term "origin" is not limited to the manufacturer but also includes the distribution chain. Finally, the ITC rested its decision in part on the Fair Packaging and Labeling Act, accepting the ALJ's finding that, with the exception of CWE, no importer complied with the requirements of that federal statute. The Act requires, inter alia, that all goods sold in the United States must contain English-language statements about the nature of the goods being sold, the net quantity contained in any packages, and the name and place of business of the manufacturer. As regards the lack of English-language packaging, Duracell has a legitimate claim. The failure to disclose the name and place of business of the manufacturer can be attributed to Duracell, Belgium's parent, who presumably could insist that the foreign packages contain that information. In other words, a U.S. parent could prevent gray market trade in its product by refusing to adequately label its foreign goods. That type of manipulation of the law should be avoided.[36]

To conclude its determination that sec. 337 of the Tariff Act was violated, the ITC had to consider whether "the effect or tendency [of the unfair practices] is to destroy or substantially injure an industry, efficiently and economically operated, in the United States."[37] To satisfy this requirement, the commissioners adopted the ALJ's finding, adding their view that the "health of Duracell, USA is intertwined with the goodwill of the U.S. mark," and to the extent it lost profits on potential sales, injury was established. This conclusion harkens back to the question debated in the Lanham Act cases—whether loss of sales is the equivalent of trademark injury. That question, not finally resolved in the Lanham Act context, is more clear-cut in *Duracell*, where the statutory standard for injury is far broader.[38]

Two commissioners, including the Chair, filed an opinion that diverges markedly from that of the majority, although it does reach some of the same results. This separate opinion begins with the conclusion that the ITC lacks jurisdiction to exclude gray market goods under either sec. 526 of the Tariff Act or sec. 42 of the Lanham Act. These issues, the dissenters wrote, "are explicitly to be dealt with in the context of a congressionally created set of procedures by the Customs Service, and thus should not be considered a basis for a violation of sec. 337."[39]

The dissent, however, went on to demonstrate a further reason for disagreement with the majority. While it too held that "territoriality" was "a part of U.S. law," it took issue with whether violation of that principle is an "unfair act" under sec. 337. "The fact that two marks are legally separate does not establish that their use in any particular country or market is unfair," the dissenters wrote. "Unfairness results only when the independent marks are used to violate the rights the holder of the original mark has under the laws of the country in which the trademark is used."[40] Section 42's proscription against any copy or simulation must, in their view, be understood to include a presumption of confusion not expressly stated in the statute. Customs' interpretation, the dissenters felt, precluded application of that presumption when the foreign- and U.S.-trademark owners are related. And even though that interpretation has been "questioned," the minority commissioners concluded that it would "choose to defer to Customs' regulations as they currently exist"[41]

The dissenters thus would hold that the principle of territoriality "cannot be 'violated,' " but they were prepared to consider whether the gray market DURACELLs nevertheless infringe a U.S. trademark by virtue of sec. 32 of the Lanham Act. To so hold, they would have to find that the use of the mark by the gray market sellers is likely "to cause confusion, or to cause mistake, or to deceive."[42] The dissenters thus begin their analysis with the observation that "a foreign-made 'DURACELL' battery is the same battery as a domestically produced

'DURACELL' alkaline battery."[43] They agree with the majority, however, that the foreign-marked DURACELLs contain "copies" of the U.S. mark, a legal conclusion dictated by the rule of territoriality.

The more difficult issue, in the dissent's view, is the question of confusion, and the fact that the batteries in question are genuine and "identical or virtually so" is confounding. The dissent concludes, however, that there can be no confusion of source because Duracell, Inc. produces both sets of batteries and is responsible for the quality of production by both its foreign and domestic subsidiaries. But the dissenters agreed with the majority that there could be a confusion of sponsorship that could harm the local goodwill of Duracell, USA, especially in view of the fact that freshness is a desired characteristic in batteries, and, in view of Duracell, USA's efforts, the domestic batteries are more likely to be fresh than are the gray market counterparts.

The dissent thus relies on this variation of the product differences theme to reach its conclusion that harm from gray market batteries is likely. The conclusion is akin to Judge Debevoise's reasoning (on the motion for summary judgment) about the product quality tests employed by Weil in the Lladro litigation. That issue, interestingly, was not addressed by the Third Circuit in that case. It should be remembered, however, that skepticism was raised about whether Weil's inspection was really different from that of the gray market sellers; Judge Higginbotham remanded the *Weil* case for trial, where presumably that issue could be raised again. By contrast, the dissenting commissioners in *Duracell* accepted the conclusion about differences made by the ALJ *after an evidentiary hearing*, clearly a different procedural context than that which confronted the courts in *Weil*. Because of the split decision, it is hard to view *Duracell* as endorsing a product differences test, but it is nevertheless clear that issue will not go away.

The dissent also makes an observation, seeming somewhat to motivate its conclusion, that although Belgian DURACELLs are imported at lower wholesale prices than U.S. DURACELLs, they are sold at retail at equivalent prices. "Despite the differences between the [batteries]," they write, "consumers are paying the same price[s]. They thus appear unaware of those differences. We, therefore, conclude that complainant . . . has established the requisite likelihood of confusion [for a violation of sec. 32]."[44] But the dissenters did not agree with the majority that there was also a violation for "false designation of origin" under sec. 43(a) because, as already stated, they did not see any likelihood of confusion of source.

The dissenting commissioners also expressed their belief that a finding of "unfairness" must be premised upon a violation of a specific section of the Lanham Act and not upon general principles of trademark law. Nor can such a finding be based solely upon the "exclusive rights provided to one who secures a federal registration" (sec. 33 of the Lanham Act), as the majority seems to imply. The dissenters refused to find unfairness from a violation of sec. 526 of the Tariff Act, from sec. 42 (when the foreign manufacturer is a related entity), or from sec. 33 of the Lanham Act. Rather, they rest their decision solely upon the language of sec. 32 that a mark infringes if it is a "reproduction, copy, counterfeit, or colorable imitation" *and* is likely to cause confusion.

This latter theory, however, is clearly based upon a finding of inferior goods and must be so understood. Simply put, without true corporate separateness, there can be no confusion of source. And without inferior goods, there can be no finding of confusion about the level of quality and, thus, inherent goodwill symbolized by the U.S. and foreign marks. Without these twin findings, there can be no Lanham Act violation. Thus the dissenters stress their disagreement with the majority that the mere operation of the gray market is "an inherent violation of trademark rights" and thus an automatic violation of sec. 337.

The dissenters also disagreed with the majority about the proper scope of the remedy for the violation proved. The majority recommended a broad exclusion order, finding that that was the only means of solving Duracell's problems with gray market imports. But the dissenters suggested a narrower order aimed at "[p]roper labelling which clearly indicates that the two products, while the same at the point of manufacture, are not similarly authorized and guaranteed in the United States. . . . "[45] The feeling was that once the confusion was ended, Duracell would not be injured, and "[t]he ultimate price of the foreign batteries . . . would then properly reflect the true nature of the imported product."[46] So marked, the importation would presumably have a beneficial economic effect and would seemingly fall under the penumbra of *Prestonettes v. Coty*,[47] Justice Holmes's second attempt at addressing the gray market.[48] Only if labeling would prove inadequate, a situation deemed not present in *Duracell*, would a broad exclusionary order be proper.

The majority disagreed that adequate labeling could cure the violation and distinguished *Prestonettes* as a case where "the mark was separated from the goodwill which it symbolized, [where t]he defendant. was no[t] capitalizing on the goodwill of Coty's trademark."[49] That may be a narrow reading of *Prestonettes*, but the majority also cited the

> strength of the [DURACELL mark], the low value of the product, and the fact that the imported batteries are being sold in the same trade dress, we find that labeling would not eliminate all the consumer confusion. Some consumers would still be inevitably confused.[50]

The dissenters' approach to the remedy is interesting. It suggests a consumer protection/free market approach to solving the gray market issue.[51] If the industry cannot survive without consumer deception or a dependence upon consumer ignorance, it should be outlawed. If on the other hand, it can survive once consumers know the truth, it is not detrimental, and additional competition must be viewed as beneficial. The dissenters' approach is thus a fair acid test for the viability of the gray market.[52]

This debate is an interesting one, indeed one that might have been explored further but for two facts. First, the federal courts do not have power to fashion a remedy the way the ITC does, so no federal judge will ever face the issue this way. Eventually, a federal judge might have to decide whether a disclaiming label is adequate if he or she is presented with one, but that is a question that has not yet reached the courts. Second, the issue became moot because two months after the ITC announced its recommendations in *Duracell*, President Reagan disapproved granting *any* relief to the company.

The expressed ground for disapproval of relief was that it was contrary to the Customs Service interpretation. The president thus agreed with the dissenting commissioners that Customs is the agency responsible for setting import policies under the Lanham Act.

> The Administration has advanced the [Customs Service's] interpretation in a number of pending court cases. Recent decisions of the U.S. District Court for the District of Columbia and the Court of International Trade explicitly uphold [that] interpretation. Allowing the Commission's determination in this case to stand could be viewed as an alteration of that interpretation.[53]

The president, however, was not prepared to close the door to revision of the Customs policy, and he further stated his administration has

> solicited data from the public concerning the issue of parallel market importation and are reviewing responses with a view toward formulating a cohesive policy in this area. Failure to disapprove the Commission's determination could be viewed as a change in the current policy prior to the completion of this process.[54]

As is now evident, that process was completed without significant result, and the administration successfully defended its policy before the U.S. Supreme Court.[55] At this stage, it is unlikely that any policy change will be forthcoming and even less likely that change will come through the ITC window. And even though the opinions in Duracell are articulate expressions of the differing views on gray market legality by experts in international trade, those opinions possess little precedential value for the federal courts while gray market law develops and matures. But a review of Duracell at this stage was certainly useful, because it highlights many of the themes developed elsewhere in this work and demonstrates that resolution of gray market problems is as much a matter of policy as a matter of law.

THE EFFECT OF LAWS OF FOREIGN COUNTRIES ON GRAY MARKET TRADE IN THE UNITED STATES

Many other countries' legal and political systems, like that of the United States, have had to confront the issues raised by gray market trade. These other countries, for obvious reasons, are generally unconcerned with gray market imports into the United States. They are sometimes concerned, however, with importation into their own country; that phenomenon has an effect on many U.S. companies through the practice known as "gray market exportation."

The practice of unauthorized exportation of goods, from the United States or elsewhere, into foreign markets has not been the subject of any significant legal proceedings in the United States. Nevertheless, there are a handful of cases dealing with unauthorized sale within the United States, and certain principles might be extrapolated from those cases and applied to gray market exports.

The most recent of these cases is *H.L. Hayden Co. of New York, Inc. v. Siemens Medical Systems, Inc.*[56] The case began as an antitrust action resulting from an alleged conspiratorial termination. Schein Dental Equipment was a subsidiary of the plaintiff; Schein published a catalog offering Siemens' dental x-rays, machines it obtained from its corporate parent, which held an authorized distributorship. After complaints from other authorized dealers about low prices and free-riding, Siemens refused to renew the plaintiff's distributorship unless it stopped selling to Schein. The plaintiff refused, was terminated, and sued for damages.

Siemens counterclaimed that Schein's sales violated sec. 43(a) of the Lanham Act. The antitrust complaint was dismissed by the district court, and all but one of the counterclaims were also dismissed (the exception was based on false suggestions that the manufacturer's warranty applied). Siemens appealed the dismissal of two of its claims; first, that the unauthorized sale was itself a violation of sec. 43(a) and second, a novel claim that Schein free-riding constituted tortious interference with contract. The court rejected both these claims, and that rejection is likely to benefit the gray market export trade.

Siemens argued that it did not have control over the assembly, installation, and servicing of its product, causing a loss of quality control and probable injury to itself. The court ruled that Schein's activities were not actionable because no inferior product was being sold and because Schein did not in any way suggest that it was part of the Siemens sales network. The court cited *El Greco* and Judge Cardamone's opinion in *Original Appalachian* to prove that unauthorized sales are actionable when the trademark owner has not had the right to inspect the goods prior to sale (*El Greco*) or when "there was 'a very real difference in the product itself.' "[57]

The court's reasoning on the second point, that there be no suggestion that the unauthorized seller is part of the trademark owner's organization, is quite logical. Without consumer association, failures far down the line in the distribution process cannot harm the trademark owner. Indeed, Judge Goettel, who had made the decision in the lower court, observed that even though disappointed customers of Schein sought help from Siemens, they did so "out of desperation," not because of some belief that Siemens was responsible for their troubles.

That conclusion might seem at odds with, for example, the majority decision in *Duracell* where the ITC assumed that any problem with batteries would automatically be blamed on Duracell, USA. The two cases may be harmonized, however, on the basis that buyers of dental x-ray equipment (a big-ticket item) are more knowledgeable or at least more careful than are purchasers of alkaline batteries. Additionally, it can be said that those who buy from a catalog can generally expect less personal, often less effective service. The low price of the batteries and concomitant low level of care evidenced by consumers of DURACELL batteries seemed to outweigh the foreign language packaging of most of the Belgian DURACELLs. Packaging that seemed to demonstrate that the goods were not sponsored by Duracell, USA was often overlooked by consumers.

The court in *Hayden* also rejected the other counterclaim, based upon tortious interference with contract. Siemens alleged that the plaintiffs interfered with their distribution system by inducing dealers to sell to them in violation of the distribution agreement. The district court had dismissed the claim on the ground that no loss was suffered by Siemens, which still made a profit on the sales to the plaintiffs, and that the expense incurred to track them down was a foreseeable part of policing the distribution agreement. Siemens argued that "the district court took too constrained a view of damages, failing to apply 'the more liberal rules applicable to tort actions.' "[58] The Second Circuit rejected the claim, agreeing with Judge Goettel about injury[59] and stating that Siemens was really trying only to protect its reputation because it did not have full control over the sale of its goods, a theory implicitly rejected in *El Greco*.

A third claim against Schein, made by an authorized distributor called Healthco, was also addressed by the court. The claim was that Schein's free-riding on the authorized distributor's presale and point-of-sale services constituted unfair competition under New York law. The district court rejected the claim because first, it did not believe that Schein's activities directly or indirectly encouraged consumers to take advantage of the other distributors' services, and second, "unfair competition must be grounded in either deception or appropriation of . . . property."[60]

The court of appeals rejected the district court's first conclusion but agreed with the second. It called the theory being employed "novel and interesting," but said that it was not "grounded in any New York case of which we are aware that is at all close on its facts to the counterclaim alleged here."[61] The court thus refused to expand New York law to create what it called a " 'free rider' tort." In the *Yamaha* case, the court also seemed to deny any general relief for free-riding. Even though the gray market goods were less expensive and the warranties inferior, the court refused to label the practice of the gray market as "unfair."

The judicial approach to (domestic) unauthorized sales should apply in the international context as well. Indeed, in that scenario the possibility of injury in the United States is even more remote, only occurring if the gray market exports are reimported to the United States. If they are not, any claim for infringement or false designation of origin would have to be resolved under the laws of the foreign country where the goods are sold. That result is dictated by a reverse application of the territoriality principle. Such a case could theoretically be brought in the United States, assuming personal jurisdiction over the defendants. But without economic effects in the United States, our courts are likely to be reluctant to hear the matter.

U.S. law is therefore unlikely to present a substantial impediment to gray market exports. Investigation and termination of offending distributors remain the principal weapon, action that is almost always held to be a lawful attempt to police the distribution system. But gray market sales have been the subject of such proceedings in foreign countries as well as the United States. Of course, each nation's laws differ, and no attempt will be made herein to survey the laws of every country in regard to their gray market import policies. Nevertheless, some general principles can be discerned, and, in the case of Europe, there is some established precedent worthy of discussion.

The most important general principle is that foreign countries, especially developing nations, have elaborate policies on imports, foreign investment, and foreign trade that affect the gray market and generally go beyond questions of trademark protection. These countries are generally less concerned than the United States about protecting consumer interests, guarantees of quality symbolized by trademarks, and so forth. They are more concerned with protecting home industries, generating foreign exchange, and protecting their own resources. With this in mind, their policies about gray market imports are likely to have little to do with the kind of legal issues to which U.S. citizens and lawyers are accustomed.

Foreign thirst for American-trademarked (and manufactured) products is certainly significant and on the rise, especially in the pharmaceutical and petrochemical fields where demand is high and availability overseas is limited. At the same time, foreign governments are most concerned, for the policy reasons alluded to in the previous paragraph, to prevent gray market competition in these areas. A desire to protect and develop national industries in these fields has led to steps to halt such "gray market importation." Thus, in these fields gray market trade has taken on many of the indicia of counterfeit trade (i.e., smuggling). To that extent, therefore, gray market trade has taken on an extralegal character: U.S. manufacturers and distributors undertake shady practices to gain access to these lucrative markets, and efforts are made to conceal it rather than to fight in courts for the right to import.

But the case is different in the European Economic Community, where protectionism is less overt and legal controversies over gray market goods erupt with great frequency. Most of these controversies have involved attempts to halt parallel imports (and reimports) from other member countries, a practice that in most cases[62] violates the principle of free trade that underlies the Common Market's union.[63] In these cases, parallel importation of identical goods was deemed lawful, and attempts to block such imports were deemed to be a violation of the EEC Treaty.

The case is different, however, when dealing with gray market imports from nonmember states. In these cases, the ITC's pro-competition policy comes into play. That policy encourages and places greater importance on intrabrand competition than on our own, resulting in a situation where parallel importation is often lawful.

As is the case with our own antitrust laws, the relevant provisions of the EEC Treaty require a finding of concerted behavior as a prerequisite to a violation of competition law. Unilateral action by a trademark owner to halt unauthorized importation is thus immune to legal attack. But the European court has construed even the transfer of national trademark rights to an independent company as an agreement in restraint of trade;[64] a transfer to a parent or subsidiary, however, is not deemed a conspiracy.

The open question concerns trademark licensing: Is it a violation of Article 85(1) to use an exclusive territorial licensing scheme to develop and secure restrictions against parallel imports? Can a licensee be sued or have his license terminated for engaging in parallel importation into an EC country outside his allotted territory? At first blush, such a restrictive scheme would also seem to violate the principles of Article 85(1), but recently the European Court has indicated a hesitancy to apply those principles to exclusive licenses. Although the final determination about the legality of exclusive license has not yet been made, the trend seems to indicate a permissive approach in Europe toward using licensing to bar parallel importation.

The court has also held that enforcement of national trademark rights is not an "abuse" of a dominant market position under Article 86 of the treaty because, as a matter of law, a trademark, by itself, confers no market power. This position is akin to the theories used to level criticism at Judge Edelstein's antitrust conclusions in *Guerlain*. Finally, because the treaty's free-trade provisions are generally unconcerned with import barriers directed at nonmember nations, those articles are unlikely to be construed as barring attempts to halt gray market trade from outside the European Community. One thing, however, is clear: In Europe, attempts to halt gray market trade in "equal quality" goods are likely to be viewed as competition problems, rather than intellectual property problems.

The situation is somewhat different in Japan, where the approach is more closely akin to our own. The Trademark Law of Japan was viewed initially as hostile to gray market importation.[65] But in litigation concerning gray market importation of PARKER pens, a lower court in Osaka ruled that importation of identical goods was unlikely to harm any Japanese trademark interests in view of the fact that first, the PARKER trademark had strong international recognition and second, the Japanese trademark registrant was actually trading upon the foreign appeal of the mark rather than upon any local goodwill it might have possessed. The Japanese court was also motivated by the potential for competitive benefits in prices and services, a factor too often overlooked in the United States.

In 1972 the Japanese Customs Office promulgated import rules quite similar to those in the United States, including barring relief in cases where the foreign and Japanese marks are owned by the same person or where parent–subsidiary relationships are present.[66] But the Japanese rules seem to go even further, also providing that there will be no import relief where the foreign trademark owner supplied the gray market importer directly. The regulation does provide for relief in all cases where the goods are not identical. Finally, under the Antimonopoly Act, it is deemed unlawful for one who holds an exclusive distributorship from unduly hindering parallel imports.

Gray market exports thus present interesting questions of U.S., foreign, and international law (and politics). While no definitive answer can be given, it is clear that any business wishing to engage in or combat gray market imports faces potentially complex legal problems both here and abroad. As is the case in the United States, the solution to these problems lies in future judicial decisions.

NOTES

1. 108 S.Ct. 1811 (1988).

2. 599 F. Supp. 1380 (E.D.N.Y. 1984), rev'd 806 F.2d 392 (2d Cir. 1986), cert. denied, 108 S.Ct. 71 (1987). For a full discussion of this case refer to Chapter 3.

3. 589 F.Supp. 470 (S.D.N.Y. 1984). For a full discussion of this case refer to Chapter 3.

4. N.Y.Gen.Bus.L. sec. 368–d (McKinney 1968).

5. 599 F.Supp. at 1395–96.

6. 589 F.Supp. at 476.

7. 703 F.Supp. 1398 (C.D.Calif. 1988)

8. Id. at 1403.

9. Id.

10. 218 U.S.P.Q.560 (S.D.N.Y. 1982).

11. Id. at 563. After a complaint by Seiko to the New York State Attorney General, Alexander's changed their ad to indicate in a footnote that the "suggested retail prices" were for the same model if in fact that model appeared in Seiko's U.S. catalog and were for similar models available in the United States if the precise models being advertised were not available.

12. The explanatory footnote was also deemed insufficient to save Alexander's from a determination that it had engaged in deceptive advertising.

13. 218 U.S.P.Q. at 566.

14. Similar deceptive warranty practices were present in *Osawa*, supra Ch. II.

15. N.Y. Gen.Bus.L. sec. 218-aa (McKinney 1988).

16. *California Civil Code*, sections 1797–8 et seq.

17. *In the Matter of Certain Alkaline Batteries*, 225 U.S.P.Q. 823 (ITC 1984).

18. Id. at 825.

19. Id. at 827.

20. Id. at 828.

21. Id. at 829.

22. Id. at 831.

23. Id. at 831.

24. Id. at 834.

25. Id. at 833.

26. Id. at 834.

27. 707 F.2d 1054 (9th Cir. 1983). For a full discussion of this case refer to Chapter 3.

28. In a footnote, the ITC does state that if the batteries were found to be inferior, that would have provided an additional basis for the conclusion that sec. 337 had been violated.

29. 225 U.S.P.Q. at 834.

30. Id. at 836.

31. There is reason to believe that the warranty in such a case would be honored by Duracell regardless of whether the batteries were made in Belgium. The Belgian arm of Duracell makes the same warranty as does the U.S. arm, and that warranty could be enforced in the United States by virtue of the U.S. presence of Duracell, Belgium's parent (i.e., any U.S. consumer wishing to claim under the Belgian warranty

could obtain jurisdiction over Duracell, Belgium here in the United States). Even without firm knowledge of Belgian warranty law, one is inclined to believe that the Belgian warranty is coextensive with the "limited" warranty offered by Duracell, USA.

32. 225 U.S.P.Q. at 837.

33. The ITC found that the retail price for gray market DURACELLs was often the same as for authorized goods; the finding does mean that such is always the case.

34. 548 F.Supp. 1063 (E.D.N.Y. 1982), reversed and remanded, 719 F.2d 42 (2d Cir. 1983). For a full discussion of this case refer to Chapter 2.

35. 703 F.Supp. at 1402.

36. Alone, the violation of the Packaging and Labeling Act might not rise to the level of sec. 337 violation because of the required "injury" standard, discussed presently.

37. 225 U.S.P.Q. at 838.

38. The ITC also made reference to a loss of morale in Duracell's sales force, and a deterioration of relations with retailers. The ITC, however, does not indicate whether this deterioration is the result of the mere fact that gray market goods are available or because they are available at a lower price.

39. 225 U.S.P.Q. at 847. The dissenters expressly adopted Judge Restani's views on the history and purpose of the Customs exclusion, calling them "compelling" and "convincing."

40. 225 U.S.P.Q. at 849–850.

41. Id. at 851.

42. Id.

43. Id.

44. Id. at 853.

45. Id. at 858.

46. Id.

47. 264 U.S. 359 (1924). For a full discussion of this case refer to Chapter 2.

48. The dissenters also cited *Bell & Howell: Mamiya Co.*, supra. Ch. 2, where the Second Circuit reasoned that "less drastic means would appear to be available to avoid the claimed confusion." 719 F.2d at 46.

49. 225 U.S.P.Q. at 839.

50. Id. at 840.

51. This approach is not dissimilar from that discussed earlier in this chapter — the consumer protection legislation passed in New York and California. That legislation, if its weaknesses had been improved, might have been a formidable weapon in minimizing the problems of the gray market.

52. Another approach that had some early appeal was a process known as demarking — gray market sellers must remove trademark from the goods before they are sold. There is little question that that practice would kill the gray market because, while significant numbers of consumers seem willing to purchase gray market goods knowing that the U.S. trademark owner does not sponsor them, it can be assumed that a far smaller number of U.S. purchasers would want goods with no markings. In any event, probably because nearly all gray market sellers are unwilling to engage in demarking, the debate about it as a remedy quickly died out.

53. 225 U.S.P.Q. at 862.

54. Id.

55. Duracell, obviously unhappy with the president's determination appealed to the Federal Circuit. That court then ruled that the president's power to disapprove relief was embedded in the statute and that it was not reviewable by the courts. *Duracell, Inc. v. U.S. International Trade Commission*, 778 F.2d 1578 (Fed.Cir. 1985). The court further held that while review may be proper when a president disapproves relief because he disagrees with "the merits of an investigation," he is free to disapprove "for policy reasons." The president's letter disapproving the relief expressly stated it was "for policy reasons," and the court declined to look behind that statement. Duracell had argued that the question of jurisdiction between the ITC and Customs over sec. 42 of the Lanham Act was a disapproval "for legal reasons." The court responded: "It is sufficient that the president disapprove the determination for *his* policy reasons. Policy is a broad concept. . . . " Id. at 1581–2.

56. No. 1239, slip op., June 12, 1989.

57. Id. at 7638 (citing *Original Appalachian*, 816 F.2d at 73).

58. Id. at 7640.

59. The court further found that injury is an element of the cause of action for tortious interference with contract and that, therefore, even injunctive relief was precluded.

60. No. 1239, slip op., at 7642, citing 672 F.Supp. at 752.

61. Id. at 7643.

62. The EEC applies an "identity/inferiority" approach, not unlike our own, to protect businesses from injury caused by lower quality trademarked goods.

63. M. Devine, "The Application of EEC Regulation 2641/84 on Illicit Commercial Practices with Special Reference to the U.S.A.," 22 *International Lawyer* 1091 (1988); H. Kersten, "'Gray Market' Exports and Imports Under the Competition Law of the European Economic Community," 78 *Trademark Rep.* 479 (1988); R. Moxon, "Piracy and Gray Markets in the European Economic Community," 10 *Hastings Comm. Ent. L.J.* 1090 (1988).

64. *Sirena v. Eda*, ECR 69 (European Ct. 2/18/71).

65. See generally K. Takamatsu, "Parallel Importation of Trademarked Goods: A Comparative Analysis," 57 *Wash. L. Rev.* 433, 440–443 (1982).

66. The 1972 rules also provide for a personal-use exemption.

9

Epilogue

When one first looks at the gray market, one sees many difficult questions. It is hoped that this book reviewed and analyzed all answers that have been given or may be given to these questions. In the last year, it has become clear that some gray imports will be permitted and some will be excluded. Thus, the principal question for the future is: Where will the law draw the line?

Some lines have already been drawn. Unauthorized goods manufactured by a foreign licensee of a U.S. trademark owner will be halted at the border. They are to be excluded regardless of quality and regardless of whether consumers want to purchase these goods with full knowledge of any defects. At bottom, this result can be justified as a legitimate attempt to protect the integrity of trademark licensing, a legitimate and well-developed industry.

Of course, the Customs prohibition still applies to *Bourjois* situations, protecting those who at arm's length purchase all the right "to do business" in a certain trademarked product. The key to this protection is that the substance of the transaction will be paramount, the form being irrelevant. Viewed as such, it becomes apparent why many courts and commentators have looked to the affiliation between the U.S.- and foreign-trademark owner as a basis for making a decision in a given case. Those advocating a corporate affiliation test simply do not believe that multinational parents with wholly owned subsidiaries should be allowed to use their trademarks to divide world markets for the products they manufacture. The predominant rationale employed to justify this often unspoken conclusion is that *Bourjois* should be limited to its facts.

Subsequent sub-rationales exist, but the skepticism about claims of trademark injury pervades the materials. When that skepticism is balanced against a perception that gray market price competition is desirable, the conclusion is inescapable: some goods should be let in. Those who share this prointrabrand competition philosophy have successfully shifted the battle to their issues (i.e., which goods should be allowed and which excluded).

These forces knew from the start that they could never realistically defeat *Bourjois*, that they could never win carte blanche for all gray market goods. If the trademark owners can be faulted in their assault, they can be faulted for putting too much behind their efforts to exclude all gray market goods. Having lost the initial battle over issues, they are losing the overall war against gray market imports. *K-Mart* and *Weil*, combined with *NEC*, provide substantial momentum for the pro-gray market forces. Added to this general momentum is the fact that the overwhelming bulk of gray market goods follow the "multinational corporate structure" as opposed to the *Bourjois* fact pattern.

It cannot be said, however, that the trademark owners won no significant battles. The exclusion for licensed goods is one victory; the use of the antifencing statute against a diverter found operating in the United States is another. But if the gray market seller is personally innocent, he is protected under the U.C.C., thus rendering the trademark owner's victory a Pyrrhic victory. On the copyright front, the pro-gray market forces also have momentum. Finally, any hope of securing change from either the executive or legislative branch seems slim, no change at Customs is likely, and the ITC route appears closed. In Congress, legislation is stalled, with little prospect of revival. Of course, the Supreme Court holds the last trump card, but after *Cartier* it appears unlikely that the court will again join the fray.

So the debate is about which gray goods are legal and which are not. That debate will continue, with more fact patterns and more cases establishing more legal distinctions. All the questions about multinationals that do not wholly own their manufacturing or distributional companies, about identical goods and material differences, and about the role of trademark law in an international economy will be resolved as we approach the year 2000.

No matter how these issues are decided, given that at least some gray market goods will enter the country and be legal, the most important consideration should be consumer education. If the trademark owners are right about those who purchase gray market goods inevitably becoming dissatisfied, why do they not attempt to educate consumers about the danger of buying gray market. Trademark owners, experts in the advertising business, instead seek a solution to their problems in the courts of law, not in the "court" of public opinion.

But the gray market importers are at fault as well. When they do not offer good warranties, when they are unable to service a product, when they sell inferior goods, and when they do not clearly inform consumers about what they are actually getting, they damage their own reputations (and perhaps that of the trademark owner) and their own long-term business (and legal) interests. When they practice full disclosure to consumers and provide an equivalent product at a lower price, they attain the moral and legal high ground from which a winning battle can be fought.

The federal government missed a grand opportunity to make an impact in this area when it refused to grant the modified relief suggested by the dissenting commissioners in the *Duracell* case before the U.S. ITC. The dissenting opinion suggested that a "truth-in-trademark" approach would produce a useful acid test for the viability of the gray market in an economy filled with knowledgeable consumers. That opinion expressed an important theme that should be considered by all who analyze gray market law:

[W]e believe that the general issue of operation of the gray market is not strictly a legal issue but a policy issue which should be addressed by the appropriate policy making bodies. Courts which have examined the right of a single international enterprise to preclude the fairly traded imports of its own foreign operations have not generally found adequate basis for such exclusion or have avoided the substantive issues on procedural grounds.

In view of the abdication of the political parties, Congress, and the president to create a cohesive policy toward gray market imports, the courts have no choice but to resolve the controversies. The states could relieve some of the burden by passing and enforcing effective consumer legislation, thereby informing their citizens about gray market imports. The legislation that was attempted in New York and California fell short of being successful, but that fact should not deter new attempts. Congress and the president could also assist by rethinking their approach and positions on the law of the gray market.

If the government can assure that consumers are well informed about gray market goods, it will diminish the chance for injury to consumers *and* business goodwill, and simultaneously provide consumers with more economic choices, a broader range of prices, and the benefits of competition. Commissioners Stern and Rohr defended their "truth-in-trademark" answer to the gray market problem in *Duracell*, believing that it would not eliminate the gray market, only the injury to trademark owners. They wrote,

> Because consumers enjoy paying less for similar goods, retailers and wholesalers would also discover that there is a demand for the fairly traded product. Not only would consumers benefit from having the option of purchasing such fairly traded gray market goods, but [the international trademark owners] would benefit by the resulting expansion of the market for lower-priced [goods]. Because of these concomitant benefits on the welfare of the U.S. consumer and the competitive condition of the U.S. economy, we believe the public interest is better served by [the "truth-in-trademark" approach].

This compromise approach, more beneficial to all concerned than is the status quo, is thus far the most rational way to deal with the gray market. Unfortunately, at present it appears to have too few adherents.

It is clear that the gray market is assured of a future; exactly what that future holds, however, one can only project. Cases continue at a steady pace. Without the guidance of the Supreme Court or Congress, the result will continue to be phenomenological — dependent upon which court decides which case on what facts. Although no unified theory has yet been expressed, gray market law thus continues to develop in the tradition of the common law: judges decide the case before them, careful not to divulge too much about how they will decide the next case. This is the path the gray market will travel for the foreseeable future.

Appendix I: Statutes

TRADEMARK ACT OF 1946

§ 1056   USE BY RELATED COMPANIES (amended 1988) [LANHAM ACT-§ 5]

Where a registered mark or a mark sought to be registered is or may be used legitimately by related companies, such use shall inure to the benefit of the registrant or applicant for registration, and such use shall not affect the validity of such mark or of its registration, provided such mark is not used in such manner as to deceive the public. If first use of a mark by a person is controlled by the registrant or applicant for registration of the mark with respect to the nature and quality of the goods or services, such first use shall inure to the benefit of the registrant or applicant, as the case may be.

§ 1114   INFRINGER LIABLE IN CIVIL ACTIONS [LANHAM ACT - § 32]

(1) Any person who shall, without the consent of the registrant -
(a) use in commerce any reproduction, counterfeit, copy, or colorable imitation of a registered mark in connection with the sale, offering for sale, distribution, or advertising of any goods or services on or in connection with which such use is likely to cause confusion, or to cause mistake, or to deceive; or
(b) reproduce, counterfeit, copy or colorably imitate a registered mark and apply such reproduction, counterfeit, copy or colorable imitation to labels, signs, prints, packages, wrappers, receptacles or advertisements intended to be used in commerce upon or in connection with the sale, offering for sale, distribution, or advertising of goods or services on or in connection with which such use is likely to cause confusion, or to cause mistake, or to deceive,
shall be liable in a civil action by the registrant for the remedies hereinafter provided. . . .

§ 1125.   FALSE DESIGNATIONS OF ORIGIN AND FALSE DESCRIPTIONS FORBIDDEN [LANHAM ACT - § 43]

(a) Any person who, on or in connection with any goods or services, or any container for goods, uses in commerce any word, term, name, symbol, or device, or any combination thereof, or any false designation of origin, false or misleading description of fact, or false or misleading representation of fact, which -
(1) is likely to cause confusion, or to cause mistake, or to deceive as to the affiliation, connection, or association of such person with another person, or as to the origin, sponsorship, or approval of his or her goods, services, or commercial activities by another person, or
(2) in commercial advertising or promotion, misrepresents the nature, characteristics, qualities, or geographic origin of his or her or another person's goods, services, or commercial activities,
shall be liable in a civil action by any person who believes that he or she is or is likely to be damaged by such act.
(b) Any goods marked or labeled in contravention of the provisions of this section shall not be imported into the United States or admitted to entry at any customhouse of the United States. The owner, importer, or consignee of goods refused entry at any customhouse under this section may have any recourse by protest or appeal that is given under the customs revenue laws or may have the remedy given by this Act in cases involving goods refused entry or seized.

CHAPTER 4

SHERMAN ACT

§1   TRUSTS, ETC., IN RESTRAINT OF TRADE ILLEGAL

Every contract, combination in the form of trust or otherwise, or conspiracy, in restraint of trade or commerce among the several States, or with foreign nations, is declared to be illegal:

§2   MONOPOLIZING TRADE

Every person who shall monopolize, or attempt to monopolize, or combine or conspire with any other person or persons, to monopolize any part of the trade or commerce among the several States, or with foreign nations, shall be deemed guilty of a misdemeanor, and, on conviction thereof, shall be punished by fine not exceeding fifty thousand dollars, or by imprisonment not exceeding one year, or by both said punishments, in the discretion of the court.

CHAPTER 5

TRADEMARK ACT OF 1946

§ 1124   IMPORTATION OF GOODS BEARING INFRINGING MARKS OR NAMES FORBIDDEN [LANHAM ACT - § 42]

Except as provided in subsection (d) of section 526 of the Tariff Act of 1930 [19 USC § 1526(d)], no article of imported merchandise which shall copy or simulate the name of any domestic manufacturer, or manufacturer, or trader, or of any manufacturer or trader located in any foreign country which, by treaty, convention, or law affords similar privileges to citizens of the United States, or which shall copy of simulate a trademark registered in accordance with the provisions of this Act [15 USC § § 1051 et seq.] or shall bear a name or mark calculated to induce the public to believe that the article is manufactured in the United States, or that it is manufactured in any foreign country or locality other than the country or locality in which it is in fact manufactured, shall be admitted to entry at any customhouse of the United States; and, in order to aid the officers of the customs in enforcing this prohibition, any domestic manufacturer or trader, and any foreign manufacturer or trader, who is entitled under the provisions of a treaty, convention, declaration, or agreement between the United States and any foreign country to the advantages afforded by law to

citizens of the United States in respect to trademarks and
commercial names, may require his name and residence, and the
name of the locality in which his good are manufactured, and a
copy of the certificate of registration of his trademark, issued
in accordance with the provisions of this Act [15 USC §§ 1051 et
seq.], to be recorded in books which shall be kept for this
purpose in the Department of the Treasury, under such regulations
as the Secretary of the Treasury shall prescribe, and may furnish
to the Department facsimiles of his name, the name of the
locality in which his goods are manufactured, or of his
registered trademark, and thereupon the Secretary of the Treasury
shall cause one or more copies of the same to be transmitted to
each collector or other proper officer of customs.

§ 1127   CONSTRUCTION AND DEFINITIONS [LANHAM ACT - § 45]
           (amended 1988)

                              *   *   *
     Related Company.   The term "related company" means any
person whose use of a mark is controlled by the owner of the mark
with respect to the nature and quality of the goods or services
on or in connection with which the mark is used.

                           TARIFF ACT

§ 1526   MERCHANDISE BEARING AMERICAN TRADEMARK

(a) Importation prohibited
     Except as provided in subsection (d) of this section, it
shall be unlawful to import into the United States any
merchandise of foreign manufacture if such merchandise, or the
label, sign, print, package or wrapper, or receptacle, bears a
trademark owned by a citizen of, or by a corporation or
association created or organized within, the United States, and
registered in the Patent and Trademark Officer by a person
domiciled in the United States, under the provisions of section
81 to 109 of title, 15, and if a copy of the certificate of
registration of such trademark is filed with the Secretary of the
Treasury, in the manner provided in section 106 of said title 15,
unless written consent of the owner of such trademark is produced
at the times of making entry.
(b) Seizure and forfeiture
     Any such merchandize imported into the United States in
violation of the provisions of this section shall be subject to
seizure and forfeiture for violation of the customs laws.
(c) Injunction and damages
     Any person dealing in any such merchandise may be enjoined
from dealing therein within the United States or may be required
to export of destroy such merchandise or to remove or obliterate

such trademark and shall be liable for the same damages and profits provided for wrongful use of a trade-mark, under the provisions of sections 81 to 109 of title 15.
(d) Exemptions; publication in Federal Register; forfeitures; rules and regulations
(1) The trademark provisions of this section and section 1124 of title 15, do not apply to the importation of articles accompanying any person arriving in the United States when such articles are for his personal use...
(e) Merchandise bearing counterfeit mark; seizure and forfeiture; disposition of seized goods
Any such merchandise bearing a counterfeit mark (within the meaning of section 1127 of the title 15) imported into the United States in violation of the provisions of section 1124 of title 15, shall be seized and, in the absence of the written consent of the trademark owner, forfeited for violations of the customs laws. Upon seizure of such merchandise, the Secretary shall notify the owner of the trademark, and shall, after forfeiture, obliterate the trademark where feasible and dispose of goods seized. . .

CODE OF FEDERAL REGULATIONS

§ 133.12   APPLICATION TO RECORD A TRADE NAME.

* * *
(d) The identity of any parent or subsidiary company, or other foreign company under common ownership or control which uses the trade name abroad (see § 133.2(d); and . . . .

§ 133.21   RESTRICTIONS ON IMPORTATION OF ARTICLES BEARING RECORDED TRADEMARKS AND TRADE NAMES.

(a) Copying or simulating marks or names. Articles of foreign or domestic manufacture bearing a mark or name copying or simulating a recorded trademark or trade name shall be denied entry and are subject to forfeiture as prohibited importations. A "copying or simulating" mark or name is an actual counterfeit of the recorded mark or name or is one which so resembles it as to be likely to cause the public to associate the copying or simulating mark with the recorded mark or name.
(b) Identical trademark. Foreign-made articles bearing a trademark identical with one owned and recorded by a citizen of the United States or a corporation or association created or organized within the United States are subject to seizure and forfeiture as prohibited importations.
(c) Restrictions not applicable. The restrictions set forth in paragraphs (a) and (b) of this section do not apply to imported articles when:
(1) Both the foreign and the U.S. trademark or trade name

are owned by the same person or business entity;
(2) The foreign and domestic trademark or trade name owners
are parent and subsidiary companies or are otherwise subject
to common ownership or control (see §§ 133.2(d) and
133.12(d)):
(3) The articles of foreign manufacture bear a recorded
trademark or trade name applied under authorization of the
U.S. owner;
(4) The objectionable mark is removed or obliterated prior
to importation in such a manner as to illegible and
incapable of being reconstituted, for example by:
    (i) Grinding off imprinted trademarks wherever they
    appear;
    (ii) Removing and disposing of plates bearing a
    trademark or trade name;
(5) The merchandise is imported by the recordant of the
trademark or trade name or his designate;
(6) The recordant gives written consent . . . .
(7) The articles of foreign manufacture bear a recorded
trademark and the personal exemption is claimed and allowed
under § 148.55 of the chapter.
(d) Exceptions for articles bearing counterfeit trademarks. The
provisions of paragraph (c)(4) of this section are not applicable
to articles bearing counterfeit trademarks at the time of
importation (see § 133.24).

CHAPTER 6

UNIFORM COMMERCIAL CODE

§ 1 - 201   DEFINITIONS

* * *
(19) "Good faith" means honesty in fact in the conduct or
transaction concerned.

§ 2 - 103   DEFINITIONS

(1) In the Article unless the context otherwise requires
    (b) "Good faith" in the case of a merchant means honesty in
fact and the observance of reasonable commercial standards of
fair dealing in the trade.

§ 2 - 403   POWER TO TRANSFER; GOOD FAITH PURCHASE OF GOODS

(1) A purchaser of goods acquires all title which his
transferor had or had power to transfer except that a purchaser

of a limited interest acquires rights only to the extent of the interest purchased. A person with voidable title has power to transfer a good title to a good faith purchaser for value. When goods have been delivered under a transaction of purchase the purchaser has such power even though

(a) the transferor was deceived as to the identity of the purchaser, or

(b) the delivery was in exchange for a check which is later dishonored, or

(c) it was agreed that the transaction was to be a "cash sale", or

(d) the delivery was procured through fraud punishable as larcenous under the criminal law.

THEFT, ROBBERY, AND RELATED CRIMES
FLORIDA ANTIFENCING ACT

§ 812.005   SHORT TITLE

Sections 812.012-812.037 shall be known as the Florida Anti-Fencing Act.

§ 812.012   DEFINITIONS

As used in §§ 812.012-812.037:

(1) "Dealer in property" means any person in the business of buying and selling property.

(2) "Obtains or uses" means any manner of:

(a) Taking or exercising control over property.

(b) Making any unauthorized use, disposition, or transfer of property.

(c) Obtaining property by fraud, willful misrepresentation of a future act, or false promise;

(d) 1. Conduct previously known as stealing; larceny; purloining; abstracting; embezzlement; misapplication; misappropriation; conversion; or obtaining money or property by false pretenses, fraud, or deception; or

2. Other conduct similar in nature.

(3) "Property" means anything of value, and includes:

(a) Real property, including things growing on, affixed to, and found in land.

(b) Tangible or intangible personal property, including rights, privileges, interests, and claims. . . .

(4) "Property of another" means property in which a person has an interest upon which another person is not privileged to infringe without consent, whether or not the other person also has an interest in the property. . . .

(6) "Stolen property" means property that has been the subject of any criminally wrongful taking.

(7) "Traffic" means:
    (a) To sell, transfer, distribute, dispense, or otherwise dispose of property.
    (b) To buy, receive, possess, obtain control of, or use property with the intent to sell, transfer, distribute, dispense, or otherwise dispose of such property.
(8) "Enterprise" means any individual, sole proprietorship, partnership, corporation, business trust, union chartered under the laws of this state, or other legal entity, or any unchartered union, association, or group of individuals associated in fact although not a legal entity.

§ 812.016   POSSESSION OF ALTERED PROPERTY

Any dealer in property who knew or should have known that the identifying features, such as serial numbers and permanently affixed labels, of property in his possession had been removed or altered without the consent of the manufacturer, shall be guilty of a misdemeanor of the first degree. . . .

§ 812.019   DEALING IN STOLEN PROPERTY

(1) Any person who traffics in, or endeavors to traffic in, property that he knows or should know was stolen shall be guilty of a felony of the second degree. . . .
(2) Any person who initiates, organizes, plans, finances, directs, manages, or supervises the theft of property and traffics in such stolen property shall be guilty of a felony of the first degree. . . .

§ 812.022   EVIDENCE OF THEFT OR DEALING IN STOLEN PROPERTY

* * *

(2) Proof of possession of property recently stolen, unless satisfactorily explained, gives rise to an inference that the person in possession of the property knew or should have known that the property had been stolen.
(3) Proof of the purchase or sale of stolen property at a price substantially below the fair market value, unless satisfactorily explained, gives rise to an inference that the person buying or selling the property knew or should have known that the property had been stolen.

CHAPTER 7

COPYRIGHT ACT OF 1976

§ 102   SUBJECT MATTER OF COPYRIGHT: IN GENERAL

(a)   Copyright protection subsists, in accordance with this title, in original works of authorship fixed in any tangible medium of expression, now known or later developed, from which they can be perceived, reproduced, or otherwise communicated, either directly of with the aid of a machine or device. Works of authorship include the following categories:
     (1)   literary works;
     (2)   musical works, including any accompanying words;
     (3)   dramatic works, including any accompanying music;
     (4)   pantomimes and choreographic works;
     (5)   pictorial, graphic, and sculptural works;
     (6)   motion pictures and other audiovisual works; and
     (7)   sound recordings.
(b)   In no case does copyright protection for an original work of authorship extend to any idea, procedure, process, system, method of operation, concept, principle, or discovery, regardless of the form in which it is described, explained, illustrated, or embodied in such work.

§ 106   EXCLUSIVE RIGHTS IN COPYRIGHTED WORKS

Subject to sections 107 through 118, the owner of copyright under this title has the exclusive rights to do and to authorize any of the following:
     (1)   to reproduce the copyrighted work in copies or phonorecords;
     (2)   to prepare derivative works based upon the copyrighted work;
     (3)   to distribute copies or phonorecords of the copyrighted work to the public by sale or other transfer of ownership, or by rental, lease, or lending;
     (4)   in the case of literary, musical, dramatic, and choreographic works, pantomimes, and motion pictures and other audiovisual works, to perform the copyrighted work publicly; and
     (5)   in the case of literary, musical, dramatic, and choreographic works, pantomimes, and pictorial, graphic, or sculptural works, including the individual images of a motion picture or other audiovisual work, to display the copyrighted work publicly.

§ 109   LIMITATIONS ON EXCLUSIVE RIGHTS: EFFECT OF
           TRANSFER OF PARTICULAR COPY OR PHONORECORD

(a)   Notwithstanding the provisions of section 106(3), the
owner of a particular copy or phonorecord lawfully made under
this title, or any person authorized by such owner, is entitled,
without the authority of the copyright owner, to sell or
otherwise dispose of the possession of that copy or phonorecord.
(b)   Notwithstanding the provisions of section 106(5) the
owner of a particular copy lawfully made under this title, or any
person authorized by such owner, is entitled, without the
authority of the copyright owner, to display that copy publicly,
either directly or by the projection of no more than one image at
a time, to viewers presents at the place where the copy is
located.

§ 602   INFRINGING IMPORTATION OF COPIES OR PHONORECORDS

(a)   Importation into the United States, without the
authority of the owner of copyright under this title, of copies
or phonorecords of a work that have been acquired outside the
United States is an infringement of the exclusive right to
distribute copies of phonorecords under section 106, actionable
under section 501.   This subsection does not apply to -
                         *   *   *
(2) importation, for the private use of the importer and not
for distribution, by any person with respect to no more than
one copy or phonorecord of any one work at any one time, or
by any person arriving from outside the United States with
respect to copies or phonorecords forming part of such
person's personal baggage; or
(3) importation by or for an organization operated for
scholarly, educational, or religious purposes and not for
private gain, with respect to no more than one copy of an
audiovisual work solely for its archival purposes, and no
more than five copies or phonorecords of any other work for
its library lending or archival purposes, unless the
importation of such copies or phonorecords is part of an
activity consisting of systematic reproduction or
distribution, engaged in by such organization in violation
of the provisions of section 108 (g) (2).
(b)   In a case where the making of the copies or phonorecords
would have constituted an infringement of copyright if this title
had been applicable, their importation is prohibited.   In a case
where the copies or phonorecords were lawfully made, the United
States Customs Service has no authority to prevent their
importation unless the provisions of section 601 are applicable.
In either case, the Secretary of the Treasury is authorized to
prescribe, by regulation, a procedure under which any person
claiming an interest in the copyright in a particular work may,

upon payment of a specified fee, be entitled to notification by the Customs Service of the importation of articles that appear to be copies or phonorecords of the work.

CHAPTER 8

NEW YORK GENERAL BUSINESS LAW

§ 368-d   INJURY TO BUSINESS REPUTATION; DILUTION

Likelihood of injury to business reputation or of dilution of the distinctive quality of a mark or trade name shall be a ground for injunctive relief in cases of infringement of a mark registered or not registered or in cases of unfair competition, notwithstanding the absence of competition between the parties or the absence of confusion as to the source of goods or services.

NEW YORK GENERAL   BUSINESS LAW

§ 218-aa.   WARRANTY DISCLOSURE

1. As used in this section, the term "grey markets merchandise" means any brand-name consumer product normally accompanied by a warranty valid in the United States of America which is imported into the United States through channels other than the manufacturer's authorized United States distributor, for sale to the public in this state, and which, by reason of this manner of distribution, may not be accompanied by a manufacturer's express written warranty valid in the United States. Grey markets merchandise shall be limited to products purchased by a consumer for use primarily for personal, family or household purposes.

2. Every retail dealer who knowingly offers for sale grey markets merchandise shall conspicuously post, in the following manner, the information required by subdivision three of this section:
   a. On a sign attached to the items itself; or
   b. On a sign affixed to each cash register or point of sale at which such goods are offered for sale; or
   c. On a sign so situated as to be clearly visible to the buyer from the register.

3. Every retail dealer who offers for sale grey markets merchandise shall disclose, as applicable, that either some of the products or a specific product are not:
   a. accompanied by the manufacturer's warranty valid in the United States; or
   b. accompanied by instructions in English; or
   c. eligible for a rebate offered by the manufacturer.

4. Every retail dealer or dealer engaged in a mail-order

business who offers for sale grey markets merchandise shall include the disclosure required by subdivision three of this section in any written advertisement relating to such product. Such disclosure shall be made in type of a conspicuous size.

5. Any retail dealer who violates any provision of this section shall be liable, for a period of up to twenty days from the date of purchase, to the buyer for a refund or credit on credit-card purchases provided the product purchased has not been used or damaged by the buyer.

6. Whenever there shall be a violation of this section an application may be made by the attorney general in the name of the people of the state of New York to a court or justice having jurisdiction by a special proceeding to issue an injunction, and upon notice to the defendant of not less than five days, to enjoin and restrain the continuance of such violations; and if it shall appear to the satisfaction of the court or justice that the defendant has, in fact, violated this section, an injunction may be issued by such court or justice, enjoining and restraining any further violation, without requiring proof that any person has, in fact, been injured or damaged thereby. In any such proceeding, the court may make allowances to the attorney general as provided in paragraph six of subdivision (a) of section eighty-three hundred three of the civil practice law and rules, and direct restitution. Whenever the court shall determine that a violation of this section has occurred, the court may impose a civil penalty of not more than five hundred dollars for each violation. In connection with any such proposed application, the attorney general is authorized to take proof and make a determination of the relevant facts and to issue subpoenas in accordance with the civil practice law and rules.

7. Provided, however, that it shall be an affirmative defense that the consumer is provided with a written warranty which offers equal or greater protection than the manufacturer's warranty through a warrantor demonstrated to be a financially responsible retailer, distributor, importer or other third person capable of fulfilling warranty obligations.

CALIFORNIA GREY MARKET
CONSUMER DISCLOSURE ACT

Cal. Civ. Code § 1793.1 FORM OF EXPRESS WARRANTIES

(a) (1) Every manufacturer, distributor, or retailer making express warranties with respect to consumer goods shall fully set forth such warranties in simple and readily understood language, which shall clearly identify the party making such express warranties, and which shall conform to the federal standards for disclosure of warranty terms and conditions set forth in the federal Magnuson-Moss Warranty Federal Trade

Commission Improvement Act, and in the regulations of the Federal Trade Commission adopted pursuant to the provisions of that act.

§ 1797.8   DEFINITIONS

(a) As used in this chapter, the term "grey market goods" means consumer goods bearing a trademark and normally accompanied by an express written warranty valid in the United States of America which are imported into the United States through channels other than the manufacturer's authorized United States distributor and which are not accompanied by the manufacturer's express written warranty valid in the United States.

(b) As used in this chapter, the term "sale" includes a lease of more than four months.

§ 1797.81   DISCLOSURES BY RETAIL SELLERS

(a) Every retail seller who offers grey market goods for sale shall post a conspicuous sign at the product's point of display and affix to the product or its package a conspicuous ticket, label, or tag disclosing any or all of the following, whichever is applicable:

(1) The item is not covered by a manufacturer's express written warranty valid in the United States (however, any implied warranty provided by law still exists).

(2) The item is not compatible with United States electrical currents.

(3) The item is not compatible with United States broadcast frequencies.

(4) Replacement parts are not available through the manufacturers' United States distributors.

(5) Compatible accessories are not available through the manufacturer's United States distributors.

(6) The item is not accompanied by instructions in English.

(7) The item is not eligible for a manufacturer's rebate.

(8) Any other compatibility or nonconformity with relevant domestic standards known to the seller.

(b) The disclosure described in paragraph (1) of subdivision (a) shall not be required to be made by a retail seller with respect to grey market goods that are accompanied by an express written warranty provided by the retail seller, provided that each of the following conditions is satisfied:

(1) The protections and other benefits that are provided to the buyer by the express written warranty provided by the retail seller are equal to or better than the protections and other benefits that are provided to buyers in the United States of America by the manufacturer's express written warranty that normally accompanies the goods.

(2) The express written warranty conforms to the requirements of Section 1793.1.

(3) The retail seller has posted a conspicuous sign at the product's point of sale or display, or has affixed to the product or its package a conspicuous ticket, label, or tag that informs prospective buyers that copies of all of the warranties applicable to the products offered for sale by the retail seller are available to prospective buyers for inspection upon request.

§ 1797.82   DISCLOSURES IN ADVERTISEMENTS

Every retail dealer who offers for sale grey market goods shall be required to disclose in any advertisement of those goods the disclosures required by Section 1797.81. The disclosure shall be made in a type of conspicuous size.

§ 1797.83   USE OF EQUIVALENT LANGUAGE IN MAKING DISCLOSURES

In making the disclosures prescribed by this chapter, the retail seller may use reasonably equivalent language if necessary or appropriate to achieve a clearer, or more accurate, disclosure.

TRADE ACT OF 1974
UNFAIR IMPORT PRACTICES

Sec. 341   AMENDMENT TO SECTION 337 OF THE TARIFF ACT OF 1930

(a) Section 337 of the Tariff Act of 1930 (19 U.S.C. 1337) is amended to read as follows:

Sec. 337. Unfair Practices in Import Trade

(a) UNFAIR METHODS OF COMPETITION DECLARED UNLAWFUL. - Unfair methods of competition and unfair acts in the importation of articles into the United States, or in their sale by the owner, importer, consignee, or agent of either, the effect or tendency of which is to destroy or substantially injure an industry, efficiently and economically operated, in the United States, or to prevent the establishment of such an industry, or to restrain or monopolize trade and commerce in the United States, are declared unlawful, and when found by the Commission to exist shall be dealt with, in addition to any other provisions of law, as provided in this section.   ★ ★ ★

(c) DETERMINATIONS;   REVIEW. - The Commission shall determine, with respect to each investigation conducted by it under this section, whether or not there is a violation of this section. Each determination under subsection (d) or (e) shall be made on the record after notice and opportunity for a hearing in conformity with the provisions of subchapter II of chapter 5 of title 5, United States Code.   All legal and equitable defenses may be presented in all cases.   Any person adversely affected by a final determination of the Commission under subsection (d) or (e) may appeal such determination to the United States Court of Customs and Patent Appeals.   Such court shall have jurisdiction to review such determination in the same manner and subject to the same limitations and conditions as in the case of appeals from decisions of the United States Customs Court.

(d) EXCLUSION OF ARTICLES FROM ENTRY. - If the Commission determines, as a result of an investigation under this section, that there is violation of this section, it shall direct that the articles concerned, imported by any person violating the provision of this section, be excluded from entry into the United States, unless, after considering the effect of such exclusion upon the public health and welfare, competitive conditions in the United States economy, the production of like or directly competitive articles in the United States, and United States consumers, it finds that such articles should not be excluded from entry.   The Commission shall notify the Secretary of the Treasury of its action under this subsection directing such exclusion from entry, and upon receipt of such notice, the Secretary shall, through the proper officers, refuse such entry.

* * *

(g) REFERRAL TO THE PRESIDENT. -
    (1)   If the Commission determines that there is a violation of this section, or that, for purposes of subsection (e), there is reason to believe that there is such a violation, it shall -
        (A) publish such determination in the Federal Register, and
        (B)   transmit to the President a copy of such determination and the action taken under subsection (d), (e), or (f), with respect thereto, together with the record upon which such determination is based.
    (2) If, before the close of the 60-day period beginning on the day after the day on which he receives a copy of such determination, the President, for policy reasons, disapproves such determination and notifies the Commission of his disapproval, then, effective on the date of such notice, such determination and the action taken under subsection (d), (e), or (f) with respect thereto shall have no force or effect.
    (3)   Subject to the provisions of paragraph (2), such determination shall, except for purposes of subsection (c), be effective upon publication thereof in the Federal Register, and the action taken under subsection (d), (e), or (f) with respect thereto shall be effective as provided in such subsections,

except that articles directed to be excluded from entry under subsection (d) or subject to a cease and desist order under subsection (f) shall be entitled to entry under bond determined by the Commission and prescribed by the Secretary until such determination becomes final.

(4) If the President does not disapprove such determination within such 60-day period, or if he notifies the Commission before the close of such period that he approves such determination, then, for purposes of paragraph (3) and subsection (c) such determination shall become final on the day after the close of such period or the day on which the President notifies the Commission of his approval, as the case may be.

FEDERAL FAIR PACKAGING AND LABELING PROGRAM

§ 1451   CONGRESSIONAL DECLARATION OF POLICY

Informed consumers are essential to the fair and efficient functioning of a free market economy. Packages and their labels should enable consumers to obtain accurate information as to the quantity of the contents and should facilitate value comparisons. Therefore, it is hereby declared to be the policy of the Congress to assist consumers and manufacturers in reaching these goals in the marketing of consumer goods.

§ 1452   UNFAIR AND DECEPTIVE PACKAGING AND LABELLING; SCOPE OF PROHIBITION

(a)   It shall be unlawful for any person engaged in the packaging or labeling of any consumer commodity (as defined in this chapter) for distribution in commerce, or for any person (other than a common carrier for hire, a contract carrier for hire, or a freight forwarder for hire) engaged in the distribution in commerce of any packaged or labeled consumer commodity, to distribute or to cause to be distributed in commerce any such commodity if such commodity is contained in a package, or if there is affixed to that commodity a label, which does not conform to the provisions of this chapter and of regulations promulgated under the authority of this chapter.

(b)   The prohibition contained in subsection (a) of this section shall not apply to persons engaged in business as wholesale or retail distributors of consumer commodities except to the extent that such persons (1) are engaged in the packaging or labeling of such commodities, or (2) prescribe or specify by any means the manner in which such commodities are packaged or labeled.

§ 1453   REQUIREMENTS OF LABELING; PLACEMENT, FORM, AND CONTENTS
          OF STATEMENT OF QUANTITY; SUPPLEMENTAL STATEMENT OF
          QUANTITY

(a) No person subject to the prohibition contained in section
1452 of this title shall distribute or cause to be distributed in
commerce any packaged consumer commodity unless in conformity
with regulations which shall be established by the promulgating
authority pursuant to section 1455 of this title which shall
provide that -
     (1) The commodity shall bear a label specifying the identity
     of the commodity and the name and place of business of the
     manufacturer, packer, or distributor;
     (2) The net quantity of contents (in terms of weight,
     measure, or numerical count) shall be separately and
     accurately stated in a uniform location upon the principal
     display panel of that label;
     (3) [A] separate label statement of net quantity of contents
     appearing upon or affixed to any package . . .

Appendix II: Vivitar Corp. v. United States, 593 F. Supp. 420 (CIT 1982)

RESTANI, J.:

Congress first restricted importation of merchandise bearing trademarks in 1871. 16 Stat. 580 (1871). This act and a number of subsequent acts restricted importation of merchandise bearing a trademark that "copied or simulated" a domestic trademark. These restrictions were put in their current form by the Trademark Act of 1905, Pub.L. No. 58–84, 33 Stat. 724 (1905). Section 27 of the act [Now 15 U.S.C. sec. 1124 (1982)] provides in relevant part that "no article of imported merchandise ... which shall copy or simulate a trade-mark registered in accordance with the provisions of this Act ... shall be admitted to entry...."

After enactment of this section, a pair of Second Circuit cases tested the meaning of the term "copy or simulate." *Fred Gretsch Mfg. Co. v. Schoening*, 238 F. 780 (2d Cir. 1916); *A. Bourjois & Co., Inc. v. Katzel*, 275 F. 539 (2d Cir. 1921), rev'd, 260 U.S. 689 (1923). ...

In both cases, the Second Circuit held that the trademark on the challenged imports did not copy or simulate the plaintiffs' marks. The court decided that section 27 was not intended to bar imports bearing a trademark if the trademark accurately described the manufacturing source for the goods. ...

Legislative History

Section 1526 (a) was enacted in response to the Second Circuit decision in *Katzel*. As Judge Hand noted, it "was intended only to supply the casus omissus, supposed to exist in section 27 of the Act of 1905 . . ., because of the decision of the Circuit Court of Appeals in *Bourjois v. Katzel*. . . . Had the Supreme Court reversed that decision [earlier], it would not have been enacted at all." *Coty, Inc. v. LeBlume Import Co., Inc.*, 292 F. 264, 269 (S.D.N.Y. 1923), aff'd, 293 F. 344 (2d Cir. 1923). The section was added as a floor amendment to the Tariff Act of 1922, Pub.L. No. 67–318, sec. 526, 42 Stat. 975 (1922). The legislative history is sparse, consisting of a short floor debate and a brief paragraph in the Conference Report. But the history makes very clear that the purpose of sec. 1526(a) was to reverse the Second Circuit *Katzel* decision. The Conference Report notes:

> A recent decision of the circuit court of appeals holds that existing law does not prevent the importation of merchandise bearing the same trade-mark as merchandise of the United States, if the imported merchandise is genuine and if there is no fraud upon the public. The Senate amendment makes such importation unlawful without the consent of the owner of the American trade-mark.

H. R. rep. no. 1223, 67th Cong., 2d Sess. 158 (1922).

In the floor debates, both proponents and opponents of the section note that the purpose of the section was to give trademark owners the protection denied them by the Second Circuit. One of the section's sponsors, Senator McCumber, noted "the courts have held that we cannot prevent any product being shipped into the United States if it is in violation of a trade-mark where the foreign maker has sold trade-mark and all, patent and everything in the United States." 62 Cong. Rec. 11604 (1922). Another proponent, Senator Sutherland noted that

> [A]ll that this paragraph does is to prevent fraud, and I believe that the Senate is in favor of protecting the property rights of American citizens who have purchased trade-marks from foreigners, and when these foreigners deliberately violate the property rights of those to whom they have sold these trade-marks by shipping over to this country goods under identical trade-marks.

Id. at 11603. Senator Moses objected to the section because "[a] case involving its entire principle has been heard in the circuit court of appeals and is now on its way to the Supreme Court of the United States for final determination." Id. [footnote omitted]

The floor debate was brief, [footnote omitted] but far-ranging. A number of examples where the section would apply were discussed. In all of them, the sponsors made clear that the purpose of the amendment was to protect an American trademark owner who had purchased the right to use a trademark in America from an independent foreign company. Senator McCumber illustrated the limited scope intended for the section:

> Suppose not only the patent but the trade-mark, which is "Bayer's Aspirin" with a red cross, is sold to an American concern outright. The patent will defend against any importations so long as the patent lasts; but suppose, now, the patent expires. Then the German firm, notwithstanding that they have sold all rights, including the trade-mark, begins to ship in Bayer's Aspirin with the same kind of a trade-mark that they had before, although the right is owned in the United States. According to the decision that was read by the Senator from West Virginia the American purchasers of these rights are entirely unprotected, and this is to give the opportunity to protect the American purchaser. That is all there is to it. . . .

Id. at 11604; see remarks of Senator Sutherland, supra.

At the end of the debate, Senator Lenroot expressed a concern as to whether the section would apply in a case involving facts similar to the facts at issue here. Senator Lenroot wanted to know whether an international corporation could designate an American agent to register its trademark in the United States and then use that registration to bar unauthorized imports. "I want to inquire whether any American could purchase [the product] abroad and import it without the written consent of [the] agent here in the United States, and if not, why not? There is no fraud, no deceit." Id. at 11605. Senator McCumber clearly did not believe that the section applied to these facts. "[I]f there has been no transfer of trade-mark, that presents an entirely different question. . . . The mere fact of a foreigner having a trade-mark and registering that trade-mark in the United States, and selling the goods in the United States through an agency, of course, would not be affected by the provision." Id. Apparently Senator Lenroot was unconvinced that the language proposed was sufficiently narrow to achieve the stated purpose. He restated his example, making clear that the agent registering the trademark was domiciled in the United States, and stated that under the section the product "could not be bought in the markets of the world and sold here without written consent of the [trademark owner] or [its] agent domiciled here in America." Id.

However, the sponsors of the section apparently did not believe that the section created these rights. And all concerned with the debate believed that the purpose of the section was to reverse the result in *Katzel.*

Shortly after sec. 1526(a) became law the Supreme Court reversed the Second Circuit decision in *Katzel.* In *Katzel,* the Supreme Court held that the Trademark Act of 1905 outlawed importation of trademark goods from a foreign manufacturer when the foreign manufacturer had sold the American trademark to the plaintiff. The court held that this followed from the law governing assignment of trademarks [citations omitted]. In a similar case, the Supreme Court held that sec. 27 of the 1905 act (sec. 1124) required the same result. *A. Bourjois & Co., Inc. v. Aldridge,* 263 U.S. 675, 44 S.Ct. 4, 68 L.Ed. 501 (1923) answering questions certified at 292 F. 1013 (2d Cir. 1922).

Since Congress passed sec. 1526(a) to provide rights that the Supreme Court held were already provided by the Trademark Act of 1905, it is not surprising that the Bureau of Customs issued one set of regulations to implement both statutes. Customs Regulations of 1923, Articles 475–480. These regulations offer little insight into the Bureau of Customs' interpretation of sec. 1526(a). The relevant language notes that "[t]rade-marks owned by an American citizen . . . are entitled to the protection of section 526 . . . if the mark has been registered." Id. at Article 476. But the regulations do not describe what does or does not constitute a violation of the section.

Section 1526(a) was reenacted without change in the Tariff Act of 1930. Congress debated the section at length in the context of a proposed amendment which would have drastically altered the section. (fn. — The proposed amendment would have outlawed importation of all goods bearing a trade-mark registered by an American citizen. The amendment was intended to compel American trademark owners to produce their goods domestically. 71 Cong.Rec. 3871 [1929]). The debate contains only brief references to the existing scope of sec. 1526(a), but it seems to reflect the views of the original sponsors. Senator Reed noted:

At the present time the tariff laws forbid the importation of an article bearing a trade-mark registered in America unless the owner of that trade-mark consents in writing to the importation. Obviously the purpose of that provision is to protect the American owner of the trade-mark against importations of articles which have been stamped with his mark without his consent.

71 Cong.Rec. 3873 (1929).

Administrative Policy and Practice

Customs Regulations issued shortly after the reenactment of sec. 1526(a) could be read as suggesting that the Bureau of Customs would apply the section broadly.

Prohibition of entry. Entry is prohibited of imported merchandise bearing a genuine trade-mark when such trade-mark is recorded with the Treasury Department and registered under the trademark law of February 20, 1905, if compliance is had with all provisions of section 526 of the tariff act of 1930, provided the period of protection for such trade-mark has not expired.

Customs Regulations of 1931, Article 518(a).

If the Bureau of Customs did intend a sweeping result, that view was short lived. In 1936, the Bureau of Customs issued a new regulation setting out its interpretation of sec. 1124 and sec. 1526(a). T.D. 48537 (1936). Article 518 was amended to read

Prohibition of importation.

(a) Merchandise of foreign or domestic manufacture is prohibited importation when it bears a name or mark which copies or simulates a trade-mark or trade name entitled to the protection of the Trade-Mark Act of 1905 or the Trade-Mark Act of 1920, unless such merchandise is imported by or for the account of, or with the written consent of, the owner of the protected trade-mark or trade name.

(b) A name or mark (including a name or mark which is a genuine trade-mark or trade name in a foreign country) on an article of foreign manufacture identical with a trade-mark or trade name protected by the trade-mark laws of the United States, as well as a name or mark on an article of foreign or domestic manufacture counterfeiting such protected trade-mark or trade name, or so resembling such protected trade-mark or trade name as to be likely to cause confusion or mistake in the minds of the public or to deceive purchasers, shall be deemed for the purposes of these regulations to copy or simulate such protected trade-mark or trade name. *However, merchandise manufactured or sold in a foreign country under a trade-mark or trade name, which trade-mark is registered and recorded, or which trade name is recorded under the trade-mark laws of the United States, shall not be deemed for the purpose of these regulations to copy or simulate such United States trade-mark or trade name if such foreign trade-mark or trade name and such United States trade-mark or trade name are owned by the same person, partnership, association, or corporation.*

T.D. 48537 (1936) (emphasis added).

The new regulation appears to respond to the concerns raised by Senator Lenroot in the initial debate over sec. 1526(a). Goods of foreign manufacture bearing a genuine trademark were prohibited imports absent the American Trademark owner's consent. [footnote omitted]. But this protection was not extended if the same entity owned the foreign and domestic trademarks. Thus, the plaintiff in *Katzel* that bought the United States trademark rights to a product was protected. Imports of genuine goods bearing the trademark of the foreign company that sold its U.S. rights were outlawed. But the 1936 regulation bars a company from registering a trademark in both the United States and abroad, selling the trademarked goods in both markets, and restricting the importation of the goods it sells abroad. [footnote omitted].

The essential thrust of this regulation has remained unchanged since 1936.

In 1953, the Bureau of Customs expanded its construction of the limits on sec. 1526(a). T.D. 53399 (1953). The new regulations, 19 C.F.R. sec. 11.14, denied trade-mark owners the right to prohibit imports if the American and foreign trademarks were owned by related companies as defined by sec. 45 of the Lanham Act, Pub.L. No. 79–489, 60 Stat. 443 (1946). Section 45 of the Lanham Act provides in relevant part:

The term "related company" means any person who legitimately controls or is controlled by the registrant or applicant for registration in respect to the nature and quality of the goods or services in connection with which the mark is used.

This regulation was consistent with Customs' policy in the application of the prior regulation. Commissioner of Customs Frank Dow explained Customs' policy in a 1951 letter to Senator Paul Douglas.

> As interpreted by the Bureau, section 526 prohibits importation of genuine articles of foreign origin bearing a genuine trade-mark valid in the foreign country which articles were not produced by or with the authority of the United States owner of such mark. . . .
>
> However, if the United States trade-mark owner and the owner of the foreign rights to the same mark are one and the same person, articles produced and sold abroad by the foreign owner may be imported by anyone for the reason that the trade-mark owner has himself introduced the articles into commerce or authorized such introduction and may not unreasonably restrict the use of the product thereafter. For this purpose a foreign subsidiary or licensee of the United States trade-mark owner is considered to stand in the same shoes as such trade-mark owner.

In 1959, the Bureau of Customs amended 19 C.F.R. sec. 11.14 to eliminate the provisions for related companies. T.D. 54932 (1959). There is no evidence that this amendment reflected a substantive change in Customs' policy, especially since the amendment retained the limitation based on ownership of the foreign and domestic trademark by the same person, partnership, association, or corporation.

The Bureau of Customs reaffirmed its interpretation of sec. 1526(a) in a pair of letters in 1962 and 1963, a series of letters in 1968 and 1969, and a 1969 Treasury decision. Deputy Commissioner Flinn wrote in 1963:

> It has been the Bureau's position for many years that in permitting anyone to import merchandise manufactured or sold by the foreign parent or subsidiary corporation of an American trademark owner is the correct interpretation of section 526 of the tariff act and section 42 of the trademark law.

And in 1962 he wrote:

It is the Bureau's opinion that a foreign wholly owned subsidiary and its United States parent corporation are the same corporation within the meaning of section 11.14(b) of the Customs Regulations. This interpretation has been consistently applied for some years before insertion of the "related companies" provision in the customs regulations and since the "related companies" provision was deleted from the regulations in 1959.

In 1968, Paul K. McCarthy, Assistant Director (Restricted Merchandise) for Customs wrote Peter Gray, the Managing Director for plaintiff's predecessor corporation:

[I]t is our position that only trademarks, on foreign-made products, which were unauthorized when introduced into foreign commerce are prohibited importation under section 1526, title 19, United States Code. Thus if any goods sold to markets abroad by a foreign branch, subsidiary, or agent should be offered for importation into the United States, those goods would be considered to bear genuine "VIVITAR" trademarks and would be admissible to entry. This position is based on the legislative and judicial history 19 U.S.C. 1526.

An in 1969, Mr. McCarthy wrote to Mr. Gray analyzing the statutory basis for Customs' interpretation.

The purpose of the relevant law, section 1526, title 19, United States Code, is to protect American firms which have bought trademarks from foreign firms, against fraudulent competition by the foreign firms. Obviously this purpose is not served when an American trademark owner authorizes foreign use of his genuine trademark, even though it is not intended that merchandise so marked will be imported into the United States.

And T.D. 69–12(2) (1969) provides:

Trademarks and Trade Names. The trademark or trade name on imported foreign-produced merchandise shall not be deemed to copy or simulate a registered trademark or trade name, if the foreign producer is the parent or subsidiary of the American owner or the firms are under a common control. Further, if a foreign producer has been authorized by the American owner to produce and sell goods abroad bearing the recorded trademark or trade name, merchandise so produced and sold is deemed admissible.

In 1972, the Bureau of Customs revised 19 C.F.R. sec. 11.14. The new regulation, 19 C.F.R. sec. 133.21, embodied the construction of sec. 1526(a) which the Customs Service (previously named Bureau of Customs) had generally maintained, from 1936. [footnote omitted]. The regulation makes clear that Customs will not restrict genuine imports bearing a trademark registered in the United States if the foreign and domestic trademark owners are the same, closely related, or the American trademark owner consented to the application of its trademark to the imported goods. The Justice Department's comments on the regulation provide a detailed analysis of, and further justification for, Customs' interpretation of sec. 1526(a). Justice analyzed the litigated history of the *Katzel* case and the legislative history of sec. 1526(a) and agreed that Congressional intent and public policy required a narrow reading of sec. 1526(a). Letter from Walker B. Coomegys, Acting Assistant Attorney General, Antitrust Division to Myles J. Ambrose, Commissioner of Customs, dated April 19, 1971. [footnote omitted].

Although Customs' stated policy seems clear, there is some evidence that the Bureau of Customs did not always apply its construction of sec. 1526(a) uniformly. In the hearings on the Lanham Act, the Justice Department objected to New Jersey Zinc Company's use of its trademark to restrict imports.

[Section 1526] obviously was designed to prevent the importation into the United States of foreign merchandise bearing counterfeit trade-marks, etc. It was the ingenuity of the New Jersey Zinc Co.'s lawyers to pervert this provisions [sic] of the Tariff Act to serve their own purposes, namely, to exclude absolutely from the United States zinc produced abroad under licenses granted by New Jersey Zinc Co. under its patents and bearing New Jersey's trade-mark as required by New Jersey.

Hearings on H.R. 82 before a subcommittee of the Senate Committee on Patents, 78th Cong., 2d Sess. 68 (1944). Also the briefs filed by the

Justice Department in an antitrust action indicated that Customs was excluding perfumes bearing American trademarks even though the foreign trademark for the perfumes was owned by companies related to the American trademark owners. *United States v. Guerlain, Inc.*, 155 F.Supp. 77, 79–80 (S.D.N.Y. 1957), vacated and remanded, 358 U.S. 915, 79 S.Ct. 285, 3 L.Ed. 2d 236 (1958), dismissed, 172 F.Supp. 107 (S.D.N.Y. 1958). [footnote omitted].

The Bureau of Customs' exclusion of goods bearing the Guerlain and the New Jersey Zinc trademarks appears contrary to Customs' policy as contained in their regulations and the letter of Commissioner Dow. It is especially difficult to see how Customs could exclude the goods in *Guerlain* if Customs knew the foreign and the domestic trademark owners were commonly controlled. This would have been directly contrary to the newly promulgated Customs regulations of 1953.

John F. Atwood, a Customs Law Specialist, provides a plausible explanation for this apparent inconsistency in practice in his comprehensive review of customs' interpretation of sec. 1124 and sec. 1526. In discussing the *Guerlain* case, he concludes that the Bureau of Customs "had always denied complete exclusionary protection to an American trademark registrant when it knew the importer to be a subsidiary or parent of the foreign user of the trademark. Prior to 1953, however, the Customs Regulations were not set up to specifically elicit this kind of information." Atwood, Import Restrictions on Trademarked Merchandise – The Role of the United States Bureau of Customs 59 Trademark Rep. 301 (1969). "[S]ome Customs trademark recordants who had recorded before 1953 undoubtedly continued to be permitted to exclude merchandise from their foreign supplier, since Customs did not know of the relationship between the two entities." Id. at 310. This interpretation is supported by the Customs Regulations governing recording of trademarks. Customs Regulations of 1936, Article 519.

Therefore, the court concludes that, since 1936, Customs, in essence, has construed sec. 1526(a) so as to deny American trademark owners the right to exclude goods manufactured abroad bearing their trademarks, when control of the foreign trademark is in the hands of the American trademark owner. Customs, in its own writings, and in the writings it gathered in the regulation promulgation process, has provided persuasive exegesis of the legal justification for this construction. See letter of Commissioner Dow [and] McCarthy and Comegys.

Thus, this construction is entitled to substantial weight. *Securities and Exchange Commission v. Sloan*, 436 U.S. 103, 117–118, 98 S.Ct. 1702, 1711–1712, 56 L.Ed. 2d 148 (1978). Customs' longstanding construction has been consistently applied since at least 1962, and, as discussed above, probably reflects Customs general practice under its regulations since 1936.

Congressional Ratification

In 1976 and 1978, Congress indicated its acceptance of Customs' interpretation of sec. 1526(a) by failing to amend sec. 1526(a) when it enacted legislation closely related to this provision. In 1976, a House Report, prepared as background for the proposed Customs Modernization Act of 1975, carefully examined the administrative practice under sec. 1526(a). The report noted that sec. 1526

has been consistently interpreted by the United States Customs Service for the past 20 years as excluding from protection foreign-produced merchandise bearing a genuine trade-mark created, owned, and registered by a citizen of the United States if the foreign producer has been authorized by the American trade-mark owner to produce and sell abroad goods bearing the recorded trade-mark.

H.R. Rep. 138, 94th Cong., 2d Sess. 54 (1976). In 1978, another House Report repeated the analysis of the 1976 report. H.R. Rep. 621, 95th Cong., 1st Sess. 27 (1978). Both reports were prepared in the context of proposals for substantial amendments to sec. 1526.

In 1978 Congress adopted two major amendments to sec. 1526. The first permitted travelers to freely import trademarked goods for personal use. Pub.L. no. 95–410, 92 Stat. 903 (1978), (19 U.S.C. sec. 1526(d)). The second specified the procedure to be followed by the Customs Service when it discovers imported goods bearing a counterfeit mark. 92 Stat. 903–904, 19 U.S.C. sec 1526(e). Congress examined Customs' administrative practice towards imports bearing both genuine and counterfeit trademarks. After this examination, Congress decided to define strict statutory standards for imports bearing counterfeit marks while not altering Customs' administrative practice concerning imports bearing genuine marks. This failure to alter sec. 1526(a) is sufficient indication of Congressional acquiescence in

Customs' administrative practice. *Haig v. Agee*, 453 U.S. 280, 301, 101 S.Ct. 2766, 2779, 69 L.Ed 2d 640 (1981). [footnote omitted].

Appendix III: Table of Statutes

Appendix IV: Table of Cases

Index

About the Author

SETH E. LIPNER is Associate Professor of Law at Bernard M. Baruch College, New York City. He is the author of a series of articles concerning gray market issues, and of the book, *Computer Law: Cases and Materials.*